The
Fear
of
God

Ngozi Joy Nwokoma

The
Fear
of
God

Ngozi Joy Nwokoma

THE FEAR OF GOD

Copyright © 2018 by Ngozi Joy Nwokoma

ISBN 978-1-907143-28-1

Unless otherwise indicated, all Scripture quotations are taken from the New King James Version of the Bible. Copyright © 1982 by Thomas Nelson, Inc., Publishers.

Published by Favour Land Publications
August 2018
5 Keswick Close
Manchester
M13 0DD
United Kingdom
www.favourbooksandmusic.com.

TABLE OF CONTENTS

ACKNOWLEDGEMENT

*I*am thankful to the Almighty God for the opportunity of working with the Holy Spirit throughout the process of writing the contents of this book. Even when I had lost hope of getting it completed, He graciously put it back in my hands and restored me to continue with it.

To my husband and best friend, Chinwe Nwokoma, thank you for your encouragement throughout the journey of writing this book.

CHAPTER 1

AN INTRODUCTION TO THE FEAR OF GOD

What Is The Fear Of God?

*T*he fear of God can be described as a godly emotion, a feeling of reverence, awe and respect toward the Almighty God.[1] This entails acknowledging God for who He is and giving Him the place that is due Him in everything.

In Isaiah 11:1-2, we read:

> There shall come forth a Rod from the stem of Jesse, and a Branch shall grow out of his roots. The Spirit of the LORD shall rest upon Him, the Spirit of wisdom and understanding, the Spirit of counsel and might, the Spirit of knowledge and of the fear of the LORD.

Here we see one of the prophecies about the coming of our Lord Jesus Christ stating that the Holy Spirit would come upon Him. In addition to being the Spirit of wisdom, understanding, counsel, might and knowledge, the Holy Spirit is also referred to as the Spirit of the fear of the

---

1 Hayford's Bible Handbook. Jack W. Hayford (Editor) 1995, Thomas Nelson Publishers. Nashville, Tennessee, USA. p. 610.

THE FEAR OF GOD

LORD.

The same Holy Spirit also equips Christians to live like Christ did, to do God's will. Romans chapter 8:13-14 tells us that being Spirit-led equates to being sons of God: "For if you live according to the flesh you will die; but if by the Spirit you put to death the deeds of the body, you will live. For as many as are led by the Spirit of God, these are the sons of God.' For the purpose of this book, the fear of God and the fear of the LORD are used interchangeably with the intention of conveying the same meaning.

In the Holy Bible, God is referred to as "the fear of Isaac." In Genesis 31:42, as part of his address to Laban, Jacob said, "Unless the God of my father, the God of Abraham and the Fear of Isaac, had been with me, surely now you would have sent me away empty-handed. God has seen my affliction and the labour of my hands, and rebuked you last night."

Again, in verse 53, Jacob concluded his speech, saying, "The God of Abraham, the God of Nahor, and the God of their father judge between us." And Jacob swore by the Fear of his father Isaac.'

To elucidate this phrase, it would be worthwhile exploring the origin of **Isaac**, the circumstances of his arrival on planet earth. Isaac was the child born to Abraham and his wife Sarah in their old age. God had visited Abram (as he was initially called) and promised that he would have a son from his legitimate wife then called Sarai.

The LORD spoke to Abram in a vision affirming His commitment to him saying, "Do not be afraid, Abram. I am your shield, your exceedingly great reward" (Genesis

15:1).

Abram's reply implied dissatisfaction with the circumstances in which he found himself since leaving his homeland and his father's household. Being very rich in livestock, silver and gold (Genesis 13:2) he had acquired a lot of wealth, but his response portrayed a lack of appreciation of his wealth since the circumstances indicated he was going to leave it all to one who was not of his blood descent.

Abram said in response to God's offer, "Lord GOD, what will You give me, seeing I go childless, and the heir of my house is Eliezer of Damascus?" – Genesis 15:2. His use of the term 'Lord GOD' to address the Almighty implied an acknowledgement that He is sovereign and capable of doing anything.

But the Lord knew these facts better than Abram himself. He goes on to tell God what He already knew, "Look, You have given me no offspring; indeed one born in my house is my heir!" – Genesis 15:3.

Without openly asking God for a child, Abram pointed out that this situation was not satisfactory and that God in blessing him seemed to have overlooked that very important detail. God then lets him in on His plan. His heir was not whom he thought it would be. No, his heir would rather come from his own body, innumerable, just like the stars. Abram believed in the LORD, and He accounted it to Him for righteousness (Genesis 15:6).

In Chapter 16 of Genesis, Sarai, who had being childless, convinces Abram to have a child with Hagar, her handmaid. After a turbulent time of some family strife that accompanied the resultant pregnancy, Hagar had a son whom she called Ishmael according to the instructions from the Angel of the LORD. Abram was 86 years old at this time.

As the narrative continues, thirteen years later, God steps in again. He gives Abram a new name – Abraham, promising to multiply him exceedingly into kings that will extend to endless generations.

At this point, God also formalises their relationship with an everlasting covenant, marked with circumcision of all male members of his family. Abraham seemed happy with the plan until God mentioned Sarai. In Abram's mind, you could say… 'been there, done that, not going to work!!'

God changed Sarai's name to Sarah – mother of nations, promising that she would have a son for Abraham and that kings of peoples were to come from her. Abraham had a secret laugh at this point. His assessment of the situation was that having a son at the age of 86 was something extra-ordinary, but to have one at a hundred, born by a ninety year old woman – that seemed a bit too far-fetched.

Both Abraham and Sarah were well advanced in age and in Abram's words, which he said in his heart (Genesis 17:17) - "Shall a child be born to a man who is one hundred years old? And shall Sarah who is ninety years old bear a child?"

His reply essentially told God that this miracle was not even necessary. A bird in hand is worth ten in the woods one might say. "Oh, that Ishmael might live before You!" he said to God (Genesis 17:18). But the Almighty had His own plans that He gently affirmed to Abraham in Genesis

17:19-21:

> "No, Sarah your wife shall bear you a son, and
> you shall call his name Isaac; I will establish My
> covenant with him for an everlasting covenant, and
> with his descendants after him. As for Ishmael, I
> have heard you. Behold, I have blessed him, and
> will make him fruitful, and will multiply him
> exceedingly. He shall beget twelve princes, and I
> will make him a great nation. But my covenant I
> will establish with Isaac, whom Sarah shall bear to
> you at this set time next year."

When God returned to Abraham, Sarah's response also showed that she had become satisfied or at least accepted that Abraham's heir would be Ishmael. Like Abraham, she also laughed at the prospect saying within herself, "After I have grown old, shall I have pleasure, my lord being old also?" - Genesis 18:12.

From the foregoing, it is easy to arrive at the conclusion that Isaac's arrival was not because of his parents' desire for a child; that desire had gone, as they settled for what they had. They did not ask God for him, but he was in God's plan from the beginning and was only going to come at God's timing.

His origin had no reason except that God wanted him to be there, chose him to be the carrier of His covenant with Abraham. When his older brother Ishmael made fun of him, scoffing (Genesis 21:9), Sarah was instrumental to the removal of his brother from the household, giving Isaac an environment in which to flourish. He had his father's sole attention, being raised up to take over the estate that God had given Abraham.

Then another turn of events, God lays claim on Isaac. He requested of Abraham to sacrifice Isaac. Reasons were not given to Abraham why this turn of events was necessary. God declared that Isaac belonged to Him even though He had given him to Abraham in fulfillment of His own promise. At this point, Ishmael was away from home, his whereabouts unknown to Abraham.

In fact, so far was he gone from Abraham's life that when God spoke to him, he said, "Take now your son, your only son Isaac, whom you love, and go to the land of Moriah, and offer him there as a burnt offering on one of the mountains of which I shall tell you" (Genesis 22:2).

Abraham obeyed God and Isaac encountered an unusual situation. The fire – check; the wood – check; the lamb ... question time!! "Look, the fire and the wood, but where is the lamb for a burnt offering?" he asked his father Abraham who calmly replied, "God will provide for Himself the lamb for a burnt offering" (Genesis 22:7b-8).

Then they arrive at God's chosen place for the offering. Isaac watches Abraham build an altar and observes the arrangement of the wood in order; perhaps he even helps set up the altar, then .... stop for a minute here and put yourself in Isaac's position. This man was his own father, married to his mother. His legitimacy was not in question. His father's love for him was unquestionable.

In fact, a big party was thrown earlier to celebrate his progress. The Holy Bible does not tell us how old Isaac was at this point but certainly old enough to carry the wood for the burnt offering, old enough to have observed the family's previous sacrifices, and notice that the supposed lamb for the offering was absent on this occasion.

I don't imagine that Abraham would have told him that God had demanded he be sacrificed. So, for reasons unknown to Isaac, he was bound by his father and laid down on the altar upon the wood where the lamb should have been. He must have seen exactly what happened to the lamb in previous offerings, from selection to slaughter to roasting and the portion that was eaten by the family.

I don't know about you but I find it hard to imagine, my mind cannot even conjure up an imitation of what Isaac could have experienced at that time. There was no dialogue involved here.

No one asked his opinion whether it was alright with him for this to go ahead. No explanation that we are told of was given to him before hand, but as the story is reported, one can imagine that he eventually got to find out that God had asked for him to be put on the altar.

I wonder why he did not ask a further question, like, "Why are you tying me up and putting me on the wood? Are you alright, father? Did God fail to provide the lamb? Will I see you again? Will you cut up my body, will it hurt? My mind is full of questions at the moment but we are not told of any such utterance or resistance from Isaac.

The movies made from this Bible story often show Isaac's eyes covered with a blindfold. The fact that he was "bound" implies his hands and feet were tied together. If his eyes were open, he would have seen Abraham's arm raised with the knife in it to slay him.

THE FEAR OF GOD

Up until this point, he would have been receiving instructions from his father as the heir, on how to look after the estate in preparation for when the time came that his father was unable to do so himself. 'What went wrong?' he must have thought. Had he done something so terrible as to completely disqualify him even though his father had no other son? At this point, he was as good as dead, at the mercy or non-mercy of his own father who loved him.

Then, yet another turn of events – the Angel of the LORD called out to Abraham from heaven, "Do not lay your hand on the lad, or do anything to him; for now I know that you fear God, since you have not withheld your son, your only son, from Me" (Genesis 22:12).

This is God's description of the fear of God: a heart that gives Him first place and withholds nothing from Him. Isaac watched as his father untied him; took him off the altar, took a ram from the nearby bush and offered it for a burnt offering instead. God did provide after all, but Isaac had no idea about the coming provision of the ram while he was on the altar.

The Bible does not say anything about Isaac's response to this experience except to say that his son Jacob referred to God as "the fear of my father Isaac" – Genesis 31:42 and 53. It is noteworthy that there is no record of Isaac being afraid of Abraham. I can imagine that the relationship took a new angle as Isaac found out that his father's love for him was subject to the fear of God in Abraham.

Some of the lessons from this account are discussed below:
• God was the source, the sole proposer and

originator of Isaac's very being.
- He allowed the environment to favour
  Isaac's development.
- God was in control of Isaac's continuing existence,
  even those who loved him could not stand against
  God accomplishing His desire upon Isaac.
- Isaac's future only had meaning with reference
  to God, he only had what God permitted him to have.

A life that embraces the fear of God is one that embraces these principles. If we could see ourselves in this light, we would have less cause for concerns about everyday life. We would do well to acknowledge the role of God Almighty in these four aspects concerning our own lives.

Nobody but God alone has given us all we have – life, intelligence, health, power and indeed every ability. We owe our abilities to nobody else but Him alone. No one else deserves first place honour, attention and awe but God Almighty.

He instructed Isaiah in these words – "Do not say, 'A conspiracy,' concerning all that this people call a conspiracy, nor be afraid of their threats, nor be troubled. The LORD of hosts, Him you shall hallow; let Him be your fear and let Him be your dread." (Isaiah 8:12 -13)

As was the case with Isaac, God should be our fear. We should look to God for all that comes to us from those we relate to and from all issues in life. I often wonder about myself and the fear of God. The Bible commands that we love Him with all our heart, with all our soul, with all our strength (Deuteronomy 6:5).

THE FEAR OF GOD

The fear of God demands our all to be subject to Him. Abraham had riches but yearned for a son for many years. Then when he got Isaac, he valued him so much. Yet when God asked for Isaac, he obliged without murmuring or grumbling. This obedience required of Abraham to give God prime position in his heart, soul and strength.

If this be the fear of God, I need to do some work on my attitude to the things that God has given me; many of the things I resist to yield to God are not even of so much value. To give up few hours of sleep to wait on Him on behalf of another; to give up some comfort in other to minister His love and grace to another; the list goes on and on. Things I do not even consider doing because my heart just turns away from the sacrifice involved.

Ponder Time

Pause – your turn: how are you doing with giving God and His will prime position in your heart, soul and strength?

The LORD's grace is sufficient and as He instructs me even at this very moment, I can look forward to yielding to Him what He has given me so that I can bless Him in the way I live and through blessing those around me.

Yes Abraham valued Isaac but God valued Isaac even more. In our everyday life, we should pray that the person in authority over us has the fear of God as the determinant of the threshold for their decisions and actions.

We need to constantly pray for this to be the case for those that the LORD has placed around us to be our 'helpers,' whether they are in our immediate vicinity, for example, spouses, friends, children, work colleagues, supervisors, teachers, pastors, and mentors; or people far from us such as government officials and leaders of nations who make decisions and formulate laws that affect our lives directly or indirectly.

One can see from the experience of Adam and Eve that the enemy, Satan, went to the one who was sent to Adam to be his 'help' – Genesis 2:18. Satan tried same tactics by trying to go through the helpers of our Lord Jesus, particularly through Peter, to suggest that He turn away from the agony of the cross.

Concluding his exposition on wisdom, the writer of the book of Ecclesiastes wrote in the thirteenth verse of the twelfth chapter – 'Let us hear the conclusion of the whole matter: Fear God and keep His commandments, for this is man's all.' My observation is that even among Christians today, God's commandments are treated like 'suggestions' that one can choose to obey, modify, edit or completely ignore.

I recall listening to a teaching along same line of thought by renowned Bible teacher **Pastor John Hagee** sometime ago. One of the great things about the commandments of God is that they are like a manual for having a good life, in them one can see that God meant them to bless us and not to cause pain or problems; they are essentially for our own good.

However, the short-sightedness that has plagued

man from the very start - considering the life and fall of Adam and Eve, continues to pose a significant problem. Commandment is not a commonly used term I must say. In the military, where similar terms are used, one can see that a soldier knows to obey the commander's last command even at the risk of losing his own life.

God deserves that we give due respect to His word even, and especially, when it does not make sense to us. God desires an undiluted uncontaminated regard for whom He is. The passage in 2 Kings 17:33-41 gives some insight into this and interestingly reflects practices observed across the nations today:

> They feared the LORD, yet served their own gods—according to the rituals of the nations from among whom they were carried away. To this day they continue practising the former rituals; they do not fear the LORD, nor do they follow their statutes or their ordinances, or the law and commandment which the LORD had commanded the children of Jacob, whom He named Israel, with whom the LORD had made a covenant and charged them, saying: "You shall not fear other gods, nor bow down to them nor serve them nor sacrifice to them; but the LORD, who brought you up from the land of Egypt with great power and an outstretched arm, Him you shall fear, Him you shall worship, and to Him you shall offer sacrifice. And the statutes, the ordinances, the law, and the commandment which He wrote for you, you shall be careful to observe forever; you shall not fear

other gods. And the covenant that I have made with you, you shall not forget, nor shall you fear other gods. But the LORD your God you shall fear; and He will deliver you from the hand of all your enemies." However they did not obey, but they followed their former rituals. So these nations feared the LORD, yet served their carved images; also their children and their children's children have continued doing as their fathers did, even to this day.

One may not appreciate the immediate or long-term consequence of not doing things according to God's specifications and instructions.

When the people of Israel went to get the Ark of God from Abinadab's house, they set it on a new cart driven by Uzzah and Ahio, sons of Abinadab. When the oxen stumbled, Uzzah reached out and held the Ark of God. This roused the anger of God and He struck him dead. Following this, the Bible reports that King David was afraid of the LORD that day; and he said, "How can the ark of the LORD come to me?" - 2 Samuel 6:9.

They were forced to give the LORD His due place and regard. King David acknowledged that moving or relocating the Ark of God was not a small issue; it required that appropriate care be taken and the LORD's terms and conditions be adhered to.

Equally, living according to the fear of God demands that He is given due regard and respect, that attitudes and actions are tempered to live according to His ways and desires. As we read the above account, one considers: these days, immediate judgment - at least in the natural sense - does not appear to follow sin; yet it shall be well with those who fear the LORD.

On the other hand the Holy Bible teaches that the ultimate outcome for those who choose not to fear the LORD is eternity in hell as it carries the risk of spiralling down a path that turns away from salvation through Christ Jesus. Now, that is not at all to be ignored. I perceive that in reality, many Christians live, or desire to live, by the fear of God but do not grasp its meaning. Consequently, they do not ask the LORD for it or embrace it whole-heartedly.

Living by the fear of God should be a way of life for the Christian - a twenty-four-seven (24/7) issue; and not something one practises when suitable. In Jonah 1:9-10, Jonah identified himself saying, "I am a Hebrew; and I fear the LORD, the God of heaven, who made the sea and the dry land."

The implication of the statement is that, being a Hebrew, he should fear the LORD or give Him prime position in his life. The other people on the ship with Jonah gave due regards to their gods; and so, could be said to 'fear' those gods.

Essentially, Jonah was saying that if the seas were calm or rough, it was up to his God who made them. The men were afraid; they believed what Jonah said about his God. 'Why have you done this?' - they asked him. It was as if they were saying, 'If you knew your God to be as you have said, why have you tried to run from His assignment? You should have known better.'

It would appear that Jonah had an awareness of the fear of God. It may even have been his tool for deciding how he lived his life on an average day but the challenges posed by his attitude towards the people of Nineveh got the better of him.

What This Fear Of God Is Not

In Exodus chapter 20, we read that as the LORD prepared to meet with Israel, He descended on Mount Sinai which became covered in smoke. The smoke ascended like the smoke of a furnace and the whole mountain quaked greatly. There were thunderings and lightnings and loud trumpet sounds. The people were afraid; they trembled and stood afar off (Exodus 20:18).

This is not the fear of God that the Spirit of God births and develops in His children; it certainly is not what God our Father wants. He does not want us to have a fear that drives us away from Him.

In Exodus 20:20 we read: And Moses said to the people, "Do not fear for God has come to test you, and that His fear may be before you, so that you may not sin." The latter is the real purpose of the fear of God - that one may not sin or live contrary to God's ways. Compare this with the situation of Adam and Eve.

In Genesis 3:10, Adam replied God from where himself and Eve were hiding from His presence, "I heard Your voice in the garden, and I was afraid because I was naked; and I hid myself." The fear of God on the other hand should draw us to God rather than away from Him. It is noteworthy that this ungodly fear was first mentioned after the fall of man.

THE FEAR OF GOD

The New Oxford American Dictionary describes fear, in its noun form, as an unpleasant emotion caused by the belief that someone or something is dangerous, likely to cause pain, or a threat. Fear as an emotion should not be allowed to oppress or dominate the Christian life.

Romans chapter 8 verse 15 puts it this way, 'For you did not receive the spirit of bondage again to fear, but you received the Spirit of adoption by whom we cry out, "Abba, Father." ' Note the difference, the spirit of bondage to fear is written in lower case letter in the Bible version to differentiate it from the Spirit of adoption written in upper case letter.

Healthy fear keeps one from harm in everyday living. For example, fire burns – get away from it! The horse is made fearless, a character that makes it suitable to be used for battle – it does not care if it dies in it. Job 39:19-25 reads:

> Have you given the horse strength? Have you clothed his neck with thunder? Can you frighten him like a locust? His majestic snorting strikes terror. He paws in the valley, and rejoices in his strength; he gallops into the clash of arms. He mocks at fear, and is not frightened; nor does he turn back from the sword. The quiver rattles against him, the glittering spear and javelin. He devours the distance with fierceness and rage; nor does he come to a halt because the trumpet has sounded. At the blast of the trumpet he says, 'Aha!' He smells the battle from afar, the thunder of captains and shouting.

To be effective in battle, we must master the unhealthy ungodly fear so that our advance in battle is not hindered by it. Thank God that He saves us from our fears. Psalm 34:4 states, 'I sought the LORD, and He heard me, and delivered me from all my fears.' It is not God's purpose that we should have a fear that torments. All unhealthy ungodly fears are to be given over to God to deliver us from them.

Fear given to us by God therefore ought to drive us to God and not from Him. He is the answer to ungodly fear. Personally, I found in my faith journey, the closer I am to God, the less fearful I am of issues and circumstances I encounter as part of daily living.

The Bible speaks of the nations fearing God as they see His blessings on His people. In Psalm 67:7 we read, 'God shall bless us, and all the ends of the earth shall fear Him.' Essentially this passage implies that the nations have to acknowledge that our God is, and give Him due regard; that He is mighty as they see His work manifest in our lives.

In Deuteronomy 2:25, God said to Israel as they began to possess the land of other nations, 'This day I will begin to put the dread and fear of you upon the nations under the whole heaven, who shall hear the report of you, and shall tremble and be in anguish because of you.' This sort of fear is involuntary, like the fear and trembling of the enemy, not out of his choice.

Again, this is not what we are discussing in this book; rather, the focus is on the fear of God that is mediated by the Holy Spirit. The fear of God imparted by His Holy Spirit has to be chosen and yielded to. It develops as we

17

yield to Him and let Him lead us into all truth as we get to know God better, a process which continues beyond our earthly journey.

In 2 Chronicles 14:2, the Bible records that Asa, King of Judah did what was good and right in the eyes of the LORD his God. Reading further in 2 Chronicles 14:14, we find that at war, King Asa and his army 'defeated all the cities around Gerar, for the fear of the LORD came upon them; and they plundered all the cities, for there was exceedingly much spoil in them.' For the enemies of God or enemies of God's people, an encounter with the fear of the LORD and His power brings a sense of defeat as they see themselves as no match for Him.

In the absence of the Holy Spirit, this sort of fear is a weapon of warfare that God uses against His enemies. This is different from what we are discussing here as the focus is on its effect on those who acknowledge Him as Lord and embrace the fear of God.

Similarly, in 2 Chronicles 20, we read that during the reign of Jehoshaphat king of Judah, the fear of the LORD was on all the kingdoms of those countries when they heard that the LORD had fought against the enemies of Israel.

When the people of Ammon, Moab and Mount Seir came against Israel in battle, King Jehoshaphat called a fast across the nation. They cried to the Lord who responded by saying in verse 15b, "Do not be afraid nor dismayed because of this great multitude, for the battle is not yours, but God's." They were not to take God's place by fighting the battle themselves.

Thereafter, the Lord made Israel's enemies to destroy

themselves and the result recorded in verses 29-30:

> And the fear of God was on all the kingdoms of
> those countries when they heard that the LORD
> had fought against the enemies of Israel. Then the
> realm of Jehoshaphat was quiet, for his God gave
> him rest all around.

Hearing what God had done brought the fear of God on
the kingdoms – they acknowledged who the God of Israel
is and because they were on the opposing side, they knew
what it meant for them.

The situation is different for the one who is on the
LORD's side. Amen. Reminding Timothy of his inheritance,
being part of a family of faith-filled people in generations
before him, Paul encouraged him to stir up the gift of God
in him which he had received following the laying on of
Paul's hands.

He further advised Timothy to do away with the fear
that was hindering this - 'For God has not given us a spirit
of fear, but of power and of love and of a sound mind' (2
Timothy 1:7). This spirit of fear does not however refer to
the fear of God, which the Holy Spirit imparts, which we
have seen repeatedly referred to as an indispensable part of
Christian living.

The fear of God we are discussing in this book can be
seen to be more like a virtue or akin to the gifts of the Holy
Spirit discussed in the twelfth chapter of 1 Corinthians.
While the Holy Spirit imparts these gifts to the children
of God as He sees fit; Paul the apostle encourages that one
earnestly desire these gifts - 1 Corinthians 12:31.

THE FEAR OF GOD

Similarly, the fear of God can be imparted by the Holy Spirit and increasingly developed as He leads us into all truth. Equally, one should actively seek after and embrace a life that is ordered according to the fear of God. Moreover, a revelation of the love of God, which is also given by the Holy Spirit, drives away ungodly fear but develops the fear of God.

First John chapter 4 verses 17-19, which gives a detailed analysis of this, states that:

> Love has been perfected among us in this: that we may have boldness in the day of judgment; because as He is, so are we in this world. There is no fear in love; but perfect love casts out fear, because fear involves torment. But he who fears has not been made perfect in love. We love Him because He first loved us.

The fear that torments we are told, is eliminated as God's love is perfected in us. This is something that happens as we mature in Him. Just like we have not been perfected in other aspects of our Christian living, we have not been perfected in the love that drives away the tormenting fear.

Again, the fear of God we are talking about here develops, not diminishes, as one grows or increases in the knowledge of who He is. It is definitely not a tormenting fear either. Certainly as I have drawn closer to the LORD, I can testify that His love has grown in me and given me the confidence that His forgiveness of my sins through Christ Jesus has saved me from His wrath.

The Bible says in Ephesians 2:3b - 9:

We …were by nature children of wrath, just as the others. But God, who is rich in mercy, because of his great love with which He loved us, even when we were dead in trespasses, made us alive together with Christ (by grace you have been saved), and raised us up together, and made us sit together in the heavenly places in Christ Jesus, that in the ages to come He might show the exceeding riches of His grace in His kindness toward us in Christ Jesus. For by grace you have been saved through faith, and that not of yourselves; it is the gift of God, not of works, lest anyone should boast.

Have you heard a person comment that the discipline received from a parent or teacher for example, though not pleasant at the time, had actually helped them to turn out better? To examine this issue further, let us read some passages on the love of God. 1 John 3:16 says, 'By this we know love, because He laid down His life for us. And we also ought to lay down our lives for the brethren.'

First John chapter 4 verses 9-10 reads, 'In this the love of God was manifested toward us, that God has sent His only begotten Son into the world, that we might live through Him. In this is love, not that we loved God, but that He loved us and sent His Son to be the propitiation for our sins.'

Also, in John 3:16 our Lord Jesus says, 'For God so loved the world that He gave His only begotten Son, that whoever believes in Him should not perish but have everlasting life.' God's love led to the death of His Son

THE FEAR OF GOD

Jesus to procure salvation for those who would believe and follow His ways with the promise of spending eternity with Him and not in hell.

Second Peter chapter 3:9 adds that, 'The Lord is not slack concerning His promise, as some count slackness, but is longsuffering toward us, not willing that any should perish but that all should come to repentance.' However, much as I do not like the sound of it, many people loved by God are dying and going to hell without God. The fear of God, like the cross of Jesus, is another of God's tools aimed at stopping man from ending up in hell.

In Biblical days, the state of the fig tree was used to ascertain seasonal changes. In Luke 21:29-30, explaining the times and events surrounding His return to earth, Jesus Christ used the fig tree to illustrate His point: "When they are already budding, you see and know for yourselves that summer is now near."

In Genesis 3:7 the season of humanity changed when Adam and Eve ate the fruit, which the LORD forbade them to eat. To mark this new season, they sewed fig leaves for covering their newly discovered nakedness. In verse 10, when God called Adam, he replied, "I heard Your voice in the garden, and I was afraid because I was naked; and I hid myself."

Sin brought about the kind of fear that makes man to run away from God. By dying on the cross, Jesus Christ restores our place with God, doing away with sin and all its accompaniments, including fear.

Living out God's blessings can only be achieved through Jesus and only those who are specially blessed and privileged get to discover this mystery. Yes, that is the truth. In Colossians 1:27 we read, 'To them God willed to make known what are the riches of the glory of this mystery among the Gentiles: which is Christ in you, the hope of glory.'

In his letter to the Galatians, Paul the apostle put it in yet another way, 'I have been crucified with Christ; it is no longer I who live, but Christ lives in me; and the life which I now live in the flesh I live by faith in the Son of God, who loved me and gave Himself for me' – Galatians 2:20.

Clothing one's self with the Lord Jesus is the sure way to living a victorious life: 'But put on the Lord Jesus Christ, and make no provision for the flesh, to fulfil its lusts' - Romans 13:14.

The salvation package of God to restore man to fellowship with Himself eternally is packaged in the Lord Jesus. In Acts 4:12 we read, "Nor is there salvation in any other, for there is no other name under heaven given among men by which we must be saved."

The man in Matthew 25:24-25, who received a talent from his master said, 'Lord I knew you to be a hard man, reaping where you have not sown, and gathering where you have not scattered seed. And I was afraid, and went and hid your talent in the ground. Look, there you have what is yours.'

It is clear from this servant's words that he had little if any reverence for his master. He essentially called his master a thief in saying that he gathered where he had not scattered – thereby taking what rightfully belonged to another. He said he was afraid – of what?

THE FEAR OF GOD

Afraid of doing what his master would have him do at the expense of displeasing himself which would have led to his master's goods prospering in his hands. He sounded as though he would be displeased to see his master benefit from the talent that was put in his care.

In response to his account, his master is reported to have called him 'wicked and lazy' sentencing him to the outer darkness where there would be weeping and gnashing of teeth. What we have just explored in that story is not a godly fear.

Just as Satan twisted God's word and added a false perspective, which led to the first sin in the Garden of Eden, he may present a twisted version of the fear of God for his purpose, which is the opposite of the purpose of the fear of God administered by the Holy Spirit.

It is not God's intention to draw man away from Himself; rather, to draw man to God. The word of God teaches in Romans 8:15-17 that:

> For you did not receive the spirit of bondage again to fear, but you received the Spirit of adoption by whom we cry out, "Abba, Father." The Spirit Himself bears witness with our spirit that we are children of God, and if children, then heirs – heirs of God and joint heirs with Christ, if indeed we suffer with Him, that we may also be glorified together.

Addressing the Israelites in Exodus 20:20, Moses advised them, "Do not fear; for God has come to test you, and that His fear may be before you, so that you may not sin." It seems almost like a contradiction but here Moses explains that the fear of God is to keep the people loyal to Him and not to frighten them away from Him.

Again, in Matthew 14:27 when the disciples became afraid on seeing the Lord Jesus walking on the sea, He dissuaded them from being afraid saying, "Be of good cheer! It is I; do not be afraid." In Isaiah 41 the LORD repeatedly told Israel that His presence with them should remove fear as He would help and strengthen them.

In Luke 8:22-25 we read of when, having told His disciples to cross over by boat to the other side of the lake, Jesus fell asleep on the journey. When the disciples felt jeopardised by a fierce wind storm, they woke Him up saying, "Master, Master, we are perishing!" He rebuked the storm and asked where there faith was.

In verse 25 we read, 'And they were afraid and marvelled, saying, "Who can this be? For He commands even the winds and water, and they obey Him!"' Having a limited knowledge and understanding of who God is breeds the wrong or unhealthy form of fear towards Him.

Should A Christian Have The Fear Of God?

Our Lord Jesus Himself had the fear of God endowed upon Him by the Holy Spirit as seen previously in Isaiah 11:1-2. In reality, every person who has the Spirit of God in him or her, has the fear of God as this is one of His attributes.

The question, 'Should a Christian have the fear of God?' then comes close to asking 'Should a Christian have or live by the Holy Spirit?' It follows then that a Spirit-filled

Christian cannot really say he or she does not have the fear of God.

If one were averse to the fear of God, that person would have to ask the Holy Spirit to leave his or her being, a dangerous thought. However, just as we are encouraged to ask God for wisdom, an attribute of the Holy Spirit, if we feel deficient in that area (James 1:5), we should also ask Him for the development of the fear of God to maximally benefit from this equally important attribute of His Holy Spirit.

Reading further in verse 3 of the same chapter we see that our Lord Jesus Christ took delight in the fear of the LORD. I was sharing the Word of God on the Fear of God at a Christian meeting sometime ago and asked if anyone had ever asked God for the gift or impartation of the fear of God in prayer.

Out of about ten adults, one person said that he had done so at some point in his journey of faith. It takes a good appreciation of what the fear of God is and our deep need for it to be able to take delight in it or ask the Father to endow us with it. I believe that through this book, the LORD wants to give His people insight into this subject.

Like other attributes of the Holy Spirit, He is the best teacher on the subject of the fear of God; and, He will lead you into the deeper truths about it if you open yourself to His instruction.

If you my reader have never asked the Father to develop the fear of God in you, read on and, hopefully before you get to the end of this book, I hope that you will earnestly desire it enough to seriously contemplate doing so.

Talking about the experiences of our Lord Jesus Christ on earth, the writer of Hebrews stated:

> ..who, in the days of His flesh, when He had offered up prayers and supplications, with vehement cries and tears to Him who was able to save Him from death, and was heard because of His godly fear, though He was a Son, yet He learned obedience by the things which He suffered - Hebrews 5:7-8.

God's children are encouraged to develop the fear of God. Psalm 22:23-24 encourages us:

> You who fear the LORD, praise Him! All you descendants of Jacob, glorify Him, and fear Him, all you offspring of Israel! For He has not despised nor abhorred the affliction of the afflicted; nor has He hidden His face from Him; but when He cried to Him, He heard.

In Psalm 34:11, the LORD gives this open invitation, "Come, you children, listen to me; I will teach you the fear of the LORD." This implies that the fear of God can be learnt from His Spirit when we submit ourselves to His instruction. Every child of God is encouraged to avail him or her self of this.

In Deuteronomy 4:10 Moses reminds Israel of the day they stood before the LORD at Mount Horeb when the LORD said, 'Gather the people to Me, and I will let them hear My words, that they may learn to fear Me all the days they live on the earth, and that they may teach their children.' Again, this affirms that the children of God are called to learn to 'fear' Him, just like one would learn to live the life He has called us to live in many other respects.

The fear of God was among the criteria for choosing leaders of God's people. When the wall of Jerusalem was being rebuilt, Nehemiah appointed people who had the fear of God to do the job.

'Then it was, when the wall was built and I had hung the doors, when the gatekeepers, the singers, and the Levites had been appointed, that I gave the charge of Jerusalem to my brother Hanani, and Hananiah the leader of the citadel, for he was a faithful man and feared God more than many' - Nehemiah 7:1-2.

This suggests that as one grows in grace, love, patience and the other aspects of the fruit of the Spirit, one would be expected to grow in the expression of the fear of God. Hence, the term 'feared God more than many' is used to represent someone whose life expressed this more than others.

Jesus lived a life of godly fear; He is an example for us to follow and emulate. It is right to conclude that the fear of God should be sought after and be a delight of every Christian; that is, one who has willingly relinquished the authority over his or her life to Jesus Christ, making Him Lord over himself and committed to following in His footsteps.

In 1 Peter 1:17-19, encouraging Christians to embrace godly conduct, the apostle Peter wrote:

> And if you call on the Father, who without partiality judges according to each one's work, conduct

yourselves throughout the time of your stay here in fear; knowing that you were not redeemed with corruptible things, like silver or gold, from your aimless conduct received by tradition from your fathers, but with the precious blood of Christ, as of a lamb without blemish and without spot.

This instruction is specifically directed towards those who already believe in God. 1 Peter 2:17 also encourages us to 'Honour all people. Love the brotherhood. Fear God. Honour the king.'

In 2 Corinthians 7:1, recounting the covenant blessings of God to the Corinthians, Paul continues in saying, "Therefore, having these promises, beloved, let us cleanse ourselves from all filthiness of the flesh and spirit, perfecting holiness in the fear of God."

The fear of God here is being portrayed as a tool for perfecting holiness. In James 2:19-20 we are given a warning: "You believe that there is one God. You do well. Even the demons believe – and tremble! But do you want to know, O foolish man, that faith without works is dead?" In encouraging believers to live out their faith through their works or actions,

James drew attention to the fact that the demons also believe not just in God, but in one God; and even tremble, though they chose to be defiant to His rule and authority. It would appear then that to believe alone is not enough, and one ought to go beyond that to pursue the perfection of our holiness through living by the fear of God.

This is especially important even as the Bible warns that

without holiness no one will see the Lord (Hebrews 12:14). Furthermore, persisting wilfully in sin leads to eternal death in hell – see 1 Corinthians 6:9-10; Galatians 5:19-21; Ephesians 5:5-7.

Our Lord Jesus rounds up this discussion in Revelations 22:13-15:

> I am the Alpha and the Omega, the Beginning and the End, the First and the Last." Blessed are those who do His commandments, that they may have the right to the tree of life, and may enter through the gates into the city. But outside are dogs and sorcerers and sexually immoral and murderers and idolaters, and whoever loves and practices a lie.

Note the Lord says whoever "loves and practices," a lie, hence they have not accidentally or through weakness fallen into sin, but have chosen to love the sin. In Romans 11:20-22, Paul in addressing the Gentiles reminds them of the condition of the Jews:

> Because of unbelief they were broken off, and you stand in faith. Do not be haughty, but fear. For if God did not spare the natural branches, He may not spare you either. Therefore consider the goodness and severity of God: on those who fell, severity; but toward you, goodness, if you continue in His goodness. Otherwise you also will be cut off.

Again, note the qualifying phrase – 'if you continue.' Before going on, let us take a look at Jude verse 24, 'Now to Him who is able to keep you from stumbling, and to present you faultless before the presence of His glory with exceeding joy.' This passage refocuses us on God as the One we should look to whose strength will preserve those who are earnest in their faith in Jesus Christ.

Ponder Time

What is the opinion of heaven on the fear of God?

Heaven speaks of the fear of God. In Revelation 15:3-4 the apostle John wrote of a revelation of heaven where those who were victorious over the beast sang the song of Moses, which he also referred to as the song of the Lamb:

> "Great and marvellous are Your works, Lord God Almighty! Just and true are Your ways, O King of the saints! Who shall not fear You, O Lord, and glorify Your name? For You alone are holy. For all nations shall come and worship before You, for Your judgments have been manifested."

Revelations 14:6-7 speaks of an angel preaching the fear of God to those on the earth:

> Then I saw another angel flying in the midst of heaven, having the everlasting gospel to preach to those who dwell on the earth—to every nation, tribe, tongue, and people—saying with a loud

voice, "Fear God and give glory to Him, for the hour of His judgment has come; and worship Him who made heaven and earth, the sea and springs of water."

Again, in Revelation 19:5, in response to the worship rendered by the twenty-four elders and four living creatures, a voice came from the throne of God saying, "Praise our God, all you His servants and those who fear Him, both small and great!" This instruction, which was followed by the voice of the praise from a great multitude, did not appear to be directed to the people on earth; rather, to those in heaven.

He deserves to be honoured by the fear of God as the holy One above all. In agreement with the afore-going, Psalm 89:7 teaches that, 'God is greatly to be feared in the assembly of the saints, and to be held in reverence by all those around Him.'

As a manifestation of regard for who He is and submission to His authority, heaven could not be without the fear of God. This implies that the fear of God is also applicable in the life to come, for those who make it to heaven. It is reasonable to believe that heaven is the largest gathering of the saints of God though the assembly referred to in the passage seems to include His saints on earth who are sanctified in Christ Jesus (1 Corinthians 1:2).

I believe the fear of God originated from heaven as the Bible says – adherence to His will should be on earth as it is in heaven (Matthew 6:10). God's will, taught or revealed to us – is already established in heaven.

The passage above (Psalm 89:7), by saying, "all those around Him," seems to extend the requirement of the fear of God beyond the saints, perhaps to include His angels, elders, living creatures and the host of heaven. In addition, Psalm 15:4 says that the one who abides in the LORD's tabernacle is one who among other things, 'honours those who fear the LORD.'

The Almighty God also demonstrates His power among His people to reveal Himself to all and cultivate the fear of God in His people, so that they can give Him His rightful place and honour. Joshua 4:23-24 gives an example:

> "for the LORD your God dried up the waters of the Jordan before you until you had crossed over, as the LORD your God did to the Red Sea, which He dried up before us until we had crossed over, that all the peoples of the earth may know the hand of the LORD, that it is mighty, that you may fear the LORD your God forever."

He does the same today. Acknowledging Him as the source of our miracles, rather than attributing them to luck, chance, our strength or others, would strengthen the fear of God in our lives.

In addition, the fear of God is a tool given to His people to enable them walk in His ways. Rebuking the people for their bad conduct, Nehemiah encouraged them to rather walk in the fear of God: Then I said, "What you are doing is not good. Should you not walk in the fear of our God because of the reproach of the nations, our enemies?" - (Nehemiah 5:9).

THE FEAR OF GOD

In Psalm 119:120 the Psalmist wrote, 'My flesh trembles for fear of You, and I am afraid of Your judgments.' Something that makes the flesh tremble! That should be good for 'flesh-discipline.'

Fear is not a pleasant feeling, so we may not want to embrace it. In the current climate, one has increasingly observed the manifestation of the time written of in the scriptures when men's ears tune in to hear what they like to hear as prophesied in 2 Timothy 4:3-4, 'For the time will come when they will not endure sound doctrine, but according to their own desires, because they have itching ears, they will heap up for themselves teachers; and they will turn their ears away from the truth, and be turned aside to fables.'

It is easier to recognise false teaching when it comes from another person, but when your own heart twists the truth to excuse your weakness or the wickedness of your heart, that is more difficult to detect.

This is where we need the word of God to be the light to our path every moment, every day. I do not like what the LORD tells me sometimes; and, He knows and understands that. The foregoing does not mean that He would let me settle for less or compromise on the issue at hand.

I remember once hearing in my spirit an instruction to get up for prayers in early hours of the morning. I promptly rebuked the 'evil voice.' Later, the LORD gently led me to see that the enemy had nothing to gain from calling me into a time of focused prayer and seeking God's face. I could see the point then. Same question applies to the fear of God.

Ponder Time

Who stands to gain and who loses if you embrace the fear of God in your life?

Worth a thought; would you not agree? Undoubtedly, God blesses the life that embraces the fear of God, as we will see in greater details in later sections of this exploration.

What Did The Lord Jesus Christ Have To Say About The Fear Of God?

In Matthew 6:9-13 we read about how, having observed Jesus' prayer pattern, His disciples asked Him to instruct them accordingly. His response is what is now popularly referred to as the Lord's Prayer:

> In this manner, therefore, pray: Our Father in heaven, hallowed be Your name. Your kingdom come. Your will be done on earth as it is in heaven. Give us this day our daily bread. And forgive us our debts, as we forgive our debtors. And do not lead us into temptation, but deliver us from the evil one. For Yours is the kingdom and the power and the glory forever. Amen.

The entire prayer embraces the fear of God as He is given His due place in the life of the person saying the prayer, demonstrating one's willingness to hand over everything to His control and submit to His authority.

Similar to the pattern of the Ten Commandments,

acknowledgement of who God is and our relationship with Him is given first place as Jesus Christ opened the prayer with – Our Father in heaven. This is then followed by a desire to see His name hallowed.

This has to come before one can go on to ask to have His authority established over any situation as indicated in the subsequent phrase, 'Your kingdom come. Your will be done ..'

The Merriam-Webster dictionary describes the word 'hallowed' as holy, sacred, revered, consecrated. The Collins dictionary describes it as respect, to admire because it is old, important or has good reputation. The same word 'hallow' is used in another passage where God Almighty commands that we fear Him.

In Isaiah 8:13, the LORD's instruction states, "The LORD of hosts, Him you shall hallow; let Him be your fear, and let Him be your dread." In Leviticus 19:32 He gives this instruction, 'You shall rise before the grey headed and honour the presence of an old man, and fear your God: I am the LORD.' He commands it.

A teaching by our Lord Jesus Christ about the fear of God is recorded in Matthew 10:28, 'And do not fear those who kill the body but cannot kill the soul. But rather fear Him who is able to destroy both soul and body in hell.' This is also recorded in Luke 12:4-5. It is great to know that no other being, human or spirit, has been given the power to destroy the soul but God alone to whom one should look.

Also, in Psalm 22:23 we read, 'You who fear the LORD, praise Him! All you descendants of Jacob, glorify Him, and fear Him, all you offspring of Israel!' King Solomon is still reputed to have unequalled wisdom according to God's promise to him in 1 Kings 3:12b, "...see, I have given you a wise and understanding heart, so that there has not been anyone like you before you, nor shall any like you arise after you."

This wisdom is evident in Ecclesiastes 5:7 where King Solomon gave this advice: "For in the multitude of dreams and many words there is also vanity. But fear God." In Proverbs 23:17-18, he further advised, 'Do not let your heart envy sinners, but be zealous for the fear of the LORD all the day; for surely there is a hereafter, and your hope will not be cut off.'

Here, he takes it a step forward in mentioning God's promise of a reward beyond life here on earth with a hope that endures forever when we fear the LORD. In Ecclesiastes 12:13, at the end of the recording of his words of wisdom King Solomon concluded, 'Let us hear the conclusion of the whole matter: Fear God and keep His commandments, for this is man's all.' This implies that the entirety of God's purposes for mankind is wrapped up in the concept of the fear of God and obedience to His commandments. One must pay close attention to these.

King David who was acknowledged by God Himself as a man after His heart (1 Samuel 13:14; Acts 13:22), also taught the fear of God; declaring in Psalms 34:9, 'Oh, fear the LORD, you His saints! There is no want to those who fear Him.'

The saints are those who through faith have been sanctified in Christ Jesus – also today known as Christians as written in 1 Corinthians 1:2, 'To the church of God which is at Corinth, to those who are sanctified in Christ Jesus, called to be saints, with all who in every place call on the name of Jesus Christ our Lord, both theirs and ours.'

There is evidence that the early Church or first Christians lived by the fear of God. In Acts 9:31 we read, 'Then the churches throughout all Judea, Galilee, and Samaria had peace and were edified. And walking in the fear of the Lord and in the comfort of the Holy Spirit, they were multiplied.'

When we ask - 'where is the God of the Acts of the apostles?' - let us not forget the ways they honoured Him. Acts 10:1-2 gives a description of a man called Cornelius who honoured God: 'There was a certain man in Caesarea called Cornelius, a centurion of what was called the Italian Regiment, a devout man and one who feared God with all his household, who gave alms generously to the people, and prayed to God always.

In Acts 10:34b-35, Peter expressed his surprise that God would honour Cornelius and his household; he declared, "In truth I perceive that God shows no partiality. But in every nation whoever fears Him and works righteousness is accepted by Him." In yet another recording in a different setting, Peter also taught that one should: 'Honour all people. Love the brotherhood. Fear God. Honour the king' (1 Peter 2:17).

God Deserves It, He Delights In It

He formed us – He is the reason for our being – He gave us existence. There is no creature without a creator. Many refer to God as the uncreated Creator and the Bible indeed

38

records God's statement in Isaiah 43:10b – 'Before Me there was no God formed, nor shall there be after Me.' Therefore He earns the sole right of being the One to whom we owe allegiance.

Genesis 2:7 records how God created man from dust and by the breath of life from His nostrils, He made man a living being. In Isaiah 40:28 we read that the LORD is the everlasting God, the Creator of the ends of the earth who neither faints nor is weary and whose understanding is unsearchable.

In Malachi 2:10 we read, 'Have we not all one Father? Has not one God created us? Why do we deal treacherously with one another by profaning the covenant of the fathers?' In Isaiah 44, the LORD repeatedly states that He formed Israel and created all things.

In verse 21 He says, "Remember these, O Jacob, and Israel, for you are My servant; I have formed you, you are My servant; O Israel, you will not be forgotten by Me!"

In verse 24 He again says, "Thus says the LORD, your Redeemer, and He who formed you from the womb: I am the LORD, who makes all things, who stretches out the heavens all alone, who spreads abroad the earth by Myself."

King David in Psalm 139:13 put it this way – 'For You formed my inward parts; You covered me in my mother's womb.' This gave him the boldness to declare in the verse that followed – 'I will praise You, for I am fearfully and wonderfully made; marvellous are Your works, and that my soul knows very well.'

Interestingly, no one else has ever claimed to have

created the world. In spite of anti-Christian theories such as the evolution theory, the issue of creation is not claimed by or attributed to any other being. Satan is the main being who was noted to have challenged God and wanted to take God's place as the Most High. Still the original place belongs to God; we know that Satan failed in his ploy (Isaiah 14:12-21).

Even when Satan claimed he could give Jesus Christ the kingdoms of the world and their glory during the temptation in the wilderness (Luke 4:1-13), he said that it had been delivered to him, meaning that it was not his to start with. In addition, Satan acknowledged that there was a God and a Son of God before going on to challenge our Lord Jesus to prove that He was the Son of God. Again, the Bible records that, 'The earth is the LORD's, and all its fullness, the world and those who dwell therein' - Psalm 24:1.

Having been a tenant in another person's property, I can recall how one would make sure everything was in as good a state as possible whenever the house owner was coming to do a house check.

Relating this to God who formed us and therefore has rightful claim of ownership over us, it is only right that we should live the life He has given in the way that is pleasing to Him, making this the core principle of our lives. We know that He is the God of the spirits of all flesh as Moses stated in Numbers 27:16, "Let the LORD, the God of the spirits of all flesh, set a man over the congregation."

Satan who was recorded to challenge God of His place and got evicted from the heavenlies, still today strives to make men and women not to give God His rightful place in their lives. There are various modalities and tactics employed by Satan; however, that is not the focus of this book and I will not delve too much into that area. There are many books out there inspired by the Holy Spirit that tell of some of these tactics. One such book is 'The Placebo' by Howard O. Pittman.

Isaiah chapter 33 verse 6 states, 'Wisdom and knowledge will be the stability of your times, and the strength of salvation; the fear of the LORD is His treasure.' The Lord treasures and values the fear of Him. Affirming that God delights in the fear of God, speaking of the Lord Jesus, Isaiah wrote, 'His delight is in the fear of the LORD' (Isaiah 11:3a).

In Jeremiah 10:7, we read 'Who would not fear You, O King of the nations? For this is Your rightful due. For among all the wise men of the nations, and in all their kingdoms, there is none like You.' With the Almighty God being unequalled in any and every way, Jeremiah wrote that the fear of God is rightfully due Him.

Psalm 76:11 also describes God as 'Him who ought to be feared.' The enemy who strives to oppose God and divert the glory due Him would also seek to distract God's people from giving Him the fear that is due Him. When we do not fear God, we tend to fear others, whether people or circumstances. Calling His people Israel to order, the LORD commented that by forgetting Him, they opened the door to the fear of the oppressor:

> "I, even I, am He who comforts you. Who are you
> that you should be afraid of a man who will die,

and of the son of a man who will be made like grass? And you forget the LORD your Maker, who stretched out the heavens and laid the foundations of the earth; you have feared continually every day because of the fury of the oppressor, when he has prepared to destroy. And where is the fury of the oppressor?" Isaiah 51:12-13.

In the book of Job chapter 1 verse 8, God provoked Satan by boasting about the man Job who feared God and shunned evil: 'Then the LORD said to Satan, "Have you considered My servant Job, that there is none like him on the earth, a blameless and upright man, one who fears God and shuns evil?"'

Satan did not counter the claim that Job was blameless and upright; he knew that if he could break through Job's fear of God everything else would go.

Through the chapters in the book of Job, we see how God used Satan to show that when we hold on to the fear of God, even through tough times, disregarding the advice or taunting or accusations of those around us, even our close friends and family, He will come through and bring a restoration beyond what we appear to lose in the process.

The fear of God is part of His covenant package for His people. In Jeremiah 32:38-41, we read of God's restoration plan for His people when they return to Him:

They shall be My people, and I will be their God; then I will give them one heart and one way, that they may fear Me forever, for the good of them and their children after them. And I will make an everlasting covenant with them, that I will not turn away from doing them good; but I will put My fear in their hearts so that they will not depart from Me. Yes, I will rejoice over them to do them good, and I will assuredly plant them in this land, with all My heart and with all My soul.'

In His matchless wisdom, our Father God, knowing that we need the fear of God to keep us faithful to His calling, included this in the package available to Christians through the work of the Holy Spirit.

Speaking to Israel about the commandments he received from God on their behalf, Moses said in Deuteronomy 6:2, "that you may fear the LORD your God, to keep all His statutes and His commandments which I command you, you and your son and your grandson, all the days of your life, and that your days may be prolonged." In Deuteronomy 8:6, this is further emphasized: "Therefore you shall keep the commandments of the LORD your God, to walk in His ways and to fear Him."

The law and the commandments represent a guide of what is expected of the life that is lived according to the fear of God. However, as Christians, the Holy Spirit teaches us and helps us to live the life that is yielded to the will of God, even beyond the provisions of the law. In Philippians 2:12-13, the apostle Paul wrote:

Therefore, my beloved, as you have always obeyed, not as in my presence only, but now much more in my absence, work out your own salvation with fear and trembling; for it is God who works in you both to will and to do for His good pleasure.

Here, we find that living out the salvation we receive from God involves embracing the fear of God, which enables us to yield our lives to Him. This is required for one to have his or her will aligned with God's will and so, to live for His pleasure. Before the writing of this book, I had thought that the fear of God would be done away with after life on earth.

However, I have since come to appreciate that, like the aspects or attributes of God revealed in the gifts and fruit of the Holy Spirit; for example righteousness, peace and joy, the fear of God will also be manifest in heaven.

In Revelation 19:5 we read: Then a voice came from the throne, saying "Praise our God, all you His servants and those who fear Him, both small and great!" Interesting to observe that heaven expects God's people to fear Him.

In Revelation 14:7, we read of how John the apostle saw an angel having an everlasting gospel to preach to the people of the earth saying in a loud voice, "Fear God and give glory to Him, for the hour of His judgment has come; and worship Him who made heaven and earth, the sea and springs of water." Compare the foregoing to the passage in Malachi 3:5 - the LORD said to Israel at a time when they had turned away from His ways:

> "And I will come near you for judgment; I will be a
> swift witness against sorcerers, against adulterers,
> against perjurers, against those who exploit wage
> earners and widows and orphans, and against those
> who turn away an alien – because they do not fear

Me, says the LORD of hosts."

It was not just their sin but also their disregard of God that brought judgment upon them. Quite possibly, it was their lack of the fear of God that led them to disregard Him in their way of life.

Speaking of a time when Israel would leave idolatory and return to Him, the Lord God says in Hosea 3:5, 'Afterward the children of Israel shall return and seek the LORD their God and David their king. They shall fear the LORD and His goodness in the latter days.' Here the Lord is saying that the fear of the LORD would be a sign of their return to Him.

Repentance needs to be accompanied by the fear of God which is important for keeping us in line with His Holy Spirit. In fact, the fear of God is a part of the identity of the children of God. Furthermore, it is noteworthy that in Acts 13:16,

Paul the apostle addressed the people of God in the synagogue on the Sabbath day as "Men of Israel, and you who fear God." One's fear of God is reflected in the quality of things or service that he or she gives to Him or how one regards God-given responsibilities.

In bemoaning the poor quality offerings being brought to the altar as sacrifice to Him, God chides Israel His people saying "A son honours his father, and a servant his master. If then I am the Father, where is My honour? And if I am a Master, where is My reverence? Says the LORD of hosts to you priests who despise My name. Yet you say, 'In what way have we despised Your name?'" (Malachi 1:6). He concludes that chapter by saying "My name is to be feared among the nations" (verse 14b).

Different levels of professionals are paid different amounts to speak or teach at conferences. People pay the price to go because, having evaluated the program, contents or calibre and expertise of the speakers, they have reached a conclusion that it is worth the expense and their time. Some people can not be bothered to buy a season's ticket to go to the football matches, others think their life is not worth much if they do not go to the matches.

For some they have to cut out some other expenditure to fund it and for others, it is not worth the sacrifice. All a question of the value one places on these things. When we develop our relationship with God, we get to know Him better and then we are more likely to make the sacrifice to spend time with Him, though in truth, it is always a great privilege to do so. The Bible says that God reveals His secrets to those who fear Him (Psalm 25:14a).

On the human level, if someone does not value you, you would tend to not want to reveal much of yourself to that person because the tendency is that they may even ridicule your person with disregard.

Similarly, as we give the LORD the place due Him in the outworking of the fear of God, then the tendency that we would make mockery of the secrets He reveals to us is eliminated. Jesus Himself advises us in Matthew 7:6, "Do not give what is holy to the dogs; nor cast your pearls before swine, lest they trample them under their feet, and turn and tear you in pieces."

Examining this loaded statement would reveal how it

relates to the afore-discussed. How much appreciation does a dog have of what is holy? None at all. Consequently, the dog would have no regard for it and may even destroy it. Thus, we need to actively embrace the fear of God and as we give Him His due place He can trust us with His holy things and His pearls.

In the times that Jesus is talking about, as should be in our times but sadly not the case, holy objects were treated with much regard. They could only be touched by those the LORD appointed to do so, and even those people had to adhere to the LORD's instructions on handling these stuff. The dog however would do no such thing.

When we do not appreciate who God is or we do not give Him His due place in everything, we may well treat His word or gift or presence with disdain to our own peril. One may think, 'I don't do any of that.' Consider for a minute though, when we treat those the LORD has brought to us with disdain or unfairly, or grumble at what He has asked us to do, it is a disregard for Him. Indirectly we are saying that if we were God, we would do that differently.

Paul the apostle discourages complaining, "....nor complain, as some of them also complained, and were destroyed by the destroyer (1 Corinthians 10:10).

In Philippians 2:14-15, we are encouraged to, 'Do all things without complaining and disputing, that you may become blameless and harmless, children of God without fault in the midst of a crooked and perverse generation, among whom you shine as lights in the world.'

Also, Jude expressed disapproval of complaining in verse 16, 'These are grumblers, complainers, walking according to their own lusts; and they mouth great swelling words, flattering people to gain advantage.'

Continuing with the Lord Jesus' advice, let us now consider pearls. They are not easy to come by and precious to those who know their value, but what does a pearl mean to a swine or a dog? Again, nothing much. The result of giving the much-valued articles to these two animals is they would trample upon the articles; that is, they would destroy them.

They do not just put them to no use like the servant who buried his talent and was punished though he preserved it, but they destroy the pearls. Moreover, the LORD adds that they may well turn around and destroy the one who gave it to them.

This is the case with someone who defames the LORD's name and makes jokes of other people's spiritual experience or testimony, or uses these testimonies against the one who has shared it with them.

Have you experienced this? It is not you that they revile but the LORD and He is the enemy's target in using such persons; so, do not take it personally. In contrast, the LORD puts premium price on us, on the entire human race. He gave His best, none other than His only begotten Son, so that He can adopt us into His family.

The enemy sought to disrupt the works of the Lord Jesus by turning people against Him. Jesus says that if we would follow Him we would be persecuted and this is part of it all. So one should not be surprised that the enemy would use those around you who do not value God to persecute you for your faith in Him.

Furthermore, as the Creator of all things, God alone has claim of ownership over it. In Deuteronomy 10:14 we read, "Indeed heaven and the highest heavens belong to the LORD your God, also the earth with all that is in it." Speaking of our Lord Jesus Christ as the One through whom all things were made, in Colossians 1:15-18, Paul the apostle wrote:

> He is the image of the invisible God, the firstborn over all creation. For by Him all things were created that are in heaven and that are on earth, visible and invisible, whether thrones or dominions or principalities or powers. All things were created through Him and for Him. And He is before all things, and in Him all things consist. And He is the head of the body, the church, who is the beginning, the firstborn from the dead, that in all things He may have the preeminence.

The LORD is the authority above all authorities and the power above all powers as we read in Isaiah 41:1-4:

> "Keep silence before Me, O coastlands, and let the people renew their strength! Let them come near, then let them speak; let us come near together for judgment. "Who raised up one from the east? Who in righteousness called him to His feet? Who gave the nations before him, and made him rule over kings? Who gave them as the dust to his sword, as driven stubble to his bow? Who pursued them, and passed safely by the way that he had not gone with

his feet? Who has performed and done it, calling
the generations from the beginning? 'I, the LORD,
am the first; and with the last I am He.'"

The Almighty God has pre-eminence over all His creation
and uses them for is own desires or purposes. A few
examples are mentioned here. Recall that God allowed
a spirit that took on the nature of a lying spirit, speaking
through the mouths of prophets in 1 Kings 22:22, to be
used for His purpose against the defiant King Ahab. We
are told that hell and destruction are before the LORD, as
is also the case for the hearts of every individual (Proverbs
15:11).

In addition, in Isaiah 45:7 God says, 'I form the light
and create darkness, I make peace and create calamity; I,
the LORD, do all these things.' Ecclesiastes 7:14 instructs
us further as follows – 'In the day of prosperity be joyful,
but in the day of adversity consider: Surely God has
appointed the one as well as the other, so that man can find
out nothing that will come after him.' Job's life reflected
acknowledgement of these attributes of God Almighty in a
spectacular way.

In response to his wife's suggestion that he should curse
God and die in the midst of his troubles, Job said, "You
speak as one of the foolish women speaks. Shall we indeed
accept good from God, and shall we not accept adversity?"
- (Job 2:9-10). God puts one down and elevates the other.
First Samuel chapter 2 verses 6-8 reads:

"The LORD kills and makes alive; He brings down
to the grave and brings up. The LORD makes poor

and makes rich; He brings low and lifts up. He raises the poor from the dust and lifts the beggar from the ash heap, to set them among princes and make them inherit the throne of glory. For the pillars of the earth are the LORD's, and He has set the world upon them."

We are therefore admonished not to rejoice over or take undue advantage of the misfortune of others. In Proverbs 17:5 we read, 'He who mocks the poor reproaches his Maker; he who is glad at calamity will not go unpunished.' Proverbs 14:31 also adds, 'He who oppresses the poor reproaches his Maker, but he who honours Him has mercy on the needy.'

And Proverbs 19:17 says, 'He who has pity on the poor lends to the LORD, and He will pay back what he has given.' The terms poor or needy are not limited to the availability of finances, clothing or housing facilities. One could be poor in mannerisms, knowledge, expertise, wisdom to mention but a few.

Helping people who are lacking in the area of one's strength is an expression of giving due regard to God. He seems to take responsibility for these as He indicates by stating that He would be the One to repay any person who lends a helping hand to those who need it.

Can We Afford To Live The Christian Life Without The Fear Of God?

In a prayer of repentance the Prophet Isaiah wrote, "O Lord, why have You made us stray from Your ways, and hardened our heart from Your fear?" - Isaiah 63:17a.

The lack of the fear of God in a Christian is a recipe for falling away from faith as the heart is left prone to hardening against God. The prophet seems to suggest that God made the people stray but later he acknowledged that they started it all themselves. Rather, God gave His people the fear of God to keep them from falling away.

A look at Romans 1:20-25 sheds more light on this, implying that persisting in sin without repentance hardens one's heart against the fear of God, against God. It reads:

> For since the creation of the world His invisible attributes are clearly seen, being understood by the things that are made, even His eternal power and Godhead, so that they are without excuse, because, although they knew God, they did not glorify Him as God, nor were thankful, but became futile in their thoughts, and their foolish hearts were darkened. Professing to be wise, they became fools, and changed the glory of the incorruptible God into an image made like corruptible man—and birds and four-footed animals and creeping things. Therefore God also gave them up to uncleanness, in the lusts of their hearts, to dishonour their bodies among themselves, who exchanged the truth of God for the lie, and worshiped and served the creature rather than the Creator, who is blessed forever. Amen.

Jeremiah 5:23-24 reads:

But this people has a defiant and rebellious heart; they have revolted and departed. They do not say in their heart, "Let us now fear the LORD our God, who gives rain, both the former and the latter, in its season. He reserves for us the appointed weeks of the harvest."

Here, the Bible says that rebellion and defiance to God's ways stems from the absence of the fear of God. In summary, the absence of the fear of God results in a life that provides a breeding ground for sin to grow and multiply.

While the presence of the fear of God identifies the people of God; the absence of it identifies the person who has rejected His ways, often referred to in the Holy Bible as 'the wicked.' In Psalm 36:1-4 King David exclaimed:

An oracle within my heart concerning the transgression of the wicked: There is no fear of God before his eyes. For he flatters himself in his own eyes, when he finds out his iniquity and when he hates. The words of his mouth are wickedness and deceit; he has ceased to be wise and to do good. He devises wickedness on his bed; he sets himself in a way that is not good; he does not abhor evil.

In Exodus 20 and Deuteronomy 5, Moses recounted the time on Mount Sinai when the LORD marked His covenant with Israel by giving them the Ten Commandments. As they witnessed the thunderings, the lightning flashes, the sound of the trumpet and the mountain smoking, they trembled and stood afar off (Exodus 20:18).

THE FEAR OF GOD

They asked Moses to stand on their behalf before God and whatever God asked of them they would do – rather than for God to speak to them, afraid that they would die (Exodus 20:19 and Deuteronomy 5:25-27).

The LORD agreed with Israel's reasoning and expressed His desire that they had His fear in their hearts: 'Oh, that they had such a heart in them that they would fear Me and always keep all My commandments, that it might be well with them and their children forever!' - Deuteronomy 5:29.

This has been and remains God's desire for His people. They were afraid of God but had no fear of Him in their hearts. Being afraid of God therefore does not help a person to live according to His will; rather the fear of God, developed with the power and enablement of the Holy Spirit, does this for us. Moses in Exodus 20:20 concurred that God's desire was for His fear to be before His people: "Do not fear; for God has come to test you, and that His fear may be before you, so that you may not sin.

Fear – not a verb or an activity but a noun – an entity to be possessed, a quality. Compare this with the earlier discussion of how the demons believe in God and tremble but yet defiantly go against God – not having the fear of God in them.

Similarly, in Deuteronomy 6:1-2, as he continued with pronouncing the requirements of the covenant of God with Israel, Moses stated, "Now this is the commandment, and these are the statutes and judgments which the LORD your God has commanded to teach you, that you may observe them in the land which you are crossing over to possess, that you may fear the LORD your God, to keep all His statutes and His commandments which I command you, you and your son and grandson, all the days of your life, and that your days may be prolonged."

In Deuteronomy 10:12-13 we read, "And now, Israel, what does the LORD your God require of you, but to fear the LORD your God, to walk in all His ways and to love Him, to serve the LORD your God with all your heart and with all your soul, and to keep the commandments of the LORD and His statutes which I command you today for your good?"

Deuteronomy 10:20 also admonishes further: "You shall fear the LORD your God; you shall serve Him, and to Him you shall hold fast, and take oaths in His name."

When one's values are not developed based on the fear of God, they become based on the wisdom of men. The Bible already says that His ways are not our ways – Isaiah 55:8-9. Commenting on the people's lukewarm attitude towards revelation, the LORD stated in Isaiah 29:13-14:

"Therefore the Lord said: "Inasmuch as these people draw near with their mouths and honour Me with their lips, but have removed their hearts far from Me, and their fear toward Me is taught by the commandment of men, therefore, behold, I will again do a marvellous work among this people, a marvellous work and a wonder; for the wisdom of their wise men shall perish, and the understanding of their prudent men shall be hidden."

A person who does not abhor evil invariably embraces

evil; that is, everything goes. There is essentially no set limit to how far such a person would go in pursuit of evil. This is affirmed by Paul's writing in Romans 3:10-18:

> As it is written: "There is none righteous, no, not one; there is none who understands; there is none who seeks after God. They have all turned aside; they have together become unprofitable; there is none who does good, no, not one." "Their throat is an open tomb; with their tongues they have practised deceit"; "The poison of asps is under their lips"; "Whose mouth is full of cursing and bitterness." "Their feet are swift to shed blood; destruction and misery are in their ways; and the way of peace they have not known." "There is no fear of God before their eyes."

Hence, certain things one may consider humanly inconceivable like mindless murders, the consumption of human flesh or blood, mindless cruelty or injustice are examples of behavioural patterns that manifest in the absence of the fear of God.

This is what the passage above is referring to. The phrase, 'the way of peace they have not known,' implies that the person who does not have the fear of God would find it difficult to embrace peace. This would make way to a difficult personality and strife or stress in relationships. Such a person would find it difficult to establish long lasting relationships with other people in a family setting or otherwise.

So what about 2 Timothy 1:7 which says, 'For God has

not given us a spirit of fear, but of power and of love and of a sound mind' and 1 John 4:18 which says, 'There is no fear in love; but perfect love casts out fear, because fear involves torment. But he who fears has not been made perfect in love.'

These passages have been discussed in detail in a previous paragraph under the sub-heading 'What the fear of God is not.' My experience has been that many Christians shy away from the fear of God using these two passages to overrule the numerous others that encourage one to embrace the fear of God; the result being that they miss out on the amazing benefits therein.

God is love (1 John 4:8b). What a powerful statement! He enables us to love Him. In 1 John 4:19 we read, 'We love Him because He first loved us.' In fact, one of the functions of the Holy Spirit as stated in Romans 5:5b is that '... the love of God has been poured out in our hearts by the Holy Spirit who was given to us.' This is the same Spirit that works through the fear of God as we have considered earlier (Isaiah 11:2). All that the LORD does seems to flow from His love, even the need to discipline us which He encourages us to see as a mark of His fatherhood in Hebrews 12:5-8 (referring to Proverbs 3:11-12):

And you have forgotten the exhortation which speaks to you as to sons: "My son, do not despise the chastening of the LORD, nor be discouraged when you are rebuked by Him; for whom the LORD loves He chastens, and scourges every son whom He receives." If you endure chastening, God deals with you as with sons; for what son is there whom a father does not chasten? But if you are without chastening, of which all have become partakers, then you are illegitimate and not sons.

In Jeremiah 2:19, rebuking Israel for their backsliding, the Lord God of hosts said, "Your own wickedness will correct you, and your backslidings will rebuke you. Know therefore and see that it is an evil and bitter thing that you have forsaken the LORD your God, and the fear of Me is not in you." Here we see that the Lord pointed out that their backsliding was manifest evidence that they did not have the fear of Him in them.

God asks us to keep away from sin and in fact to rule over it. Genesis 4:7 reads - "If you do well, will you not be accepted? And if you do not do well, sin lies at the door. And its desire is for you, but you should rule over it." Can one overstate the danger of sin?

God tells us that He detests sin. Habakkuk 1:13a speaking of God says, 'You are of purer eyes than to behold evil, and cannot look on wickedness.' It follows that embracing sin or wickedness equates to asking that the eyes of God be removed from the person's life, not an enviable position.

Psalm 66:16-19 tells us that sin itself hinders one's prayers: 'Come and hear, all you who fear God, and I will declare what He has done for my soul. I cried to Him with my mouth, and He was extolled with my tongue. If I regard iniquity in my heart, the LORD will not hear. But certainly God has heard me; He has attended to the voice of my prayer.'

This is in line with what Samuel the prophet said to

King Saul in 1 Samuel 15:22, 'So Samuel said: "Has the LORD as great delight in burnt offerings and sacrifices, as in obeying the voice of the LORD? Behold, to obey is better than sacrifice, and to heed than the fat of rams.'

Refusing to give up sinful pleasures and pursuing after God in good deeds, fasting, giving of offerings and tithes, praying, bible study, attending church meetings or conferences - these do not impress Him as moreover, they would end in one being eternally separated from Him in hell.

He would not be identified as love if He turned a blind eye to sin knowing its devastating eternal consequences. Compare the foregoing to God's response to Israel when they assumed that because they were fasting, it was okay to continue their wickedness (Isaiah 58).

As the fear of God helps us detest sin, we can have increasing confidence that our prayers are heard. Moreover, sin withholds good from us - Jeremiah 5:20-25:

> Declare this in the house of Jacob and proclaim it in Judah, saying. 'Hear this now, O foolish people, without understanding, who have eyes and see not, and who have ears and hear not: Do you not fear Me?' says the LORD. 'Will you not tremble at My presence, who have placed the sand as the bound of the sea, by a perpetual decree, that it cannot pass beyond it? And though its waves toss to and fro, yet they cannot prevail; though they roar, yet they cannot pass over it. But this people has a defiant and rebellious heart; they have revolted and departed. They do not say in their heart, "Let us

now fear the LORD our God, who gives rain, both the former and the latter, in its season. He reserves for us the appointed weeks of the harvest." Your iniquities have turned these things away, and your sins have withheld good from you.

The fear of the Lord is related to our revelation of Him. This is a spiritual issue because the physical eyes or mind cannot perceive God. The tendency of our senses is to uphold the natural, that is, what our natural senses perceive.

The revelation of God by His Spirit enables us to obey the most important commandment of all – to love the LORD our God with all (of our being) our heart, with all our soul, and with all our strength (Deuteronomy 6:5).

Just like other commandments can only be obeyed with the help of the Holy Spirit, loving God comes from Him as previously noted in Romans 5:5. In agreement, Matthew 22:37 records the words of our Lord Jesus Christ when He was asked which is the greatest commandment in the law, "You shall love the LORD your God with all your heart, with all your soul, and with all your mind." The same is recorded in Mark 12:30. In Luke 10:28 Jesus affirmed this principle when it was also given by the lawyer who enquired about the requirements for inheriting eternal life with His response, 'You have answered rightly; do this and you will live.'

In Exodus 20, God gave the Ten Commandments to Israel after they had accepted His covenant (Exodus 19). In the first 3 commandments, God teaches them what is summarised above as the most important commandment without which, the other commandments cannot be fulfilled anyway.

Loving God comes before you can apply the requirements of loving your neighbour. The 4th to 10th commandments deal with our love for our neighbour. Our neighbour essentially translates into other people we encounter in everyday living, including parents and siblings, as appropriately illustrated by Jesus in Luke 10:29-37.

The fear of God is what the first 3 commandments address. First, that God's people should have a revelation of Him, without which the fear of God cannot be fully appreciated or sustained.

In Exodus 20:2, God says, "I am the LORD your God, who brought you out of the land of Egypt, out of the house of bondage." After revealing Himself to Israel as the LORD their God, He asked that His people:

- Have no other gods before Him.
- Not make carved image for themselves to bow down to or serve.
- Not take the name of the LORD their God in vain.

The revelation of Him as the LORD – over all – over everything, and also as our God is the first thing He wants to establish in relationship with His people; this precedes our obedience to Him. Without the fear of God these three commandments cannot be honoured, as one would belittle God in one's heart. This in turn has a negative impact on one's attitude to the rest of the commandments.

In the seventeenth chapter of the gospel of Matthew, when the apostles Peter, James and John witnessed the transfiguration of Jesus Christ and heard God the Father declaring Jesus to be His beloved Son in whom He is well-pleased, they were greatly afraid.

In verse 7, Jesus said to them, "Arise, and do not be afraid." Again in Isaiah 41:10, God says, 'Fear not, for I am with you; be not dismayed, for I am your God. I will strengthen you, yes, I will help you, I will uphold you with My righteous right hand.' The basis of our not being afraid of things or issues in life is revelation – an understanding of the situation or of the people we are working with allays our anxiety and calms our fear.

Have you been startled by the presence of someone you knew but they sneaked up on you, "Oh, it's you, you made me jump." The same person but in a setting with better view or revelation brings a different response. This was what these three apostles were learning. The greater the revelation they had of the Lord Jesus as they went along with Him, the less of the unhealthy fear they had towards Him.

Conversely, knowing the One who is with us, knowing the strength and power that is within us or available to us would also allay anxiety about situations that we may find ourselves in. In Psalm 23:4, David wrote, 'Yea, though I walk through the valley of the shadow of death, I will fear no evil; for You are with me; Your rod and Your staff, they comfort me.'

Imagine you and a friend are walking along a path you knew was frequently occupied by dangerous gangs. You have only recently met this friend and did not know his or her strengths. You worry about how you would make it through the dangerous path. Suddenly, the gang surrounds you both. Your friend fights them off with great kickboxing skills to your amazement.

Later on when you are alone with your friend you discover that he had won several kickboxing championships. You then decide that whenever you had the need to go through the rough dangerous path in the future, you would ask your friend along.

Each time he came with you, you went through the path fearlessly, trusting that your friend would fend off the gangsters, that is, if they dared to attack you again. You then found out that as long as your friend was with you, the gang did not bother with you; in fact, they seemed to keep well away from you. This analogy reflects the growth of our trust in God as we walk with Him and see His deliverance in different situations.

Also imagine you had read about this same friend's achievements and awards but not yet seen him demonstrate his skills, you may go along with him but only hoping that he would be strong enough to defend himself and you if the event necessitated it. However, seeing your friend actually fight off the gang boosts your confidence to trust his abilities to fend off evil along the path.

Daniel 11:32b affirms this, 'The people who know their God shall be strong, and carry out great exploits.' As the Holy Spirit reveals God to us, and as we walk through the paths of life with Him, we would give Him His rightful place, trusting in Him rather than being afraid.

The more we can live the life that God promises us in Isaiah 41:10 – not being afraid, not being dismayed; rather,

THE FEAR OF GOD

knowing that He will strengthen us, He will help us and uphold us with His righteous right hand.

In addition, knowing what is at God's disposal adds to our faith and giving Him His rightful place. The shepherd's analogy used by David refers to the shepherd's rod and staff as a comfort to him.

For those who fear God, they can know that He has a whole lot of things at His disposal. Our God has everything in the universe at His disposal to do whatever He chooses:

The angels (Psalm 91:11; Daniel 6:22; Luke 1:28-37); the wind (Jonah 4:8); the sun and moon (Joshua 10:12-14); kings (Revelations 19:16); authorities (Romans 13:1-5); plant (Jonah 4:6); rain and fountains from the deep (Genesis 7:4, 10-12 and Genesis 8:2); the agents of nine of the ten plagues of Egypt: frogs, lice, flies (Exodus 8); pestilence, skin eruptions and hail (Exodus 9); locusts (Exodus 10:21-23); brimstone and fire (Genesis 19:24; 1 Kings 18:38) and even death and destruction (Exodus 12).

By Him all things were created that are in heaven and that are on earth, visible and invisible, whether thrones or dominions or principalities or powers. All things were created through Him and for Him (Colossians 1:16).

Even the devil was roped into the crucifixion plan when he entered Judas (Luke 22:3-5) and lying spirits were used to accomplish God's purpose in 1 Kings 22:20-23). Check out these creatures in the Maker's employment: fish – Jonah 1:17, ravens – 1 Kings 17:3-4 and serpents – Numbers 21:6. God Almighty has the ability to create anything out of nothing by the power of His creative word – Genesis 1. He does not need anything to create something!

In Job chapters 38 to 41, God enumerated to Job the control that He has over creation, living and non-living. At the end of it Job's revelation of God was beyond his imagination. God revealed Himself to Job in his steadfastness. This brought Job's confession and declarations in Job 42:1-6:

> Then Job answered the LORD and said: "I know that You can do everything, and that no purpose of Yours can be withheld from You. You asked, 'Who is this who hides counsel without knowledge?' Therefore I have uttered what I did not understand, things too wonderful for me, which I did not know. Listen, please, and let me speak; You said, 'I will question you, and you shall answer Me.' "I have heard of You by the hearing of the ear, but now my eye sees You. Therefore I abhor myself, and repent in dust and ashes."

In verse 12, Job is reported to have become blessed beyond his losses. The fear of God in us gives God His due place. The Church is the bride of Jesus Christ our Lord. One should not interfere with the Church in a way that turns the bride's attention from Him to one's self. He is a jealous God.

Consider the celebrities who want to go out for a quiet stroll down the street - in a disguise, so as not to be recognised by their fans. When, for some reason, that disguise is uncovered, their fans gather around them to touch them, take a photograph or get an autograph for example. Otherwise, they carry on, lost in the crowd unrecognised.

Ponder Time

Is Jesus Christ lost in the crowded environment of our personal lives or churches? Do we still recognise Him, give Him His due place and run after Him in pursuit of His presence and fellowship? Has He even passed by unrecognised by His own bride as the focus is directed to other things?

When the due place of God is belittled, it is evidence that the fear of God is eroded; then sin finds it easy to have dominion. As the fear of God is closely related to the revelation of God, anything that tampers with that revelation, tampers with the fear of God. In the temptation that led to the fall of man in Genesis 3, the serpent's dialogue with Eve started with what God said man was not to do, but thereafter went on to diminish her revelation of God.

In Genesis 3:4-5, the serpent said to her, "You will not surely die. For God knows that in the day you eat of it (the forbidden fruit) your eyes will be opened, and you will be like God, knowing good and evil." The phrase "be like God" was aimed at blurring Eve's revelation of God, giving the impression that being like God was actually a possibility for the woman in her own power or strength.

Our God-given position among all creation, the place we have, we have in God not outside of God, that is His purpose. He fills all things. In Jeremiah 23:24 God asks, ' "Can anyone hide himself in secret places, so I shall not see him?" says the LORD. "Do I not fill heaven and earth?" says the LORD.'

Also, our Lord Jesus Christ is spoken of in Colossians 1:17, 'And He is before all things, and in Him all things consist.' Being like God was not the position God intended for man, but to be created in God's image; two different things.

The enemy himself had tried what he persuaded Eve to do and fell, lost his own original God-given position. No matter how gifted one may be, one still ought to embrace the fear of God, He is the giver of every good and perfect gift (James 1:17) and yield every manifestation or administration of such gifts to Him.

In Isaiah 14:12-14, we read of Satan's pride-originated plan to exalt himself above the position that God had given him; worse still, he coveted God's position and desired to be like the Most High (verse 14). It is noteworthy that Satan acknowledged God as the Most High, and yet desired to be like Him.

From this, it is apparent that his revelation of the Almighty God was blurred or skewed, or he would have realised that he could not be like the Most High, that his position was a privilege, which many others would have loved to be in but God chose to give it to him. Knowledge is not enough to make us give God His place, the fear of God is what makes us give Him the place we know belongs to Him.

Satan's pride is a manifest expression of a disregard for God, self-exaltation and independence from God, a lack of the fear of God. By saying in his heart that he would exalt his throne above the stars of God, Satan implied that God's wisdom, which put him in his position was flawed and that by his own strength, he could do better.

This is the same trick he played on Eve. He talked her into being dissatisfied with God's master plan and desiring a higher place achieved without God's authority, independent of God. In our lives, we may fall into similar situation when we feel our God-given position is not good enough.

One may then, not only aspire to elevate oneself, but to leave God out of this self-promotion only to get disappointed and loose what we had been given. Beware of any self-promotion that excludes God or works independent of Him. There is no fear of God in that and it only leads to demotion eventually.

Psalm 75:6-7 puts it this way, 'For exaltation comes neither from the east nor from the west nor from the south. But God is the Judge: He puts down one, and exalts another.' Along same lines, Hannah the mother of Samuel the prophet sang, "The LORD kills and makes alive; He brings down to the grave and brings up. The LORD makes poor and makes rich; He brings low and lifts up" (1 Samuel 2:6-7).

In James 4:12 we read, 'There is one Lawgiver, who is able to save and to destroy. Who are you to judge another?' The Prophet Jeremiah put it this way, 'Who is he who speaks and it comes to pass, when the Lord has not commanded it? Is it not from the mouth of the Most High that woe and well-being proceed?' - Lamentations 3:37-38.

In addition, John the Baptist in John 3:27 reinforced this

in stating that, "A man can receive nothing unless it has been given to him from heaven." In summary therefore, even if one were to desire promotion, it must not be a self-centred or self-promoting exercise but one submitted to God and attributed to Him. One should be mindful of entertaining thoughts such as these,

- I deserve a place
- I deserve better than God has given me, better than others
- I will, independent of God, or even against God's known will, exalt myself
- I will exalt myself to my own chosen place, which my heart desires.

All are manifestations of pride and are anchored on a lack of regard for the fear of God. The ultimate disregard is aspiring towards God's place, position or authority as Satan did.

When we say we want to be free to choose for ourselves, to do what we want, when and how we want it, we are inadvertently saying we want to take the place of God in our lives; to take charge and control of our lives. Today, many people still think they can attain heights and achievements beyond what God has ordained for them, but this is not possible.

Once God was belittled before Eve, the fall was settled and inevitable. She had seen the tree prior to this encounter, but following that discussion with the serpent, the boundaries were lifted and she saw what was previously "untouchable" as "good for food, pleasant to the eyes and desirable to make one wise." She then took of its fruit and ate.

It was all sorted by turning her perception of God, which made her belittle His boundaries in her heart. To avoid having a similar experience ourselves, we must regard God-ordained boundaries in everyday life with godly fear.

In Matthew 4, the account of Satan's temptation of Jesus shows us that Satan wanted to ascertain the revelation that Jesus had of Himself, the revelation of God. In verse 3 he said to Jesus, "If You are the Son of God,…"

In His response, Jesus seemed to ignore Satan's question as to this revelation of who He was. Instead He replied that the word of God, which feeds the spirit is what gives life not just that which feeds the flesh – "Man shall not live by bread alone, but by every word that proceeds from the mouth of God" – verse 4b.

Satan repeated his challenge of the identity of Jesus in the second temptation in verse 6 starting with, "If You are the Son of God…." Again Jesus responded in a manner that showed He put God first in all He did. Having no success with the previous temptations, in the third one Satan offered Jesus the kingdoms of the world and their glory in exchange for falling down to worship him. To this the Lord's response was, "Away with you, Satan! For it is written, 'You shall worship the LORD your God, and Him only you shall serve?'" – Matthew 4:10.

Interestingly, the third temptation from Satan directly challenged the first commandment: "I am the LORD your God, who brought you out of the land of Egypt, out of the house of bondage. You shall have no other gods before Me" (Exodus 20:2-3).

At this point Satan lost the permission to tempt the Son of God any further and had to be dismissed! The objective of Satan was to take the focus away from God, and then he could have been able to direct the Lord Jesus anywhere he fancied; but he underestimated the Lord.

Same way he underestimates the power of our Lord that enables us to withstand various trials and temptations. Satan seemed to have believed the lie that he could successfully bring down the Son of God in these temptations, perhaps encouraged by the fact that he had brought about the fall of the first Adam.

Having a revelation of who we are in Christ and believing it would help us put Satan in his place in all manner of temptations, particularly when he challenges the lordship and authority of God our Father. Oh I pray that we would boldly adopt the response: 'Away with you Satan, for it is written …' Jesus preached the word of God to Satan – referring to God as LORD – Satan's God, whom alone Satan should serve.

We need the revelation of God not only to stand for ourselves but also to defeat Satan and respond appropriately to his temptations. In addition, the absence of the fear of God leads to a life that is in active opposition to God's purpose including direct opposition to the activities of God's people. The reason for Amalek resisting Israel is stated to be Amalek's lack of the fear of God. In Deuteronomy 25:17-19 we read God's instructions to Israel:

"Remember what Amalek did to you on the way as you were coming out of Egypt, how he met you on the way and attacked your rear ranks, all the stragglers at your rear, when you were tired and weary; and he did not fear God. Therefore it shall be, when the LORD your God has given you rest from your enemies all around, in the land which the LORD your God is giving you to possess as an inheritance, that you will blot out the remembrance of Amalek from under heaven. You shall not forget."

How Can We Protect And Maintain The Fear Of God Within Us?

The fear of the LORD can be seen as a spiritually imparted gift. Like the other gifts of the Holy Spirit, we need to regularly stir up this gift. The natural eye cannot perceive God's revelation as already stated, but the Holy Spirit teaches and leads us into all truth.

Jesus promises us in John 14:26 that the Holy spirit will be sent as our Helper who will teach us all things in addition to bringing to our remembrance all that Jesus had said. In John 16:13-14, Jesus further emphasizes that the Spirit of truth will come to guide us into all truth for He will not speak on His own authority, but whatever He hears He will speak, telling us things to come, glorifying Jesus as He takes of what is His and declares it to us.

The first letter of Paul to the Corinthians 2:10-16, tells us of the instruction of the Holy Spirit. In verse 13, we read that His teachings compare spiritual things with spiritual. Verse 14 says that, "the natural man does not receive the things of the Spirit of God, for they are foolishness to him, nor can he know them because they are spiritually discerned."

The fear of God imparted by the Holy Spirit, the Spirit of knowledge and of the fear of the LORD (Isaiah 11:2), can only come after one's life and spirit have been opened to the Spirit of God. Furthermore, we need the Holy Spirit giving us a fresh revelation of God everyday to keep the fear of God alive in us. Likewise, it can only be understood and appreciated through His revelation and instruction, as indeed applies to the attributes of God and other gifts of the Holy Spirit.

This Spirit of truth however cannot be received by the world, reason being that the world neither sees Him nor knows Him (John 14:17). Meanwhile, the Spirit is supposed to convict the world of sin, of righteousness and of judgment.

The first obstacle to this work of the Holy Spirit is that the world does not see Him; but, they can see His works, for example, manifested in Christians who live according to the His leading. 2 Corinthians 4:3-4 says, 'if our gospel is veiled, it is veiled to those who are perishing, whose minds the god of this age has blinded, who do not believe, lest the light of the gospel of the glory of Christ, who is the image of God, should shine on them.' But Jesus is the answer to this blindness.

In Isaiah 42:6-7, we are told that Jesus is called by the LORD in righteousness, given as a covenant to the people, as a light to the Gentiles - to open blind eyes, to bring out prisoners from the prison, and those who sit in darkness from the prison house.

The restoration of man comes with the acceptance of the

THE FEAR OF GOD

free gift (free to us but paid for by the Lord) of reconciliation; giving relevance to the declaration in Galatians 2:20 which says "it is no longer I who live, but Christ lives in me; and the life which I now live in the flesh, I live by faith in the Son of God, who loved me and gave Himself for me."

Again, in Acts 17:28, Paul quotes a speech stating that "in Him we live and move and have our being." This purpose of God – to live in us - predated the creation of man and was fully achieved through Jesus. For this reason, the coming of the Lord Jesus was appointed before the foundation of the earth.

Ephesians 1:4 teaches us that God chose us in Jesus before the foundation of the world, that we should be holy and without blame before Him in love. Therefore, our God-ordained place is in Jesus and everyone who submits to this purpose of God by yielding to Jesus as his or her Lord, and Saviour – has found God's purpose for His creation.

Those who are yielded to the instruction of the Holy Spirit can see His work manifest in their lives as He promised in 2 Corinthians 3:2-3:

> You are our epistle written in our hearts, known and read by all men; clearly you are an epistle of Christ, ministered by us, written not with ink but by the Spirit of the living God, not on tablets of stone but on tablets of flesh, that is, of the heart.

In Psalm 2:8, God promises the nations to our Lord Jesus saying, "Ask of Me, and I will give You the nations for Your inheritance, and the ends of the earth for Your possession."

As the body of Christ called out of the nations, we are to ask the Father for the rest of the nations and pray for the blind eyes to be opened so that people can see the work of the Holy Spirit. Creation speaks of the glory of the LORD, but the blind eye cannot see it as such. In addition, Psalm 19:1-3 also says:

> The heavens declare the glory of God; and the firmament shows His handiwork. Day unto day utters speech, and night unto night reveals knowledge. There is no speech nor language where their voice is not heard.

Bearing this in mind we should prayerfully evangelize and intercede even more for those who do not know Jesus as Lord and Saviour, that they will receive the salvation grace.

Similarly, one who was a Christian previously and backslides would need prayers to have their perception reopened to the Holy Spirit. The fear of God can also be strengthened by our experiences and observations of events. When Israel saw the great work, they feared the LORD. Exodus 14:30-31 reads:

> So the LORD saved Israel that day out of the hand of the Egyptians, and Israel saw the Egyptians dead on the seashore. Thus Israel saw the great work which the LORD had done in Egypt; so the people feared the LORD, and believed the LORD and His servant Moses.

THE FEAR OF GOD

The natural senses and the flesh already war against the Spirit. Galatians 5:17 says, 'For the flesh lusts against the Spirit, and the Spirit against the flesh; and these are contrary to one another, so that you do not do the things that you wish.'

We must then guard against activities that feed the 'flesh' as such things would counter the work of the Spirit, including the fear of God. So, what does this mean in practical terms? Reading further in Galatians 5:19-21, we see what these works of the flesh represent:

> Now the works of the flesh are evident, which are: adultery, fornication, uncleanness, lewdness, idolatry, sorcery, hatred, contentions, jealousies, outbursts of wrath, selfish ambitions, dissensions, heresies, envy, murders, drunkenness, revelries, and the like; of which I tell you beforehand, just as I also told you in time past, that those who practice such things will not inherit the kingdom of God.

Anything that increases the manifestation of these in one's life would be detrimental to the work of the Holy Spirit, including the development of the fear of God.

God is revealed in His word, which is also called the sword of the Spirit (Ephesians 6:17b). As previously stated, our understanding of, development and growth in the fear of God is linked to our revelation of who He is. God and His word are the same.

In John 1:1 the Holy Bible says, 'In the beginning was the Word, and the Word was with God, and the Word was ˀod.' John the apostle said that we have fellowship with the Lord through His Word. In 1 John 1:1-3 he wrote:

> That which was from the beginning, which we
> have heard, which we have seen with our eyes,
> which we have looked upon, and our hands have
> handled, concerning the Word of life— the life was
> manifested, and we have seen, and bear witness,
> and declare to you that eternal life which was with
> the Father and was manifested to us— that which
> we have seen and heard we declare to you, that
> you also may have fellowship with us; and truly
> our fellowship is with the Father and with His Son
> Jesus Christ.

We therefore must expose ourselves to the privilege of the written word of God regularly, so that the revelation of God is not dimmed or blurred within us as this is dangerous considering the preceding discuss.

Factors That Hinder The Development Of The Fear Of God

Pride is an antidote to the development of the fear of God. To keep in step with the Holy Spirit, it is pertinent that one should beware of pride.

The Bible warns us that God resists the proud (1 Peter 5:5b). This means that what we do in pride, God resists – implies that He actively and intentionally sets out to make certain that it fails.

I would not want to have God Almighty opposing my activities in life. That would lead to a waste of energy and

THE FEAR OF GOD

time, not to mention frustrating lack of productivity and fruitlessness. The second part of the passage above tells us that God gives grace to the humble – a statement echoed in Proverbs 3:34b and James 4:6.

It is worth looking at some examples of the biblical perspective on pride. In Proverbs 16:18, we see that, 'Pride goes before destruction, and a haughty spirit before a fall.' Proverbs 16:5a reads, 'Everyone proud in heart is an abomination to the LORD.' Also in the book of James we read some affirmation of this, 'Humble yourselves in the sight of the Lord, and He will lift you up' (James 4:10).

Isaiah 2:11-12 says, 'The lofty looks of man shall be humbled, the haughtiness of men shall be bowed down, and the LORD alone shall be exalted in that day. For the day of the LORD of hosts shall come upon everything proud and lofty, upon everything lifted up – and it shall be brought low.'

Absence of or lack of the fear of God breeds pride, which leads to the disregard and rejection of God's word. Pride is born in the heart. In Mark 7:20-23 Jesus says:

> "What comes out of a man, that defiles a man. For from within, out of the heart of men, proceed evil thoughts, adulteries, fornications, murders, thefts, covetousness, wickedness, deceit, lewdness, an evil eye, blasphemy, pride, foolishness. All these evil things come from within and defile a man."

It all comes back to the heart. No wonder David asked God to create in him a clean heart (Psalm 51:10a). The Bible cautions us that the heart should be guarded zealously.

Proverbs 4:23 offers this advice, 'Keep your heart with all diligence, for out of it spring the issues of life.'

This implies that one should actively seek to work on this, to put in every effort and invest in activities aimed at protecting one's heart from that which does not embrace these evil things.

The capacity of the heart to yield to evil is written of in Jeremiah 17:9-10, "The heart is deceitful above all things, and desperately wicked; who can know it? I, the LORD, search the heart, I test the mind, even to give every man according to his ways, according to the fruit of his doings." In Matthew 12:33-35 (and also in Luke 6:43-45), Jesus teaches that our fruit is based on the condition of our heart:

> "Either make the tree good and its fruit good, or else make the tree bad and its fruit bad; for a tree is known by its fruit. Brood of vipers! How can you, being evil speak good things? For out of the abundance of the heart the mouth speaks. A good man out of the good treasure of his heart brings forth good things, and an evil man out of the evil treasure brings forth evil things."

The issue of the heart, and the influence of the fear of the LORD on it, will be revisited in a later chapter. Pride can creep in unnoticed, quietly, subtly.

One ought therefore be on the look out for its manifestation(s). As stated previously, the thinking that one deserves better than God has given, or trying to gain ascension without God is a manifestation of pride.

THE FEAR OF GOD

Another subtle manifestation of pride is grumbling and complaining. James 5:9 teaches, 'Do not grumble against one another, brethren, lest you be condemned. Behold, the Judge is standing at the door!' In addition, Jude verse 16 says, 'These are grumblers, complainers, walking according to their own lusts; and they mouth great swelling words, flattering people to gain advantage.'

Being so similar in principle, grumbling and complaining are often put together in the same statement. When the LORD brought Israel out of Egypt and told them to take over the land of Canaan, they heard the negative report of ten out of the twelve spies who explored the land and complained against Moses and Aaron:

> And all the children of Israel complained against Moses and Aaron, and the whole congregation said to them, "If only we had died in the land of Egypt! Or if only we had died in this wilderness! Why has the LORD brought us to this land to fall by the sword, that our wives and children should become victims? Would it not be better for us to return to Egypt?" - Numbers 14:2-3.

Israel acknowledged that it was the LORD Himself that brought them to the place where they found themselves; and, despite seeing the plagues upon Egypt that preceded their freedom from the Egyptian bondage, on the basis of the negative report from the ten spies, their judgment became clouded by fear rather than focusing on and trusting God.

In fact, they believed God meant to destroy them. One must therefore guard against ungodly fear as this can stand in opposition to giving God His due regard which is what the fear of God accomplishes. Recounting the story in Deuteronomy 1:26-33, Moses said:

> "Nevertheless you would not go up, but rebelled against the command of the LORD your God; and you complained in your tents, and said, 'Because the LORD hates us, He has brought us out of the land of Egypt to deliver us into the hand of the Amorites, to destroy us. Where can we go up? Our brethren have discouraged our hearts, saying, "The people are greater and taller than we; the cities are great and fortified up to heaven; moreover we have seen the sons of the Anakim there."' Then I said to you, 'Do not be terrified, or afraid of them. The LORD your God, who goes before you, He will fight for you, according to all He did for you in Egypt before your eyes, and in the wilderness where you saw how the LORD your God carried you, as a man carries his son, in all the way that you went until you came to this place.' Yet, for all that, you did not believe the LORD your God, who went in the way before you to search out a place for you to pitch your tents, to show you the way you should go, in the fire by night and in the cloud by day."

This was followed by God's declaration that none of those in that generation, with the exception of Caleb and Joshua, would see Canaan (Deuteronomy 1:35-38). At another stage in their wilderness journey, Israel complained about

THE FEAR OF GOD

hunger. The outcome of that is recorded in Exodus 16:6-8:

> Then Moses and Aaron said to all the children of
> Israel, "At evening you shall know that the LORD
> has brought you out of the land of Egypt. And in
> the morning you shall see the glory of the LORD;
> for He hears your complaints against the LORD.
> But what are we, that you complain against us?"
> Also Moses said, "This shall be seen when the
> LORD gives you meat to eat in the evening, and
> in the morning bread to the full; for the LORD
> hears your complaints which you make against
> Him. And what are we? Your complaints are not
> against us but against the LORD."

We see that complaints are generally against God, not man.
It is preferable to choose to pray to God, to lift one's burden
to Him, rather than complain. The word of God gives a
helpful advice on how to deal with unpleasant situations
and guard our hearts in Philippians 4:6-7:

> Be anxious for nothing, but in everything by
> prayer and supplication, with thanksgiving, let
> your requests be made known to God; and the
> peace of God, which surpasses all understanding,
> will guard your hearts and minds through Christ
> Jesus.

In addition, Philippians 2:14-16 instructs us to:

> Do all things without complaining and disputing,
> that you may become blameless and harmless,

children of God without fault in the midst of a crooked and perverse generation, among whom you shine as lights in the world, holding fast the word of life, so that I may rejoice in the day of Christ that I have not run in vain or laboured in vain.

From the foregoing, one can infer that the opposite of pride includes:
- Acknowledging God as the Almighty and the
  Most High; that He alone has that place.
  The first commandment tells us that
  having acknowledged the LORD as our God,
  we should have no gods before Him -
  we should not give another a place above God.
  Giving God's place to another is idolatry.
  The second commandment says that we should not
  make for ourselves a carved image,
  we should not bow down to them nor serve them -
  for He, the LORD our God, He is a jealous God
  (Exodus 20:1-5).
- Submitting to His will.
  This should be a natural consequence
  of acknowledging God as the Almighty and is
  affirmed by our Lord Jesus in the model prayer
  He taught in Matthew 6:10.
- Seeking the advancement of His kingdom
  in everything we are involved in;
  this also means distancing oneself from that
  which is against God's kingdom like

> David stated in Psalms 1:1-2;
> 'Blessed is the man who walks not in the
> counsel of the ungodly, nor stands in the path
> of sinners, nor sits in the seat of the scornful;
> but his delight is in the law of the LORD,
> and in His law he meditates day and night.'
> Our Lord Jesus says that, "He who is not with
> Me is against Me, and he who does not gather with
> Me scatters abroad" - Matthew 12:30.

Satan acknowledged God as the Most High, but thought of himself as being able to attain a place equal to God. It would appear that the lie he believed twisted his perception of himself and also of God.

Similarly, pride follows a distortion of perception of oneself and that of the Almighty. Being thankful for what God has ordained for one follows submission to His will. It eliminates grumbling. This is the only way a 'Joseph' can be thankful in a 'Potiphar's house'.

In brief, Joseph the eleventh of Jacob's twelve sons was treated as a prince by his father but reduced to a slave in Egypt in Potiphar's house after being sold by his brothers. In 1 Thessalonians 5:18 we read, 'in everything give thanks; for this is the will of God in Christ Jesus for you.' So, be thankful in every situation, not just the ones that gladden your heart but also that which makes your heart sorrowful

The apostle Paul in Ephesians 5:20 encourages us to be '..giving thanks always for all things to God the Father in the name of our Lord Jesus Christ.' A heart of gratitude gives value to what one is thankful for and appreciates the person to whom one is thankful. Thus, thankfulness to God appreciates Him in whatever the circumstance may be and lifts Him within our hearts, while giving us a better perception of the situation.

It is God's will for us to desire a place better than where we are at any given time. Our revelation of Him is from faith to faith (Romans 1:17) and our journey through salvation involves a continuing renewal of the mind towards being more like the Lord. Ephesians 4:23-24 reads, 'and be renewed in the spirit of your mind, and that you put on the new man which was created according to God, in true righteousness and holiness.'

Our daily experience should be that of the day-by-day renewal of the inward man (2 Corinthians 4:16). We should not be moulded to fit into the world around us. Rather we are to be transformed by the renewing of the mind, so that we may prove what the good, acceptable and perfect will of God is (Romans 12:2).

Also, Luke 6:40 teaches us that a disciple who is fully trained, would be like his teacher – encouraging us unto higher grounds of being more like our Lord Jesus.

In Genesis 12:1-3, we read God's promise to increase and bless Abraham. We have previously observed from the first book of Samuel, that promotion comes from the LORD – 1 Samuel 2:1-10.

In Philippians 2:13 we read that God seeks to partner with us, to work through our will – 'for it is God who works in you both to will and to do for His good pleasure.' But He wants us to work with Him to achieve our set goals and align them with His plans for our lives.

THE FEAR OF GOD

This reminds me of two television shows called 'You're Fired!' and 'The Dragon's Den'. In each case, contestants compete vigorously for the partnership of some rich established entrepreneurs with a great wealth of experience and acumen as well as business connections in the particular business field they are seeking to pursue. They do so because they appreciate the contribution these established entrepreneurs could bring to their work, increasing their chance of success.

The fear of God would help us appreciate the benefits of yielding to Him and seeking His partnership in every thing we do; one would not want to do anything without having Him involved in it and seeking to know that it is in line with His will, having His approval, as was the case with our Lord Jesus (John 5:19).

Proverbs 16:3 says, 'Commit your works to the LORD, and your thoughts will be established.' In addition, Proverbs 5:21 says, 'For the ways of man are before the eyes of the LORD, and He ponders all his paths.'

Living independent of God is a manifestation of pride and of the absence of the fear of God. James puts it this way:

> Come now, you who say, "Today or tomorrow we will go to such and such a city, spend a year there, buy and sell, and make a profit"; whereas you do not know what will happen tomorrow. For what is your life? It is even a vapour that appears for a little time and then vanishes away. Instead you ought to say, "If the Lord wills, we shall live and do this or that." But now you boast in your arrogance. All

An Introduction To The Fear Of God

such boasting is evil (James 4:13-16).

You may have heard some people qualify statements about future plans with phrases such as, " God-willing I will..." or "if it is God's will I will..." One may not have full knowledge of what the express will of God is but we can ask Him to reveal His will, and we may have to wait for this will to be revealed to us if the Holy Spirit leads us that way. Again, James 1:5 instructs us that, 'If any of you lacks wisdom, let him ask of God, who gives to all liberally and without reproach, and it will be given to him.'

1 Samuel 2:3b affirms that the LORD is the God of knowledge by whom actions are weighed. When we do not have the revealed will of God, committing our plans to God may be sufficient, allowing Him to lead us accordingly.

The other side of this discourse is that when we do have knowledge of the revealed will of God, we are then required to accord it due regard. There is no point asking for His will to be revealed and then intentionally going the opposite way. Going according to God's will may not be easy at all. Consider Abram who knew that it was God's will for him to leave his father's house to a destination unknown, and with no relatives; a hard call any day, would you not agree?

We know from the account of the story as recorded in Genesis chapter 12 that he took his nephew Lot along but eventually had to part ways with him to continue on his God-ordained journey.

Consider King Saul, who knew God's will was to destroy everything the Amalekites consisted of (1 Samuel 15), but he listened to his men and compromised on the mission with devastating consequences. Apart from having the kingdom authority removed from him, King Saul eventually died at the hands of an Amalekite (2 Samuel 1:6-10).

Again, consider Mary, the earthly mother of our Lord Jesus, being told that she would have a child without the involvement of a man, how does a young woman explain that to her fiancé and her family? Thankfully, God also sent also a messenger to Joseph, Mary's fiancé, although not before he had had to question her about it and started thinking of sending her away – Matthew 1:18-25.

On a personal note, I believed that I received revelation from the Lord to pursue my previous career path in the subspecialty of paediatric surgery. This proved very difficult. I received offers from well-meaning people who wanted to introduce me to other career paths with seemingly better prospects.

I was also been met with comments like, 'If God sent you to do this, He should provide all you need to do it with ease.' Eventually, after knocking on the doors and not getting as far as I had expected, I sought God's guidance as I considered a different career path, which led me to my current path. I still cannot explain why the reality I experienced was a mismatch with the direction I believed I received from God my Father; but I asked for grace to move on without regrets or being heart-broken and He graciously answered that prayer.

It is enough for me to know that He knows what went wrong and that, as He promised, He will never leave me nor forsake me. While I do not know why that path did not work out for me, I know that my God was with me all the way and is still with me now that I have moved into a different career path.

Then consider our Lord Jesus and what I regard as the most important prayer of all. He knew what God's will was - for Him to die a cruel death at the hands of men to pay the ransom for all men to be saved and reconciled to God. He had said in John 3:14-15, "And as Moses lifted up the serpent in the wilderness, even so must the Son of Man be lifted up, that whoever believes in Him should not perish but have eternal life." This was no pleasant task and after talking to God the Father in prayer and finding no suitable alternatives, He submitted to the Father's will, saying:

> "Father, if it is Your will, take this cup away from Me; nevertheless not My will, but Yours, be done." Then an angel appeared to Him from heaven, strengthening Him. And being in agony, He prayed more earnestly. Then His sweat became like great drops of blood falling down to the ground (Luke 22:42-44).

Compare this with Peter's Satan-originated opposition to the will of God the Father, recognized immediately by our Lord Jesus (Matthew 16:21-23). Once Jesus Christ knew God's will, any contrary view was an offence to Him, irrespective of whose view it was. Peter said, "Far be it from You, Lord; this shall not happen to You!" To which Jesus replied, "Get behind Me, Satan! You are an offence to Me, for you are not mindful of the things of God, but the things of men." Peter and Jesus were pretty close.

THE FEAR OF GOD

Think of a strong relationship in your own life, say a friend, spouse or family member; can you imagine replying to them in that manner? Jesus loved and valued Peter, that was not in question. Peter was not a hard shell, he was as sensitive as any other human being. The lesson here is that the relationship comes under and not above the authority of the Most High.

To walk with someone who fears God can be challenging sometimes and one should learn to yield our relationships to God and not impose ourselves in a way that puts the relationship at risk or makes the loved one go against God. We must 'live and let live' by the fear of God.

Jesus said in Matthew 10:37-38, "He who loves father or mother more than Me is not worthy of Me. And he who loves son or daughter more than Me is not worthy of Me. And he who does not take his cross and follow after Me is not worthy of Me."

When we seek to know what to do in any situation, we should put our request for insight or wisdom to God in prayer. He may choose to use people to instruct us. However, we must submit every advice to godly scrutiny, being guided by the word of God. We therefore must be rich towards God's word. The fear of God involves knowing His will and giving it due regard. Without His word, we would make mistakes, wrong decisions, equating to what God says in Hosea 4:6a 'My people are destroyed for lack of knowledge.'

Like Peter, people, including Christians and non-Christians, have the tendency to give advice that is not filtered by the fear of God. Without necessarily asking everyone who gives us an ungodly advice or advice against God's will, to 'get behind me Satan,' we can consider every advice carefully and make a decision on how to handle the issue at hand.

Moreover, when we stand before the Judge of all the earth (Genesis 18:25b, James 5:9, Acts 17:31, Romans 3:6 & Romans 2:16), stating that we acted on the advice of another would not withstand scrutiny, as it did not for neither Eve nor Adam in Genesis 3.

In line with Matthew 16:23, 'Get behind me Satan!' - should be our response when evil manifests itself through people rather than regard the people themselves as evil. Equally important is the wisdom to recognise ungodly counsel in other to respond appropriately.

THE FEAR OF GOD

CHAPTER 2

COMPLIMENTS OF THE FEAR OF GOD

*T*he fear of God creates an environment for one's trust in Him to flourish. Jesus Christ put it this way in Matthew 6:25-34:

"Therefore I say to you, do not worry about your life, what you will eat or what you will drink; nor about your body, what you will put on. Is not life more than food and the body more than clothing? Look at the birds of the air, for they neither sow nor reap nor gather into barns; yet your heavenly Father feeds them. Are you not of more value than they? Which of you by worrying can add one cubit to his stature? So why do you worry about clothing? Consider the lillies of the field, how they grow; they neither toil nor spin; and yet I say to you that even Solomon in all his glory was not arrayed like one of these. Now if God so clothes the grass of the field, which today is, and tomorrow is thrown into the oven, will He not much more clothe you, O you of little faith? Therefore do not worry, saying, 'What shall we eat?' or 'What shall we drink?' or 'What shall we wear?' For after all these things the Gentiles seek. For your heavenly Father knows that you need all these things. But seek first the kingdom of God and His righteousness, and all these things shall be added to you. Therefore do not worry about tomorrow, for tomorrow will worry about its own things. Sufficient for the day is its own trouble."

This passage compares well with the one which says, 'Let us hear the conclusion of the whole matter: Fear God and keep His commandments, for this is man's all' (Ecclesiastes 12:13). Seek to establish God's authority in all you are involved with, this is what He requires of us, promising that the things we need would be added to us. We then need to let God take care of us. The duty to provide for us is His.

Again, using the Eve example, the enemy convinced her that she needed this thing which, God was denying her and which she had the ability to get for herself. The truth rather was that God had provided all that she needed. When the place of God in our lives is crowded by things that make Him a blur to us, we start to take things into our hands and this is always accompanied by worries.

Worrying dishonours the LORD. He does not want us doing that. When I hear my own children asking where something is going to come from, 'how?' 'when?' despite explanations that it will be provided, it saddens me to think that they feel at that moment that they can not be provided for. We ought to spend the time praying to God about it rather than worrying over the situation. Worrying belittles His faithfulness, think it through for a moment.

As a consequence of the afflictions Satan brought upon

Job, with God's permission, he suffered terrible blows and lost all he had, except his life and his wife (though he lost her support in the process). Not knowing the reason or cause of his afflictions, his assessment of the situation goes something like this:

> "But He (God) is unique, and who can make Him change? And whatever His soul desires, that He does. For He performs what is appointed for me, and many such things are with Him. Therefore I am terrified at His presence; when I consider this, I am afraid of Him" - Job 23:13-15.

Earlier, his perspective when he heard the series of losses that culminated in the loss of all his children – he said falling down to the ground in worship – "Naked I came from my mother's womb, and naked shall I return there. The LORD gave, and the LORD has taken away; blessed be the name of the LORD" – Job 1:21.

This sounds like a faithless or negative confession when viewed initially. However, bear in mind that Job did not say, 'the LORD will take away.' Before this, he had placed every expectation of good and protection on God as demonstrated by his regular sacrifices (Job 1:4-5).

Today, we fight the enemy and atimes forget that nothing can come to us, which the LORD has not permitted and filtered through. The enemy cannot do whatever he wishes and when he wishes, thank God for that!

Thus, even in times of sorrow and loss, we must still acknowledge God Almighty as sovereign and the One who is in control. Such times are times we should trust Him that loved us so much as to send His only Son to a painful death on the cross just so that we may have the privilege of coming into relationship with Him. He wants the best for us at all times, including during the rough seasons of life.

In Ecclesiastes 7:14, the Bible encourages us that, "In the day of prosperity be joyful, but in the day of adversity consider: surely God has appointed the one as well as the other, so that man can find out nothing that will come after him." However, the Bible teaches that God is afflicted when His children suffer affliction as recorded in Isaiah 63:9, 'In all their affliction He was afflicted, and the Angel of His Presence saved them; in His love and in His pity He redeemed them; and He bore them and carried them all the days of old.'

The Impact Of The Fear Of God On Relationships

Man was given the desire and ability to have dominion (Genesis 1: 28) but lost the power and authority to do so at the fall (Genesis chapter 3). Submission to each other, and submission to God, can appear to be the root of many relational problems.

If you let the person you work with or do life together with take dominion over circumstance(s) that affect you, even in part, this tends to lead to a better relationship. This has been my experience and applies within the home, among extended family members, at work, in the church, on the streets - everywhere.

However, the reality is that human beings resists submission for any reason at all. When it is forcefully imposed, it becomes a violation of a person's human right to choose what to get involved in or what is done to him or her. For example, in the hospital setting, a person should only be given treatment that he or she has consented to except in the case of an emergency and when the person's level of consciousness or understanding limits the ability to give such consent.

Going contrary to this essentially constitutes an assault, even if the treatment improved the person's state of health. Even the Almighty God does not impose submission upon us except in exceptional circumstances like Jonah who was pressured into obedience. He warns us of the implications of a life lived without submission to His authority, a life lived in disregard of whom God is, a life lived without the fear of God. Still He leaves the choice to us.

Several international regulatory bodies spend a lot of time, money and effort to prevent the imposition of unlawful authority over individuals by those who have the power to do so. Despite this, several people across the world still suffer unjust imposition of submission and oppression with no assistance from regulatory bodies, sometimes continuing until someone with a strong voice speaks of their behalf, at other times endlessly as no one represents the oppressed.

This happened to the Jews who were destroyed over several months through the activities of the tyrant Hitler and his cohorts before the world got round to doing something about it. The trans-Atlantic slave trade is another example of such oppression by forced submission associated with deprivation of liberty.

Though God Almighty gives us the opportunity to

choose our ways, He overrules the authorities among men when He determines in His righteous judgment that this is the just thing to do.

Ponder Time

How can we regulate the desire to exercise dominion without causing persistent strife?

Problems arising from the desire in man to take dominion can be explored according to

1. Those who want to exercise dominion over others

2. Those who are under the dominion of others

Our power to have dominion should be yielded to God. The most significant difference between the 'good' person who refuses to submit to God but is charitable to everyone and never hurts a bird or an ant, and the Christian who embraces similar values and principles but chooses to submit to God – is the lack of desire to submit to God.

The person who wants to submit to God is not necessarily the one who has it all sorted, but the one who admits he needs sorting and is willing to ask God to help him and also willing to work with God in the process of being sorted.

Consider the experience of our Lord Jesus – more than twelve legions of angels were at His disposal but He yielded His authority to God the Father (Matthew 26:53).

According to Merriam-Webster Dictionary, a legion is defined as the principal unit of the Roman army comprising about 3000-6000 foot soldiers. So, more than twelve legions, which equate to at least 36,000 angels, were available to Jesus, more than enough to dispatch the crowd that crucified Him.

Bearing in mind that the angel of the LORD killed 185,000 Assyrian soldiers just by passing through their camp puts this in perspective (2 Kings 19:35).

Similarly, obeying God demands that we yield our ability or desire to do the opposite to His will or word, choosing rather to submit to His authority. Obedience to God's word is commanded by Jesus in Luke 11:28 where He says, "…. blessed are those who hear the word of God and keep it!"

Commenting on the Lord's humility and encouraging Christians to do the same, Paul wrote in the letter to the Philippians chapter 2 verses 5-11:

> Let this mind be in you which was also in Christ Jesus, who, being in the form of God, did not consider it robbery to be equal with God, but made Himself of no reputation, taking the form of a bondservant, and coming in the likeness of men. And being found in appearance as a man, He humbled Himself and became obedient to the point of death, even the death of the cross. Therefore God also has highly exalted Him and given Him the name which is above every name, that at the name of Jesus every knee should bow, of those in heaven, and of those on earth, and of those under the earth, and that every tongue should confess that Jesus Christ is Lord, to the glory of God the Father.

THE FEAR OF GOD

In various aspects of living, one finds that it is inevitable to encounter people who want to exert an unlawful dominion over others. I do not know about you but anytime I feel as though someone wants to 'ride over me' or 'take me for granted' or treat me as if I was nothing, (to use some of the everyday phrases) something in me wants to rebel strongly.

These days I am learning in such occasions to resist the temptation of rising to the bait of taking offence; rather, to let it go. Sometimes you have to 'take it' in the interest of peace. Turning the other cheek for the person to do the same is however; a completely different issue. Personally, I am very much a learner in that respect.

The Holy Spirit had to advise Peter or he would have responded unfavourably to the request to go down to Cornelius's house especially as Cornelius was not a Jew (Acts chapter 10). Do you look down on those around you? Do you treat your juniors like insignificant persons, or abuse those under you?

If you do, you are not alone. I have caught myself judge people and mistreat them because I felt I was better than them or because I thought I deserved better than they did due to my position within the particular establishment.

In Paul's speech to the people gathered to him in Athens at the time, he quoted an earlier speaker in Acts 17:26 saying, "'And He (God) has made from one blood every nation of men to dwell on all the face of the earth, and has determined their pre-appointed times and the boundaries of their dwellings.'"

It follows therefore that those who are around you at any

place or time have been appointed to be there by the LORD Himself. You may not like them, even for valid reasons, but for the regard you have for the One who brought them to you, you would do well to treat them respectfully and even more importantly, to find out the LORD's purpose for establishing that particular link or relationship between you and such a person. We are advised not to think of ourselves more highly than we ought. In Romans 12: 3,

Paul puts it this way, 'For I say, through the grace given to me, to everyone who is among you, not to think of himself more highly than he ought to think, but to think soberly, as God has dealt to each one a measure of faith.' This is not an instruction to devalue oneself, but to treat others as highly valued creation of the Almighty God. The fear of God should remove strife from our relationships. One way of achieving this is by removing unhealthy competition.

The Bible tells us in 2 Corinthians 10:12 that those who compare themselves are foolish: 'For we dare not class ourselves or compare ourselves with those who commend themselves. But they, measuring themselves by themselves, and comparing themselves among themselves, are not wise.'

When we acknowledge God as our source, we know that we can look to Him for anything we desire, and that it is for Him to fulfil or give us those desires, and not for us to look to another person to give them to us. So, when we do not have our heart's desire, we should look to God rather than fight with those who have it already, or blame those we thought had the power to make it possible for not making it happen.

THE FEAR OF GOD

Remember the Holy Bible's record of the case between Rachel and her sister Leah who were married to Jacob, and between Hannah and Peninnah the wives of Elkanah. In Genesis 30:1-2 we read:

> 'Now when Rachel saw that she bore Jacob no children, Rachel envied her sister, and said to Jacob, "Give me children, or else I die!" And Jacob's anger was aroused against Rachel, and he said, "Am I in the place of God, who has withheld from you the fruit of the womb?"'

Hannah on the other hand cried out to God with a vow:

> Then Elkanah her husband said to her, "Hannah, why do you weep? Why do you not eat? And why is your heart grieved? Am I not better to you than ten sons?" So Hannah arose after they had finished eating and drinking in Shiloh. Now Eli the priest was sitting on the seat by the doorpost of the tabernacle of the LORD. And she was in bitterness of soul, and prayed to the LORD and wept in anguish. Then she made a vow and said, "O LORD of hosts, if You will indeed look on the affliction of Your maidservant and remember me, and not forget Your maidservant, but will give Your maidservant a male child, then I will give him to the LORD all the days of his life, and no razor shall come upon his head."

Considering the foregoing discuss, it is good advice

that when we have what others lack, we should soberly remember that God chose to give it to us and to deny them. He could have chosen, and indeed could still choose to give it to the other person and make us the ones without the particular thing or privilege.

Bearing this in mind, one should not look down on those who are in a less privileged position as well as not giving those more privileged than us the honour due God. Rather, one should give due regard to all, acknowledging that God is the one who placed each person in their particular circumstance as He saw fit.

Consider an example with a work place scenario: a colleague seems to be getting ahead; one ought not blame or fight with the boss who promoted the person, nor with the colleague who got promoted. Rather such a person ought to reach out to God not in covetousness' but with a sincere desire to excel to His glory and to see the fulfilment of His promises; for example, that as His child whatever one lays hands on would prosper.

Here we see that giving God His rightful place brings the 'live and let live' statement alive. It makes it easier to sincerely congratulate a colleague who gets what you had worked or yearned for even before the colleague stepped into the scene; even when naturally, it seems you were unfairly bypassed while your colleague was promoted. Sounds similar to the serpent's trickery in convincing Eve that God had left her in an under-privileged position when she should have been much better placed, leading her into a most terrible mistake.

When we misplace our perception of our source, we not

only misplace the cause of our loss, but also we misplace the expectation of the maintenance of what we have. Let me explain. Take for instance, joy or happiness; if you think your joy has come from someone or something, you will focus your efforts on serving that person or thing, aligning your living or your being to make certain that the person or thing maintains your joy.

Conversely, we would also ascribe the loss of the joy to a breakdown in the structures or schemes we set up to maintain this presumed source of joy. Say for instance we take our joy to arise from a relationship; we would be inclined to give our all to maintain that relationship.

If it falls apart, so also does the joy attributed to it fall apart. Can I encourage you to re-examine this issue for yourself on a personal level. Your peace, joy, happiness, promotion, confidence and anything else you value is not sourced from anyone but God Himself. He may chose to do this through people or things but ultimately, He is the giver of every good and perfect gift – James 1:17.

Similarly, regarding any unfavourable situation including lack, sorrow, disappointment, loneliness, pain or low self-esteem; He is not unaware of one's need in these circumstances of life. If you are going to see victory in the situation, you need to look to the Almighty God, and Him alone, to make a way for you into the abundant life that is yours in Christ Jesus, as recorded in John 10:10, 'The thief does not come except to steal, and to kill, and to destroy. I have come that they may have life, and that they may have it more abundantly.'

The Bible has records of people who ascribed their

sorrows to God Almighty. Sarai said, "See now, the LORD has restrained me from bearing children" (Genesis 16:2a). When Isaac found that Rebekkah was barren, he pleaded with the LORD for her and she conceived (Genesis 25:21). As mentioned above, when Rachel, having had no children implored Jacob saying, "Give me children, or else I die!" his reply was, "Am I in the place of God, who has withheld from you the fruit of the womb?" (Genesis 30:1-2).

Later, God remembered Rachel, listened to her and opened her womb so that she conceived and bore a son. Her comment, "God has taken away my reproach," implied an acknowledgement that her situation was under God's control after all (Genesis 30:22-23). Hannah's husband Elkanah loved her, but it was the LORD who closed her womb (1 Samuel 1:5-6). Answer to prayer also belongs to God. In Psalms 65:2 we read, 'O You who hear prayer, to You all flesh will come.'

Ponder Time

For who makes you differ from another? And what do you have that you did not receive? Now if you did indeed receive it, why do you boast as if you had not received it? – 1 Corinthians 4:7.

John the Baptist said in John 3:27 that, "A man can receive nothing unless it has been given to him from heaven." In 1 Peter 4:11 we read, 'If anyone speaks, let him speak as the oracles of God. If anyone ministers, let him do it as with the ability which God supplies, that in all things God may be glorified through Jesus Christ, to whom belong the glory and the dominion forever and ever. Amen.'

Equally, when we find ourselves being a source of blessing or assistance to others, we ought not to take the glory or praise for it, but to thank God for the privilege to bless His own beloved creation.

Even as our Lord Jesus says that when we do something for those who belong to Him, we will not go unrewarded, 'For whoever gives you a cup of water to drink in My name, because you belong to Christ, assuredly, I say to you, he will by no means lose his reward' – Mark 9:41.

If we looked upon everyone and treated them as though they belonged to Jesus, the world would be a much better place. Our world will shift from asking God for a reward to thanking Him for setting us up to be a help, knowing that when we sow a blessing to another, we will reap blessing to ourselves.

Let us consider in greater detail the case of Hannah and Peninnah, the two wives of Elkanah. Peninnah, who had many sons and daughters each of whom received a portion of the family's annual offering, frequently taunted Hannah who was barren. So severe was the verbal provocation that Hannah wept and refused to eat. Peninnah's words achieved something by way of a temporary upset or depression.

Hannah got delivered out of her barrenness by turning to God (1 Samuel chapter 1). Her desperation and the taunting of Peninnah led her to promise to dedicate her son Samuel to the LORD before he was conceived. In line with God's purpose, Samuel ultimately became one of the greatest prophets in Israel.

So, should Hannah not have bothered about her barrenness and just let God work out His purpose? Well, if she did not get desperate, she would not have dedicated Samuel to the LORD; though that is not to say that he would not have become a prophet.

Our feelings, desires and fears are part of our make-up; they contribute to our personality but need to be submitted to God rather than being allowed to determine our actions in life. In Philippians 2:13 we read, 'for it is God who works in you both to will and to do for His good pleasure.' So in all unfavourable or challenging situations, we ought not to fret, but rather commit all to Him in prayer.

To the person that blesses you, by all means render thanks, but give the glory to God. For the person that betrays you, forgive and turn to God for wisdom to handle the situation, trusting Him for vindication and a favourable outcome.

Also, it is worth bearing in mind that when our times of testing come, God will work through those around us. Someone who is unknown to you, in a distant land, can hardly stretch your patience. Beware that when God wants to develop patience in you, He will not use a person without any connection to you or influence upon you.

So, say for instance, you live in the United Kingdom, a person in China may not be able to effectively put some pressure on your patience to test and develop it. It is the person in your immediate surrounding area or neighbourhood, the one you share the available everyday

local facilities with, your 'neighbour.' Just as those who
share the use of the roads with you are likely to get in your
way, and you likewise are likely to get in their way.

Sometimes it could be someone close, such as a spouse,
child, close relative or friend. We must look beyond the
offence and ask the LORD for strength and guidance to
deal with the situation while forgiving and praying for the
person.

In fact, you could get yourself to the point of thanking
the person for the opportunity to be trained or developed
in that area. Next time your spouse puts your patience
to the test, examine the situation this way: this is my
opportunity to keep my patience up to date or develop that
fruit of the Spirit. Then you can say, 'Father, have mercy
on them for they know not what they do,' just as Jesus did
when the people were used to bring about His necessary
crucifixion.

Prayer Pause

Father God, I thank You for everyone whose
actions have made me feel uncomfortable or
wronged. I forgive them completely and release
them to Your love. I trust You for a good outcome
from that experience in the name of Your Son
Jesus Christ. Amen.

I recall a revelation I had from the Lord some time ago
that I would be hurt by a certain person, so much so that
I may walk out of the relationship. I fasted for three days
asking the Lord to prevent the situation from arising. By

the third day, the Lord showed me that I had asked for the wrong thing. He let me know that the situation would still arise and the important thing was how I responded to it.

I then redirected my prayers to asking God for the grace to deal with the situation. I was amazed at my response to the situation when it finally arose and those around me were surprised as well. The comments I received included, "I don't know how you could take that quietly. I was waiting to see your reaction but till now, you have behaved as though nothing went wrong."

The person had no idea I had the privilege of asking in advance for grace specific to the situation. We can ask for grace for daily living even if we don't get the sort of revelation I had. That was just one incidence but we know that opportunities to get offended abound in everyday life and we do need God's grace to deal with them.

When Peter the apostle spoke to our Lord Jesus to discourage Him from going to the cross (Matthew 16:22-23); true, Jesus rebuked him but do you imagine that someone else in the crowd would have had the opportunity to speak the same words of challenge to Jesus? No, it had to be someone close to Him and in this case, his friend and passionate follower Peter.

When you have the misfortune of being the source of another's anguish, repent and seek to make amends, but above all, pray for God's grace to help the person come through the trial victoriously, being strengthened in and through it. Jesus needed a Judas to get to the cross, but don't hang yourself.

Look to God to restore you from the depths that caused

you to be a cause of anguish to another and pray for the betrayed person. Joseph needed someone to get him to Egypt. His father Israel inadvertently positioned him in a place where he found himself at his brothers' mercy – Genesis 37.

We read of Israel's unimaginable grief when he realised that he was responsible for his son's 'misfortune.' 'If only he had not sent him to visit his brothers that day' he must have thought. Whether through his father or his brothers or slave traders or any other means, Joseph had to go to Egypt to fulfil his God-ordained purpose.

When he realised that this was his destiny as ordained by God he told his brothers - "So now it was not you who sent me here, but God; and He has made me a father to Pharaoh, and lord of all his house, and a ruler throughout all the land of Egypt" - Genesis 45:8.

Considering the issues we see in every day life, it is clear then that we ought not blame people whose actions put us in a position of disadvantage as happened to Joseph by his brothers. In my personal experience, I went over to England (UK) when my husband got a place to undergo further postgraduate training there. I had no idea what effect the move would have on my career goal of being a paediatric surgeon.

When I found out the hurdles that I needed to pass through, coupled with the fact that my mother was repeatedly refused a VISA to visit us and help me when I had my children, I set my heart to overcoming those hurdles and achieving my objectives.

However, as I thought the time for my career to "take

off" had arrived, having obtained the required experience, passed the necessary examinations and undertaken the relevant courses, the laws in the training system changed drastically, setting me back several years once again. I had to resolve that my fate was not controlled by human factors or decisions, but rather, that God was still in full control of my life, including my career.

I decided to keep my eyes and expectations on Him and not on people. When I excel and achieve my career goals, I will know that it has been God that made it possible. He will use people to do it eventually but it will be Him that gets the credit. The problem with giving people the credit for one's achievements and excellence is that you feel indebted to them and they can tell you how to undertake the duties involved in that situation.

However, if one ascribes every opportunity and achievement to God, then it is easier to yield one's decisions to God, doing that which pleases Him, turning away from that which displeases Him even when those around you prefer that you disregard God's opinion on the issues that surround your duties or job.

This is what I want for myself, to be able to undertake my duties yielded to God's will rather than yielding to man's will in situations when it clearly goes against God. I am not indicating by any means that I will not submit to authority in my work place; on the contrary, it is my advice to anyone to obey authority in line with the instructions of the Holy Bible.

For example, in the discourse surrounding the sanctity of life, we know that doctors have been criticised for opting out of being involved in abortions of healthy fetuses, and I know that many have stood their grounds in the face of threats and oppositions because they chose to yield to God's will rather than yield to what the Bible refers to as the will of men (see Acts 5:29).

God's ways are not our ways. Isaiah 55:8-9 says, "For My thoughts are not your thoughts, nor are your ways My ways," says the LORD. "For as the heavens are higher than the earth, so are My ways higher than your ways, and My thoughts than your thoughts." Even the well-meaning get it wrong sometimes and if we remember that Peter was a disciple of Jesus, we should bear in mind that even Christians can give advice that is not in line with God's will. So when I say the 'will of men' and the 'works of the flesh,' Christians are not excluded, all advice must be put through biblical scrutiny.

The LORD invites us to ask for wisdom as already mentioned in James 1:5. Paul wrote in 1 Corinthians 13:12b, 'Now I know in part, but then I shall know just as I also am known.' No one has the capability of knowing it all on this side of eternity.

The Bible teaches us in Proverbs 29:25 that, 'The fear of man brings a snare, but whoever trusts in the LORD shall be safe.' Misplaced loyalties are a snare. Entertaining the fear of man instead of the fear of God gives to man that which belongs to God. This equates to idolatry, a practice that the Lord detests. In Deuteronomy 32:16-18 we read a report about Israel's idolatry:

> They provoked Him to jealousy with foreign gods;
> with abominations they provoked Him to anger.

They sacrificed to demons, not to God, to gods they did not know, to new gods, new arrivals that your fathers did not fear. Of the Rock who begot you, you are unmindful, and have forgotten the God who fathered you.

The marriage covenant made before God carries a different connotation that other relationships and should be given due regard in line with the fear of God. The Bible says in Mark 10:5-9:

> And Jesus answered and said to them, "Because of the hardness of your heart he wrote you this precept. But from the beginning of the creation, God 'made them male and female. For this reason a man shall leave his father and mother and be joined to his wife, and the two shall become one flesh'; so then they are no longer two, but one flesh. Therefore what God has joined together, let not man separate."

Hence, it is not up to individuals to decide after this covenant has been made before God. One should consider carefully before deciding, 'I don't want this marriage covenant anymore!' Bearing the fear of God in mind, one should therefore think carefully before entering into the marriage covenant before the Almighty God and before breaking it up.

Similarly, when one comes across a person who is already in a marriage covenant with another, and enters into a close relationship with him or her, in such a way that makes that person give to them what he or she promised to give the person they entered the marriage covenant with; whether affection, company, material wealth or such like, this is a disregard for God and a manifestation of a lack of the fear of God.

This applies irrespective of one's position in the person's life including friend, colleague, brother, sister, mother or father. The fear of God should guide one to have a healthy regard for the marriage covenant, whether one is involved in it directly or in relation with those involved in it.

Loyalty Tailored By The Fear Of God

In 1 Timothy 6:10, the Bible says, 'For the love of money is a root of all kinds of evil, for which some have strayed from the faith in their greediness, and pierced themselves through with many sorrows.'

Jesus puts it this way in Luke 16:13 – "No servant can serve two masters; for either he will hate the one and love the other, or else he will be loyal to the one and despise the other. You cannot serve God and mammon." Mammon in broad terms represents whatever we look to for the fulfilment of our needs, independent of God whether things, self or other people.

If you are like me you are probably saying, 'Not me!' However, if you could stop for a moment to consider; today's activities in your life – whose service were they for or whose purpose have they served? Commonly, one would say, 'God understands – I have to have friends.' What about saying instead, 'I will serve God, my friends will understand?'

That's the way it should be if one gives God His rightful first place. One needs to take the stance that if friends can not handle your dedication to serve God, you can pray for God to help them understand while at same time choosing not to compromise.

I find that often one gives in to what is commonly referred to as 'peer pressure' to please friends and not be left behind. Moreover, Jesus promised that whatever we give up for the sake of putting the kingdom of God first, we would get back multiples of same in this life and beyond; "And everyone who has left houses or brothers or sisters or father or mother or wife or children or lands, for My name's sake, shall receive a hundredfold, and inherit eternal life" - Matthew 19:29.

The truth is that the things we turn to instead of trusting God are often pitifully powerless to help in the circumstance anyway. When Israel chose to trust the Egyptians turning away from God, they experienced hardship; but also, being a jealous God, He made Egypt to be a shame and reproach to them. In Isaiah 30:1-5 we read:

> "Woe to the rebellious children," says the LORD, "Who take counsel, but not of Me, and who devise plans, but not of My Spirit, that they may add sin to sin; who walk to go down to Egypt, and have not asked My advice, to strengthen themselves in the strength of Pharaoh, and to trust in the shadow of Egypt! Therefore the strength of Pharaoh shall be your shame, and trust in the shadow of Egypt shall be your humiliation. For his princes were at Zoan, and his ambassadors came to Hanes. They

were all ashamed of a people who could not benefit them, or be help or benefit, but a shame and also a reproach."

All power belongs to God. He is essentially responsible for every created thing. "Before Me there was no God formed, nor shall there be after Me," He declares in Isaiah 43:10b.

Again, as He is the Beginning and the End (Revelation 1:8), there is nothing that started that He was not involved in; equally, nothing ends without Him. He is power; hence, Jesus Himself said He would be sitting at the right hand of the Power - Matthew 26:64.

With great insight, He said to Pilate who claimed to have the power to either crucify or release Him, "You could have no power at all against Me unless it had been given you from above," - John 19:11a. Every exercise of power has its origin in God. Thus, Isaiah 54:16-17 says that because He has created the makers of all forms of weapons – no weapon formed against His people will prosper. That means these weapons, produced with the intention of harming or opposing the progress of God's people, will not produce the expected results for the one who made them.

The Bible further adds in Romans 8:28, 'And we know that all things work together for good to those who love God, to those who are the called according to His purpose.' God is the One in charge of all creation. He made all things, the visible and the invisible. He is in charge of the good and the evil, including Satan.

We learnt how Satan sought God's permission to touch the blessings He had given to Job (Job 1:7-12). All things work together, including Satan. Did you ever think that the activities of evil around you work together for your good as a child of God?

The Bible says - all things. From the onset of creation, evil has worked out God's purpose not Him stumbling upon evil activities and mopping things up after Satan. Before man was created, God had prepared for Jesus to come and die to redeem us.

Without the fall, we would not be born again and God would not live within us. Since living within us and being one with us has been God's purpose from start, one can see that the serpent's temptation and Adam and Eve's fall would serve God's purpose rather than the serpent's purpose.

So, next time you start to think like I used to 'If only Eve had not listened to the serpent and eaten the apple,' stop and thank God for the way He has provided redemption through Christ, giving us a better place than we would have had without 'the fall.'

Of course, one must be mindful that on the other hand the story remains tragic for those who turn away from God's provision for this redemption plan for whom an eternal place in hell awaits; this should motivate us to witness to such people through our lives and our words, prayerfully.

Therefore, when we find ourselves in a situation where it seems the enemy has dealt us a blow, let us seek God's face and hand the situation to Him expecting a divine turn around to our good and to the glory of God. Satan's activities never take God unawares.

People create robotics, even to do operations under human control and guidance as well as to perform many complex activities. Sometimes these robots get out of control or they fail to connect and obey the instructions of the one controlling them. This is not so with God Almighty; all of His creation is under His control at all times. He gives them the power to choose and do certain things but only what He has allowed.

Similarly, consider different types of machinery that have their different parts made by their respective manufacturing firms. When a certain part malfunctions, one has to refer to the manufacturers to establish what the origin of the fault is and also to restore the normal function of that part. However, the entire universe and beyond has been created by One, that is God alone. He shares ownership of the universe with none other. When anything seems to malfunction, He is the One who knows what has gone wrong and who or what is required to set things right.

For example, a word may be spoken to put a person down, but ends up being the galvanising agent that takes that person to a place of higher privilege or authority. You may have heard someone state that they were told they would never amount to anything and that word spurred them and shook them out of their complacency with the result that they go for and achieve greater heights than they would have reached for without the challenge.

This was the case for Jabez who would not have said his prayer if he was not stirred by the name given him by his mother - 1 Chronicles 4:9-10. Several books and sermons have since been written concerning the young man's life.

Challenges in life should be seen as preparatory agents for greater victories and stepping-stones into our God-ordained place in life. David's encounter with the lion and the bear that he killed emboldened and prepared him for the battle he faced with Goliath:

> But David said to Saul, "Your servant used to keep his father's sheep, and when a lion or a bear came and took a lamb out of the flock, I went out after it and struck it, and delivered the lamb from its mouth; and when it arose against me, I caught it by its beard, and struck and killed it. Your servant has killed both lion and bear; and this uncircumcised Philistine will be like one of them, seeing he has defied the armies of the living God." Moreover David said, "The LORD, who delivered me from the paw of the lion and from the paw of the bear, He will deliver me from the hand of this Philistine." And Saul said to David, "Go, and the LORD be with you!" (1 Samuel 17:34-37).

Compare David's response to Goliath's challenge to Israel's response to the same. All the men of Israel, when they saw Goliath, fled from him and were dreadfully afraid (1 Samuel 17:24).

David's response was, "For who is this uncircumcised Philistine, that he should defy the armies of the living God?" – 1 Samuel 17:26b. Either Goliath did not recognise Israel as God's armies, or he did and chose not to give due respect to them or to their God.

Just as Satan recognised Job as God-fearing and chose not to give due respect to him, rather he sought God's permission to oppress Job. Imagine a man's enemy asking

119

his permission to strike his son; that is what happened here. Challenges in life have the same approach, why would sickness defy the LORD's armies and threaten the bodies of Christians, irrespective of the fact that they are His temple?

Why would a boss dismiss a Christian unfairly for the open expression of his or her faith? Why would Christians be killed for their faith by those who disregard their God? In Acts, our Lord Jesus clearly told Saul that in oppressing Christians he was oppressing the Lord Himself.

Let us take a look at Israel historically, why did King Nebuchadnezzar take Jerusalem captive, knowing they were God's people? God allowed him on that occasion even as Israel did not heed God's warnings and He handed them over to King Nebuchadnezzar - Jeremiah chapter 21.

In the case of the threat posed by the Moabites, the Ammonites and others who came against the people of Judah and their king, King Jehoshaphat, we see that God showed Himself strong on their behalf as the whole nation cried out to Him for help in fasting - 2 Chronicles chapter 20. Did these cities that opposed Israel have no regard for their God or did they not know about Him?

The Bible says concerning our Lord Jesus' crucifixion and glorious conclusion of His ministry as a man on earth:

> But we speak the wisdom of God in a mystery, the hidden wisdom which God ordained before the ages for our glory, which none of the rulers of this age knew; for had they known, they would not have crucified the Lord of glory - 1 Corinthians 2:7-8.

If those who were involved in the crucifixion of the Lord Jesus had recognised Him as the Son of God, they would not have laid hands on Him or even let any others do so.

Knowing who you are and knowing Your God, empowers you to thank God for the season of any oppression you experience and trust that it is working out for your good even when it seems as though it would not.

Thank God in the midst of oppression that keeps you on your knees at His feet; it always turns around for your good and to His glory! 1 Thessalonians 5:16 says, 'Rejoice always,' as do several other passages from the Bible.

Ponder Time

How much do you know about yourself?
How much do you know the LORD God?

In conducting a research for instance, you have a primary end point or outcome that is your main focus, the main issue you want to get answers for. However, you may get other results and these are called secondary outcomes.

Similarly, when the enemy stirs up trouble, he has some primary goals or end points to achieve; generally intending to kill, steal and destroy. Bear in mind that the enemy does not know God's plans in full.

Though he has an endpoint, which the Lord allows, He however works through those same circumstances to bring His ordained outcomes as we trust Him and hold on to Him. Trust God that the secondary outcomes of every unpleasant event will work out for your good to His glory. That is the message of Romans 8:28.

Interestingly, many people deny the very existence of God; let alone thank Him for every day's provisions and protection. Have you observed how people blame God for hardships but seldom or never acknowledge Him in the things that go right? For instance, one may not thank God for life on waking up to a new day, but turns to blame Him should an accident be encountered during the course of the day.

One sometimes hears comments such as, "What God would allow an earthquake that claims thousands of lives?" The truth is God was aware of the slavery that swept across the African nations, their colonisation, often by oppressive government, the continuing oppression of nations by tyrant leaders, the destruction of millions of Jews, recurring Tsunamis and hurricanes, unprovoked violent activities that claim numerous innocent lives across the nations to mention a few.

Same God who was aware of the destruction of Sodom and Gomorrah, and the destruction of man and the creatures on the earth by the flood that spared the family of the man Noah.

The last two instances are recorded in the Bible; the people were warned of the impending tragedy but disregarded the warnings and refused to accept God's offer of reconciliation, which would have averted both disasters. Same God is aware that the end for those who reject Him and His offer of reconciliation through His Son Jesus Christ will be in a place of eternal separation from Him – hell.

Today He demands of all believers to spread the good news about His love, which brought the best offering, the death of His only begotten Son, as atonement for the sins of anyone who accepts this offer. Today this good news is similarly disregarded as the devil continues the same pattern of deception he used on Eve, making people believe that they need, deserve and can have more than what God is offering.

I recall telling a friend of my deep disappointment when I had a miscarriage, how much I longed for a second child. I knew my friend was married, but I had no insight into her situation. However, she kept quiet as I moaned about my loss. I already had a son who was 3 years old at the time.

When I finished my story and looked up at my friend, there was a tear on her cheek. She said, "If only I could even have a miscarriage, it would help me feel more like a woman." She had been married for a few years but never conceived let alone miscarry a pregnancy.

When I heard her, I felt so sad at my self-centeredness. I apologised to my friend and she was understanding of the fact that I had my focus fully on my own problem and had not stopped to consider her own plight. She went on to recruit a team of praying people who joined her in calling on the LORD for a miracle as the doctors had told her that she had a less than one percent chance of having a baby by natural conception.

Today she has many lovely children without any medical assistance. To God Almighty be the glory and honour!! If she had taken a different attitude of blaming God for her childlessness and turning away from Him, she would almost certainly have ended up with a very different less favourable outcome.

While working in a hospital in Brighton, a Christian friend and colleague invited me to listen to a Jewish man's story of how he survived the holocaust. Amazing! The man had lost his entire family – brothers, sisters and parents. Along with others who moved with him, he spent long periods of time in extremely cold weather. They frequently went for prolonged periods with no food, only the occasional drink, crowded in unimaginable conditions.

He spoke of a time when God gave him favour before one of the guards who gave him portions of food, which he in turn shared with fellow prisoners. He was nearly dead by the end of the war and was in fact left for dead. After spending several days on a pile of dead bodies he found himself in hospital a month later completely unaware of how he got there. He had suffered a terrible bout of enteritis, which eventually perforated his bowel for which he required an operation.

Watching him as he told his story, then in his eighties and standing strong, with his skin showing no sign of the scars he talked about on his face, I knew that the LORD had miraculously healed him and preserved his life.

Now what do you think, should he thank God for saving his life or be angry at the loss of his family and the trauma and abuse he had undergone? Was he saved by a deliberate miraculous act of God or was he just lucky? I suppose if he died with the rest of the people, then the question would not be necessary, even as no one challenges God from the grave.

Whatever God gives us He allows us the freedom to choose whether or not to yield it to Himself. In many cases it seems that He does not get recognition as the giver of the gift but, when it all goes wrong, He gets blamed for the malfunction of the gift or for taking it away.

When asked if he had disobeyed God by eating the forbidden fruit, Adam replied, "The woman whom You gave to be with me, she gave me of the tree, and I ate" – Genesis 3:12. Rather than take responsibility for his wrongdoing, Adam blamed his fall on the fact that God had given him a wife.

This illustration also applies to today's living. Have you heard someone who refused to change his or her sinful ways say, "God made me the way I am." For example, the one who refuses to clothe himself or herself appropriately but exposes body parts indecently announces that if God wanted him or her to hide it all, He would not have given such a great body.

Similarly, one who lives according to what the Bible describes as ungodly sexual desires claims that God gave him or her those desires, creating him or her that way. It is interesting to note that God Himself made Satan beautiful and gave him everything he had. In Ezekiel 28:12-15, referring to Lucifer the Bible says:

"Son of man, take up a lamentation for the king of Tyre, and say to him, 'Thus says the Lord GOD: "You were the seal of perfection, full of wisdom and perfect in beauty. You were in Eden, the garden of God; every precious stone was your covering: the sardius, topaz, and diamond, beryl, onyx, and jasper, sapphire, turquoise, and emerald with gold. The workmanship of your timbrels and pipes was prepared for you on the day you were created. "You were the anointed cherub who covers; I established you; you were on the holy mountain of God; you walked back and forth in the midst of fiery stones. You were perfect in your ways from the day you were created, till iniquity was found in you.

In Isaiah 14:12-15, the Bible says that he even had a throne:

"How you are fallen from heaven, O Lucifer, son of the morning! How you are cut down to the ground, you who weakened the nations! For you have said in your heart: 'I will ascend into heaven, I will exalt my throne above the stars of God; I will also sit on the mount of the congregation on the farthest sides of the north; I will ascend above the heights of the clouds, I will be like the Most High.' Yet you shall be brought down to Sheol, to the lowest depths of the Pit.

However, Satan had to pay for his rebellion, having not been excused by his creator.

In contrast to the foregoing argument, our Lord Jesus instructs us that if what one has received from God would make one live a life against His requirements, to remove that from oneself, even if it is one's eyes, hands or feet (Matthew 18:8-9). When we yield our lives to God's ordained purpose and will, then whatever comes of it – the responsibility is His to sort out not ours, all we need do is yield to Him.

The Bible tells us that 'He (God) does not afflict willingly, nor grieve the children of men' – Lamentations 3:33; rather, that He is afflicted whenever His children are afflicted (Isaiah 63:9a).

Peter the apostle contributed to the discourse as follows, 'The Lord is not slack concerning His promise, as some count slackness, but is longsuffering toward us, not willing that any should perish but that all should come to repentance' – 2 Peter 3:9. In fact, the Lord God so values us that He makes creation all in order, just right - before the main guest of honour is created, that being man.

You may have several questions at this point. Some questions that I have been asked include - if God so loved us why didn't He just save us all? Why make Satan in the first instance? Couldn't He have saved the whole world without letting His precious Son Jesus die such a tragic death for that cause?

In Deuteronomy 29:29 the Holy Bible informs us that we can only know as much as it pleases God to reveal to us. It can feel frustrating to have limited knowledge and that was the challenge faced by Adam and Eve. We face the same challenge today and at best, all we can do is yield that limitation to God. The question is – what have we done with what information we have been given, never mind what is yet unrevealed.

Truth is, no one would know the answers to every question that could arise out of the intelligence God has given to the human mind. We see dimly, and we know in part ......for now (1 Corinthians 13:12). He graciously gives revelation into several issues of life. For example, today, the evidence in favour of creation is more than ever before and quite significant.

There are several books written about these including the 'Examine the Evidence' series by Ralph O. Muncaster. One of my favourite Christian teachers, Kat Kerr – a Revelator, has been taken to heaven on several occasions and taken back in time to see historical events including the process of creation; she has also written and spoken about the creation process.

Those who lived before these pieces of evidence were unearthed were still expected to believe God's account of creation as we are; and though revelation may be even deeper in the future, we are expected to believe God's word based on what is available to us, even same as those who will live in centuries to come who may have even stronger physical evidence.

The one thing that stops God is our will, we can say no to Him and He may choose to allow us take the path that is against His will. Consider for example Isaiah 1:18-20:

> "Come now, and let us reason together," says the LORD, "Though your sins are like scarlet, they shall be as white as snow; though they are red like crimson, they shall be as wool. If you are willing and obedient, you shall eat the good of the land; but if you refuse and rebel, you shall be devoured by the sword"; for the mouth of the LORD has spoken.

In Revelation 3:20 we find a similar saying from the Lord Jesus - "Behold, I stand at the door and knock. If anyone hears My voice and opens the door, I will come to him and dine with him, and he with Me."

It is amazing and mind-blowing but also terrifying that He leaves the choice to us. I recall a few times when I had been out to do some shopping with my daughter when she was eleven years old, I would usually give her a small amount of money to buy something for herself.

The intention was for her to develop the ability to make appropriate choice of clothing and jewellery for example; but also I could provide guidance on how to choose the right thing in the midst of such a wide variety of goods, especially when her desires may not be appropriate for the occasion. This was also a money saving scheme for me because, without giving her a specified amount of money,

I often found myself spending a lot more on the things she chose. Many times she would ask me to choose for her. I went through a phase where I would gladly choose something for her. Then I found out most of those articles I chose were not being used for any reasonable length of time.

Once when I asked why I had not seen her wearing something we had bought together, she replied that she did not like it and that it was my choice after all. I quickly learnt to say, 'You're the one who would be wearing it so pick what you would like to wear.'

I believe the Father leaves us to make life's decisions ourselves partly to enable us own responsibility and accept the consequences of our actions. However, when we earnestly seek His help to make choices, truly yielding our desires to Him, He is very pleased to come to our aid.

Relationship Between The Fear Of God And His Word

When one asks for proof of God's existence, the truth is usually that one has not accepted what He has revealed about Himself and is unlikely to accept even further evidence. What is required really is to have one's heart open and receptive to Him, to give Him a chance like we would give our history teachers in school.

I remember believing the accounts of my history teacher and writers of history books as though they were there when it all happened, even without questioning the evidence given. The fear of God enables us believe God's word even when our human mind fails to comprehend it. The question we should ask is – 'Is this the word of God?'

If the answer is to the affirmative, then one can confidently apply that word to supersede the word or opinion of others as the power of God is above all. Every word carries power. Proverbs 18:21 says, 'Death and life are in the power of the tongue.' Ecclesiastes 8:4a says, 'Where the word of a king is, there is power.' It then follows that the King of kings deserves the place for the power of His word to overrule that of others.

In response to the question from the elders of the people who requested of Him, "If You are the Christ, tell us" Jesus answered, "If I tell you, you will by no means believe." This was confirmed in their next breath as they accused Him of blasphemy when He replied to the next question.

They asked Jesus, "Are You then the Son of God?" to which He replied - "You rightly say that I am" - Luke 22:67-71.

The rich man in hell mentioned in the Lord Jesus' illustration asked for someone to go tell his brothers about hell in order to spare them the experience of hell. Abraham's response was that even if someone went from there to tell them, they would not believe (Luke 16:19-31).

Today, there are several accounts of people whom God has given the experience of heaven and/or of hell who came back and wrote their report. Their books are available widely but I have been met with cynical remarks when I speak of these reports. True to the story told by our Lord Jesus, people just will not receive or believe the story.

This is proof the problem is beyond what is spoken or what information is given but the important thing is the heart with which it is received.

The LORD is the only One who has the authority to reverse or amend His word. The Gethsemane prayer of our Lord Jesus recorded in Luke 22:42 reads, "Father, if it is Your will, take this cup away from Me; nevertheless not My will, but Yours, be done."

Jesus yielded His pain and anguish to God the Father in this Gethsemane prayer setting an example for us to follow in circumstances where God's will comes with a physically challenging price which we are struggling to pay.

On that occasion, the LORD maintained His stance concerning the sacrifice Jesus had to go through to see our salvation paid for in full. Compare this with the request of Hezekiah, king of Israel, whose request for an extension of his life was granted after God had said he was to die in his illness (2 Kings 20:1-11). For Jesus Christ on the other hand, there was no substitute to take His place.

A 'word' may be likened to a courtroom verdict. The enforcement agents have to execute the contents of the verdict unless a higher body within the law gives a contrary verdict and the mediator argues the case through. Lamentation 3:37-38 says, 'Who is he who speaks and it comes to pass, when the Lord has not commanded it? Is it not from the mouth of the Most High that woe and well-being proceed?'

Fear of God involves believing what He has done and what He can do - both wonderful and terrible. Psalm 40:1-4 reads:

> I waited patiently for the LORD; and He inclined to me, and heard my cry. He also brought me up out of a horrible pit, out of the miry clay, and set my feet upon a rock, and established my steps. He has put a new song in my mouth - Praise to our God; many will see it and fear, and will trust in the LORD. Blessed is that man who makes the LORD his trust, and does not respect the proud, nor such as turn aside to lies.

The manifestation of God's work makes people to give Him His rightful place; that is, if they do not doubt in their hearts that He Himself has done the things they have seen.

In Hebrews 11:7 we read of how Noah, having the fear of God, was able to give due regard to His word and do something about it: 'By faith Noah, being divinely warned of things not yet seen, moved with godly fear, prepared an ark for the saving of his household, by which he condemned the world and became heir of the righteousness which is according to faith.'

Relating The Fear Of God To The Value Of Mankind

Understanding the value that God places on mankind would develop in an individual an attitude that reflects value for others. Someone who has no understanding or appreciation of classical music may listen to it and disregard it. Many may say that such a person has poor taste.

If you look at an artist's work and disregard it, you obviously are not acquainted with that quality of work. Same applies when one disregards God's creation – it is simply because such a person's taste is poor in divine context. To disregard an object is to disregard its creator or originator.

1 Corinthians 3:16 says, 'Do you not know that you are the temple of God and that the Spirit of God dwells in you?' To live a life that is not plagued by unhealthy ungodly fear only comes from our realisation of our value in Him. Luke 12:6-7 reads Jesus' illustration:

> "Are not five sparrows sold for two copper coins? And not one of them is forgotten before God. But the very hairs of your head are all numbered. Do not fear therefore; you are of more value than many sparrows."

Whenever I find myself critical or judgmental toward

others, pondering whether they deserve my time, kindness or attention, the thought that Jesus Christ the Son of God died for such a person brings home again the fact that the person has much more value than I could possibly perceive or appreciate. In Revelation 3:18 we read,

> I counsel you to buy from Me gold refined in the fire, that you may be rich; and white garments, that you may be clothed, that the shame of your nakedness may not be revealed; and anoint your eyes with eye salve, that you may see.

It is God's plan that our nakedness, which was exposed as a consequence of the fall of Adam and Eve, should not to be revealed. His provision for this is made in the sacrifice that our Lord Jesus made of Himself on the cross about two thousand years ago because of the value that God has put on us humans. The word 'buy' from the above passage implies that this will cost us something.

The main price to pay is to lay down our pride, to accept that we need God and the covering that He offers us. To be enriched by the gold refined by fire we need to yield to the refining process of God performed in the believers by the Holy Spirit. In Malachi 3:1-3, we read of God's messenger as a refiner's fire and launderers' soap:

> "Behold, I send My messenger, and he will prepare the way before Me. And the Lord, whom you seek, will suddenly come to His temple, even the Messenger of the covenant, in whom you delight. Behold, He is coming," says the LORD of hosts.

"But who can endure the day of His coming? And who can stand when He appears? For He is like a refiner's fire and like launderers' soap. He will sit as a refiner and a purifier of silver; He will purify the sons of Levi, and purge them as gold and silver, that they may offer to the LORD an offering in righteousness."

The covering that God gives us draws us towards Him not away from Him as did the nakedness of Adam and Eve. Every Christian is encouraged to put on the full armour of God to ensure successful and victorious Christian living. This is detailed in Ephesians 6:10-18:

Finally, my brethren, be strong in the Lord and in the power of His might. Put on the whole armor of God, that you may be able to stand against the wiles of the devil. For we do not wrestle against flesh and blood, but against principalities, against powers, against the rulers of the darkness of this age, against spiritual hosts of wickedness in the heavenly places. Therefore take up the whole armor of God, that you may be able to withstand in the evil day, and having done all, to stand. Stand therefore, having girded your waist with truth, having put on the breastplate of righteousness, and having shod your feet with the preparation of the gospel of peace; above all, taking the shield of faith with which you will be able to quench all the fiery darts of the wicked one. And take the helmet of salvation, and the sword of the Spirit, which is the word of God; praying always with all prayer and supplication in the Spirit, being watchful to this end with all perseverance and supplication for all the saints.

Similar in nature to these components of the armour of God, the fear of God is like the spiritual armour that keeps us focused on God, making Him and His ways priority in our lives, keeping us from "eating of the forbidden fruit" which may look good and which the enemies of God may present before us as good.

Pause here to revisit the experience of Adam and Eve which led to the exposure of their nakedness is recorded in Genesis 3:6-8:

> So when the woman saw that the tree was good for food, that it was pleasant to the eyes, and a tree desirable to make one wise, she took of its fruit and ate. She also gave to her husband with her, and he ate. Then the eyes of both of them were opened, and they knew that they were naked; and they sewed fig leaves together and made themselves coverings. And they heard the sound of the LORD God walking in the garden in the cool of the day, and Adam and his wife hid themselves from the presence of the LORD God among the trees of the garden.

Comparing our status with the dandelion; like the dandelion's seeds on a seed head that look like a 'fur', we have the fear of God as our God-given protection from the assault of the enemy and from turning away from our relationship with Him.

The fear of God keeps us from the evil wind of disobedience, similar to the wind that blows on the dandelion making it to loose its seeds or 'fur,' and exposing its nakedness.

The Fear Of God And The Revelation Of His Nature

Being the creator of all things, God controls all things. Isaiah 10:15 says, "Shall the axe boast itself against him who chops with it? Or shall the saw exalt itself against him who saws with it? As if a rod could wield itself against those who lift it up, or as if a staff could lift up, as if it were not wood!"

In Jonah 1:9-10, Jonah identifies himself saying, "I am a Hebrew; and I fear the LORD, the God of heaven, who made the sea and the dry land." Essentially, he was saying that if the seas were calm or rough, it was up to his God who made them. The men were afraid; they believed what Jonah said about his God. 'Why have you done this?' - they asked him. It was as though they were saying, 'If you knew your God to be as you have said, why have you tried to run from His assignment? You should have known better.'

To fully develop the fear of God we need a revelation of what He does. If we see His handwork in everything that has been created, we would be able to give Him His rightful place in creation as the creator and owner of all.

'The LORD' is God's name to establish His undisputable authority over all that ever was, is, and ever will be. In Exodus chapter 20 when the LORD gave the commandments to the people of Israel, He first established who He was and that was the status that placed a requirement on them to obey His commandments.

One would not expect someone to appear from nowhere and suddenly make pronunciations like the Ten Commandments and expect the people to adopt it and abide by it without an explanation as to the reason why they should submit their will and desires for his. In verse 2 He said, "I am the LORD your God, who brought you out of the land of Egypt, out of the house of bondage." The commandments followed this introduction.

Acknowledging God as LORD and giving Him His rightful place precedes submission to His lordship or authority. The Holy Spirit helps us with this as He continually reveals God to us from one level of revelation to the next. Praise and worship embrace this principle. In many instances when God speaks of Himself, He declares the lack of grounds to compare Him to any other. In Isaiah 40:18 the Bible says: To whom then will you liken God? Or what likeness will you compare to Him?

The twenty-fifth verse of the same chapter gives a similar report: "To whom then will you liken Me, or to whom shall I be equal?" says the Holy One. In verses 13-14 of the same chapter we read:

> Who has directed the Spirit of the LORD, or as His counsellor has taught Him? With whom did He take counsel, and who instructed Him, and taught Him in the path of justice? Who taught Him knowledge, and showed Him the way of

understanding?

By His counsel a plant is a plant - stem, roots, branches, fruit and so on. By His counsel a man is a man, a woman is a woman; by His counsel the different body parts function as He has ordained them to - legs for standing and eyes in the head rather than in the feet that are the structures that move the body.

Cars have lights close to the ground but men have eyes which are at the top of the body structure, in the face – so one has to look down to see where to go or else stumble, according to the counsel of the Almighty God, by His design, anchored upon His wisdom.

Proverbs 19:21 puts it this way, 'There are many plans in a man's heart, nevertheless the LORD's counsel - that will stand.' The LORD's counsel will triumph over man's counsel, it will be the counsel that stands unchanged and unshaken in every situation. Therefore, we serve ourselves well by aligning our thoughts and plans with His counsel.

Questioning God's authenticity is not a new practice. His enemy, Satan practised this since the creation of man when as a serpent he spoke directly to Eve, having started with the opening question, "Has God indeed said ...?" – Genesis 3:1.

I have heard some people speculate that Eve was not there when God spoke the instructions to Adam; consequently, she did not know what God required of them. However, it is noteworthy that she answered by telling the serpent what God said. One can see that the serpent went on to give Eve information that God had not given her, whether it was true or not was immaterial. The fact was, his suggestion was contrary to God's instruction, irrespective of what the expected outcome was to be; in this case, the opening of her eyes, being like God and knowing good and evil – Genesis 3:5.

Similarly, today, we have the word of God that He seals by stating that we are not to add anything to it or remove from it (Revelation 22:18-19). The challenge for us then is to stay within what God reveals to us, and to ask Him for wisdom about things we do not understand.

As a consequence of this fall – over the years, man has tried to hide from God. The natural man does not desire to open himself up or expose his perceived nakedness to God. I for one wanted to paint a good picture of myself before God, forgetting that nothing is hidden from Him. Thus, He Himself invites us to come just as we are saying in Romans 3:23, 'For all have sinned and fall short of the glory of God.' In Isaiah 1:18 He invites everyone, "Come now, and let us reason together," says the LORD, "Though your sins are like scarlet, they shall be as white as snow; though they are red like crimson, they shall be as wool."

He dissuades us from trying to please Him by our own standards and ways by stating that even what we in our own mind consider good is filthy before Him. Isaiah 64:6 says, 'But we are all like an unclean thing, and all our righteousnesses are like filthy rags; we all fade as a leaf, and our iniquities, like the wind, have taken us away.' In Ecclesiastes 7:20 we read, 'For there is not a just man on earth who does good and does not sin.'

Dave Branon wrote in 'Our Daily Bread' of 1st August

2009: To know a person one needs to ascertain three things – what they say about themselves, what others say about them and what they have done. In a job interview, one is usually judged by the following: what one says about oneself, the references from the referees – this representing what others say about the person and what the person has done, as demonstrated in the Curriculum Vitae (CV). God continues to give revelations to us today through those He has chosen for that purpose. We are advised to test all spirits as a means for evaluating these revelations. 1 John 4:1-2 says:

> Beloved, do not believe every spirit, but test the spirits, whether they are of God; because many false prophets have gone out into the world. By this you know the Spirit of God: every spirit that confesses that Jesus Christ has come in the flesh is of God.

When new revelation contradicts the foundational truth and revelations in the Holy Bible, we are right to reject it. When a revelation is outside the boundaries of the word of God, we need to ask the LORD for wisdom. Recall the prophet who lied to the man of God, deceiving him to his death (1 Kings 13).

There may be occasions when what is known of the revelation of God's word is challenged beyond currently available evidence. One ought to bear in mind that we have not been given all the knowledge there is. Our generation has been given more revelations than the generations past. For example, there are more revelations of heaven and hell now than in the time our Lord Jesus Christ lived as a man on this earth.

Yet, He encouraged the people to believe even if they have not seen. In the second part of John 20:29 Jesus says, "Blessed are those who have not seen and yet have believed." The expectation on that generation is no less than the Lord put on our generation, nor will generations to come have a different requirement or expectation put on them if they have more revelations.

As already mentioned above, the Bible says in 1 Corinthians 13:12 that only at the end, we will know even as we are known and in Deuteronomy 29:29, "The secret things belong to the LORD our God, but those things which are revealed belong to us and to our children forever, that we may do all the words of this law."

So, for now we have to make do with what knowledge God gives us. Next time you have your faith challenged, pray for wisdom to give appropriate answers but do not be afraid to acknowledge that this is how much you know at the particular moment. Lean on God for what you do not understand. Consider Daniel and His friends who did not know the king's dream, they asked God in prayer and He gave the revelation to them. Moreover, we are also told that God reveals Himself in creation. Romans chapter 1 verses 16-20 says:

> For I am not ashamed of the gospel of Christ, for it is the power of God to salvation for everyone who believes, for the Jew first and also for the Greek. For in it the righteousness of God is revealed from faith to faith; as it is written, "The just shall live

by faith." For the wrath of God is revealed from heaven against all ungodliness and unrighteousness of men, who suppress the truth in unrighteousness, because what may be known of God is manifest in them, for God has shown it to them. For since the creation of the world His invisible attributes are clearly seen, being understood by the things that are made, even His eternal power and Godhead, so that they are without excuse.

THE FEAR OF GOD

CHAPTER 3

THE BENEFITS OF LIVING BY THE FEAR OF GOD

The Fear Of God Eliminates Unhealthy Ungodly Fear

*T*he fear of God endows one with several advantages as God Almighty is given His due place. Isaiah 43:1-7 says:

But now, thus says the LORD, who created you, O Jacob, and He who formed you, O Israel: "Fear not, for I have redeemed you; I have called you by your name; you are Mine. When you pass through the waters, I will be with you; and through the rivers, they shall not overflow you. When you walk through the fire, you shall not be burned, nor shall the flame scorch you. For I am the LORD your God, The Holy One of Israel, your Saviour; I gave Egypt for your ransom, Ethiopia and Seba in your place. Since you were precious in My sight, you have been honoured, and I have loved you; therefore I will give men for you, and people for your life. Fear not, for I am with you; I will bring your descendants from the east, and gather you from the west; I will say to the north, 'Give them up!' And to the south, 'Do not keep them back!' Bring My sons from afar, and

> My daughters from the ends of the earth -everyone
> who is called by My name, whom I have created
> for My glory; I have formed him, yes, I have made
> him."

The basis for one to embrace the instruction, 'fear not,'
is in knowing the One who has given that instruction, the
One by whom one has been redeemed. The One who has
engaged you in what you are doing; the One to whom you
belong and to whom you are ultimately accountable.

As a child of God, you cannot do anything that is beyond
your revelation of who God is! In Daniel 11:32b we read,
"....but the people who know their God shall be strong, and
carry out great exploits." Isaiah 43:10-13 further adds the
assurance that we have been chosen to know and believe
God:

> "You are My witnesses," says the LORD, "and
> My servant whom I have chosen, that you may
> know and believe Me, and understand that I am
> He. Before Me there was no God formed, nor shall
> there be after Me. I, even I, am the LORD, and
> besides Me there is no saviour. I have declared and
> saved, I have proclaimed, and there was no foreign
> god among you; therefore you are My witnesses,"
> says the LORD, "that I am God. Indeed before
> the day was, I am He; and there is no one who
> can deliver out of My hand; I work, and who will
> reverse it?"

In the foregoing passage, God sets Himself apart as the

unequalled and undisputed head of all creation. How many times does God state that besides Himself there is no other? In Isaiah 45:5-7, He says

> I am the LORD, and there is no other; there is no God besides Me. I will gird you, though you have not known Me, that they may know from the rising of the sun to its setting that there is none besides Me. I am the LORD, and there is no other; I form the light and create darkness, I make peace and create calamity; I, the LORD, do all these things.

Referring to the signs and wonders that God revealed in Egypt when He delivered Israel from bondage, Deuteronomy 4:35 states, 'To you it was shown, that you might know that the LORD Himself is God; there is none other besides Him.' In verses 39-40 the passage continues,

> "Therefore know this day, and consider it in your heart, that the LORD Himself is God in heaven above and on the earth beneath; there is no other. You shall therefore keep His statutes and His commandments which I command you today, that it may go well with you and with your children after you, and that you may prolong your days in the land which the LORD your God is giving you for all time."

Let us consider a few more passages that set God apart as unequalled. Deuteronomy 32:39 also reads, 'Now see that I, even I, am He, and there is no God besides Me; I kill and

147

THE FEAR OF GOD

I make alive; I wound and I heal; nor is there any who can deliver from My hand.'

In 1 Samuel 2:2 in the prayer of Hannah we read, "No one is holy like the LORD, for there is none besides You, nor is there any rock like our God." Isaiah 44:8 reads, 'Do not fear, nor be afraid; have I not told you from that time, and declared it? You are My witnesses. Is there a God besides Me? Indeed there is no other Rock; I know not one.'

Isaiah 42:5 says – 'Thus says God the LORD, who created the heavens and stretched them out, who spread forth the earth and that which comes from it, who gives breath to the people on it, and spirit to those who walk on it.' Isaiah 45:18 also says, 'For thus says the LORD, who created the heavens, who is God, who formed the earth and made it, who has established it, who did not create it in vain, who formed it to be inhabited: "I am the LORD, and there is no other."'

In Isaiah 46:5 God Almighty asks, "To whom will you liken Me, and make Me equal and compare Me, that we should be alike?" The ninth verse of the same chapter continues the discuss: 'Remember the former things of old, for I am God, and there is no other; I am God, and there is none like Me.'

This discuss further continues into the New Testament of the Holy Bible. In Mark 12:32 one of the scribes affirmed what the Lord Jesus said, "Well said, Teacher. You have spoken the truth, for there is one God, and there is no other but He."

The Heart Of Servanthood Towards God

The fear of God endows a person with the virtue of servant-hood, the grace to yield to God and the grace to commit one's cares to Him in prayer.

In Genesis 1:28 we read God's first command to man at creation, "Be fruitful and multiply; fill the earth and subdue it; have dominion over the fish of the sea, over the birds of the air and over every living thing that moves on the earth." How one carries out this command depends on what or whom one yields the spirit to: whether to God or not to God.

The Bible says that we are servant or slave to whom we submit (Romans 6:16). Everyday is an opportunity to affect the world. God is committed to each day He gives everyone of us. He waits to partner with us individually. He in fact commits on your behalf what you two – God and yourself, working as one would achieve; its outcome depends on how much you yield to Him. Doing God's will requires humility and self-denial on one's part.

An Attitude That Prefers And Values God's Will

The fear of God enables us to prioritize His will in all situations and decisions. Let us further explore to see how. 2 Corinthians 10:4-6 states:

> For the weapons of our warfare are not carnal but mighty in God for pulling down strongholds, casting down arguments and every high thing that

149

THE FEAR OF GOD

exalts itself against the knowledge of God, bringing every thought into captivity to the obedience of Christ, and being ready to punish all disobedience when your obedience is fulfilled.

We are given weapons to cast down imaginations and every high thing that exalts itself against the knowledge of God. Satan's confusion in exalting himself above the knowledge of God brought his downfall as is noted in Isaiah 14:12-14:

How you are fallen from heaven, O Lucifer, son of the morning! How you are cut down to the ground, you who weakened the nations! For you have said in your heart: 'I will ascend into heaven, I will exalt my throne above the stars of God; I will also sit on the mount of the congregation on the farthest sides of the north; I will ascend above the heights of the clouds, I will be like the Most High.'

All our God-given weapons of warfare are powered by the Holy Spirit. These include prayer, the anointing that breaks the yoke of bondage, the gifts of the Holy Spirit including the gift of healing and the working of miracles (1 Corinthians 12), wisdom, understanding, counsel, might, knowledge and the fear of the LORD (Isaiah 11:2).

Amongst other things, the fear of God also involves bringing every thought to the obedience of Christ. This is worked out practically as we make the Lord's will the measure by which every thought is judged as acceptable or unacceptable.

Essentially, if the thought is out of God's revealed will, it's out; if it is in line with His will, it's in. It is the antidote to the deception that can befall any Christian who is not watchful.

In 2 Corinthians 11:3, Paul's concern as to the possibility of Satan deceiving the believers is revealed, 'But I fear, lest somehow, as the serpent deceived Eve by his craftiness, so your minds may be corrupted from the simplicity that is in Christ.' Compare the foregoing with Peter and John's response in Acts 4:19-20 when they used the word of God to determine what to do about the instructions they had received from those in authority:

> But Peter and John answered and said to them, "Whether it is right in the sight of God to listen to you more than to God, you judge. For we cannot but speak the things which we have seen and heard."

The background was that Peter and John had healed a lame man on their way to the temple for their usual prayer meeting (Acts chapter 3).

The priests, the captain of the temple and the Sadducees arrested them for claiming the healing had been performed in the name of Jesus Christ of Nazareth and also stating, "Nor is there salvation in any other, for there is no other name under heaven given among men by which we must be saved," (Acts chapter 4).

Despite their acknowledgment that the miracle could not be denied, the leaders severely threatened them not to speak to any man in the name of Jesus. The apostle's bold response was completely out of character for the Peter we knew before the Holy Spirit descended on them with power. The same Peter who is recorded to have denied being one of the disciples of Jesus supposedly for fear of what the people would do to him (Luke 22:54-62).

Let us consider the bold ones that dared to confront the very powerful king of Israel who had erred according to the requirements of the LORD (2 Chronicles 26). The LORD had given King Uzziah victory over his enemies and made him strong. Then, he went into the LORD's temple to burn incense on the incense altar. Azariah, the chief priest, and eighty other priests went to confront the king saying (2 Chronicles 26:18), "It is not for you, Uzziah, to burn incense to the LORD, but for the priests, the sons of Aaron, who are consecrated to burn incense.

Get out of the sanctuary, for you have trespassed! You shall have no honour from the LORD God." As it happened, the king became furious, angry with the priests and was immediately struck by God with leprosy. The priests then thrust him out of the place and the Bible records that he hurried to get out because the LORD had struck him.

Next stop, Paul the apostle. Paul had been an enemy of the followers of the Lord Jesus Christ before Christ accosted him on the way to Damascus. Having received instructions from the Lord, and had the eye of his understanding opened to God's love and grace, he quickly became a preacher of the gospel himself.

Understandably, he needed to be accepted by the other apostles. In Galatians 2:9, he talks of how when James, Cephas (Peter) and John who seemed to be pillars of the early Church saw the grace that was upon him, they gave him and Barnabas the right hand of fellowship.

However, Paul did not shy away from confronting Peter openly when he was not being straightforward about the truth regarding circumcision and non-circumcision (Galatians 2:11-14). Despite the fact that Peter was among those from whom Paul had got approval to carry out his ministry, Paul still withstood him when his conduct was against the faith they had received from the Lord Jesus.

One would have thought that Paul would have let Peter get away with it to avoid offending 'one of the pillars' as he had referred to him earlier. This demonstrated Paul's understanding that though the Lord used Peter to welcome him or to commission him to his position, he was subject to God and not to Peter.

Peter on the other hand fell into the trap of fearing those who were referred to as being of the circumcision (verse 12); which made him withdraw from the Gentiles. Bringing this point home, one may feel that one's position at work or that career prospects are solely under the control of the boss and yield to the boss's ungodly request, which is clearly against God's will. It may not necessarily be easy to stand one's grounds in the face of situations that challenge our faith.

Ponder Time

Would you speak up to correct an erring leader in the church where you fellowship?

THE FEAR OF GOD

In fact we know that several people are persecuted severely within the work environment for their expressed faith in Christ Jesus.

Akin to Paul's experience is the situation where the leader of the church embraces a practice that is clearly not in line with God's will and purpose. As a person serving in the household of God under such a leader, do you keep quiet and protect your position or speak up at the risk of offending the leader and being asked to leave the congregation?

This is the reality for several people today, some speak up and bear the consequences, many times accompanied by testimony of God's promotion for their faithfulness; others keep quiet and also bear the consequences of their actions.

The question for each one of us at this point therefore is, what would you do if you were faced with a similar situation? The Bible says, 'It is a fearful thing to fall into the hands of the living God' – Hebrews 10:31. Given the choice, one should never choose to disobey God in order to please men.

I pray that we would have the wisdom, courage, boldness and strength to do the right thing because these challenges are inevitable in life. The fear of God enables us to give God's word its rightful place as the authority over our desires and decisions.

The first record of man giving in to the instruction of another creature, which was contrary to the revealed will of God, is the experience of Adam and Eve. First Eve gave in to the serpent's suggestion that the fruit, which God forbade them from eating, was good for them. She ate it and offered to Adam who also ate of it. If he had the fear of God, and hence, appropriate regard for His word, Adam should have challenged Eve's offer and her disregard for God's instruction.

On a personal note, my husband once rebuked me for suggesting to another person to take an easy way out of a crisis situation; the option I offered was one I had taken before I became a Christian and was clearly against the will of God. Thankfully, that made me rethink and offer a Bible-based advice, which resulted in a wonderful outcome.

Reverence For His Presence

God demands that we regard His presence with due reverence and honour. Leviticus 10 gives an example. When Nadab and Abihu, sons of Aaron, offered profane fire before the LORD, which He had not commanded them, fire went out from Him and devoured them.

Moses communicated God's judgment on the matter to Aaron (verse 3) saying, 'By those who come near Me I must be regarded as holy; and before all the people I must be glorified.'

I used to think that when I approached Father God in prayer or worship or praise for example, that I was doing Him a favour. I felt He should be grateful or pleased that I took time out of my busy schedule to attend His presence. Therefore, I did not consider carefully my conduct in His presence. I have since come to realise that that view was born out of my ignorance.

Thank God that He is gracious; indeed, by His mercies we are not consumed! We cannot do without Him and it is our privilege to have access to His presence, freely through

THE FEAR OF GOD

Jesus. When we approach, we ought to give due regard to His presence and this improves as the fear of God develops within us. Even keeping to the time we have agreed to meet with Him is important to Him.

On one occasion, I had said to the Lord that I would meet with Him at a set time. I recall arriving late to the meeting with my attitude of 'bless me for even making the attempt.' I felt a chill and an unease I could not explain. Then I sensed what the problem was; I couldn't quite explain it but I sensed in my spirit that He was saying something that translated into, 'You disregard me by turning up late, whenever, for no reason and without an apology.'

I fell to my face and asked for His forgiveness, which He gave instantly; the atmosphere became less tense and we had the time of fellowship together. I would never have believed it if someone told me that but I have to share that experience with you; hopefully you can learn from my experience.

I can only imagine what anyone would make of such a story; if I was not the one telling it I would have said – 'it was your imagination.' I was not going to add this story to this book but perhaps it would help someone. If I was running late and apologised, I believe it would have been no problem at all with the Lord.

Just that I showed no acknowledgement of wrongdoing or remorse or repentance or contrition. Even with humans, if someone turned up late for an appointment expecting to be applauded for bothering to show up at all, I can imagine what sort of reception that individual would receive.

Wisdom

The significance of wisdom cannot be overstated. A good example is given in Proverbs 19:8 which says, 'He who gets wisdom loves his own soul; he who keeps understanding will find good.' In Proverbs 4:7 we read, 'Wisdom is the principal thing; therefore get wisdom. And in all your getting, get understanding.'

King Solomon holds the record of being the wisest of men through all ages. As the writer of most of the biblical book of Proverbs, he made several references to the fear of the LORD being the essence of wisdom. In Proverbs 15:33 he taught that the fear of the LORD is the instruction of wisdom, and before honour is humility.

Thus, essentially the wisdom in a decision or stance is to be evaluated according to its adherence to the wisdom or word of God. I believe one would be saved from a lot of mistakes and folly by applying this test to one's decisions. In Proverbs 1:7 he wrote, 'the fear of the LORD is the beginning of knowledge, but fools despise wisdom and instruction.'

In Proverbs 1:29-31, he suggests that those who hate knowledge and do not choose the fear of the LORD would face the attendant consequences:

> Because they hated knowledge and did not choose the fear of the LORD, they would have none of my counsel and despised my every rebuke. Therefore they shall eat the fruit of their own way, and be filled to the full with their own fancies.

THE FEAR OF GOD

Proverbs 9:10, one of the most popular verses in the Holy Bible states, "The fear of the LORD is the beginning of wisdom, and the knowledge of the Holy One is understanding."

In Proverbs 2:4-5 he teaches that wisdom helps one understand the fear of the LORD: 'If you seek her as silver, and search for her as for hidden treasures; then you will understand the fear of the LORD, and find the knowledge of God.'

The writer of Psalm 111:10 agrees with the foregoing and declares: 'The fear of the LORD is the beginning of wisdom; a good understanding have all those who do His commandments. His praise endures forever.'

Ecclesiastes 8:5b-6 teaches that: A wise man's heart discerns both time and judgment, because for every matter there is a time and judgment, though the misery of man increases greatly. This means getting insight beyond the immediately obvious. The fear of God endows one with this virtue of wisdom that goes beyond the obvious. This is buttressed by this saying from the wisdom of King Solomon in Ecclesiastes 7:15-18:

> I have seen everything in my days of vanity: There is a just man who perishes in his righteousness, and there is a wicked man who prolongs life in his wickedness. Do not be overly righteous, nor be overly wise: why should you destroy yourself? Do not be overly wicked, nor be foolish: why should you die before your time? It is good that you grasp this, and also not remove your hand from the other; for he who fears God will escape them all.

Is it possible to be overly righteous? Even though the Bible says there is no one who does not sin? In Ecclesiastes 7:20 we also read that, 'there is not a just man on earth who does good and does not sin.' It is the fear of God that keeps us balanced in all things in life. It provides a safety net or boundary around us so that we do not overdo things - righteous or wicked, foolish or wise.

Divine Protection And Provision

Another great benefit of living by the fear of God is protection and provision in response to the heart that acknowledges and submits to Him for the provision of the same. An example is found in Psalm 33:18-22:

> Behold, the eye of the LORD is on those who fear Him, on those who hope in His mercy, to deliver their soul from death, and to keep them alive in famine. Our soul waits for the LORD; He is our help and our shield. For our heart shall rejoice in Him, because we have trusted in His holy name. Let Your mercy, O LORD, be upon us, just as we hope in You.

Again, Psalm 145:15-16 says, 'The eyes of all look expectantly to You, and You give them their food in due season. You open Your hand and satisfy the desire of every living thing.'

In verse 19 of the same chapter, the Bible says that God goes an extra mile for those who fear Him: 'He will fulfil the desire of those who fear Him; He also will hear their cry and save them.' This is especially so because the fear of God will surely tailor our prayers to what is approved by the LORD and reduce the risk of asking amiss or asking for the wrong thing at the wrong time.

Psalm 111 recounts some of the benefits that arise from living in accordance with the fear of God. In verse 5 we read: He has given food to those who fear Him; He will ever be mindful of His covenant.

In Psalm 119:38, the psalmist implores God to – 'Establish Your word to Your servant who is devoted to fearing You.' He lays hold of the fact that by fearing God, his prayers and cries merit special attention according to God's word. It is His word to give special attention to those who fear Him. Just as He is committed to the prayers of those who are in Christ, the righteous as is written in Psalm 34:17, 'The righteous cry out, and the LORD hears, and delivers them out of all their troubles.'

Speaking of the LORD, Psalm 90:2 states, 'Before the mountains were brought forth, or ever You had formed the earth and the world, even from everlasting to everlasting, You are God.' He predates every oppressor and every tormentor. He will also outlast them all. Halleluiah!

God promises provision to those who fear Him; even their descendants are blessed. Psalm 112 reads:

> Praise the LORD! Blessed is the man who fears the LORD, who delights greatly in His commandments. His descendants will be mighty on earth; the generation of the upright will be blessed. Wealth and riches will be in his house, and his righteousness endures forever. Unto the

upright there arises light in the darkness; he is gracious, and full of compassion, and righteous. A good man deals graciously and lends; he will guide his affairs with discretion. Surely he will never be shaken; the righteous will be in everlasting remembrance. He will not be afraid of evil tidings; his heart is steadfast, trusting in the LORD. His heart is established; he will not be afraid, until he sees his desire upon his enemies. He has dispersed abroad, he has given to the poor; his righteousness endures forever; his horn will be exalted with honour. The wicked will see it and be grieved; he will gnash his teeth and melt away; the desire of the wicked shall perish.

The Fear Of God Brings A Good Outcome

Laying emphasis on the benefits of living by the fear of God, the Holy Bible in reflecting on the fact that instant punishment no longer followed evil doing says – 'Though a sinner does evil a hundred times, and his days are prolonged, yet I surely know that it will be well with those who fear God, who fear before Him.

But it will not be well with the wicked; nor will he prolong his days, which are as a shadow, because he does not fear before God' – Ecclesiastes 8:12-13. Here, we are being encouraged that the outcome will be good when we choose to fear God.

THE FEAR OF GOD

Deliverance From Evil

God is concerned for us when we sin. Having spent time with God on Mount Sinai, Moses came down to see Israel worshipping the golden calf as their god. The Bible records the situation thus – 'Now when Moses saw that the people were unrestrained (for Aaron had not restrained them, to their shame among their enemies),' – Exodus 32:25.

When we identify ourselves as Christians and still show no restraint as should be manifested in the life of a person led by the Holy Spirit of God, we not only give cause for His name to be blasphemed (Ezekiel 36:22), but we make ourselves a ridicule before others around us, both spiritually and physically.

Imagine what would have happened in the spiritual atmosphere if Job had cursed God as Satan had boasted that he would? We need to consider this perspective when we make our decisions in life – is the kingdom of darkness hurting, groaning and disappointed because of my choices and decisions? Is there celebration in the kingdom of my Father God in heaven because of my choices and decisions?

Ponder Time

Who is celebrating your choices and decisions today?

Jesus proposed that we ask the Father for deliverance from evil in the prayer format He taught in Matthew chapter 6. The fear of God is a tool by which the LORD answers this prayer. In Proverbs 16:6 we read, 'In mercy and truth atonement is provided for iniquity; and by the fear of the LORD one departs from evil.' The Lord knows we are not able to do it by ourselves. Our Helper, the Holy Spirit helps us overcome; one of His tools for doing this being the fear of God.

Viewing Sin And Repentance Through The Eyes Of The Fear Of God

From the beginning, man has shown an inclination towards exonerating himself from guilt of wrong doing, along with a tendency to apportion blame to another person for one's mistakes. The first father, Adam, blamed God for giving him the woman whom he blamed for his downfall. In Job's situation, Satan's intention was for Job to curse God. Why not curse Satan, since he was the origin of the troubles in the first place?

Rather like today, the enemy wants us to blame God for evil in the society, even our own sins. Today, like Adam, we very often still blame God for our fall, directly or indirectly. We use phrases like, 'If I wasn't so poor, I wouldn't steal'; 'If I hadn't met that person, I wouldn't have been involved in that wrong activity' and so on.

All of God's gifts are without sorrow. Everything He does for and with us stems from His nature, which is love. It is up to us to work through and with what He has given us to bring glory to His name, working in cooperation with His Holy Spirit. If we fail at controlling what God has given us to bring it under subjection of His authority, Jesus says, it is better we remove that thing from our lives (Mark

9:43-48). Same warning is repeated in Matthew 18:8-9:

> "If your hand or foot causes you to sin, cut it off and cast it from you. It is better for you to enter eternal life lame or maimed, rather than having two hands or two feet, to be cast into the everlasting fire. And if your eye causes you to sin, pluck it out and cast it from you. It is better for you to enter into life with one eye, rather than having two eyes, to be cast into hell fire."

The value of any thing should be subject to its contribution to our life positively towards God or negatively away from Him and towards hell. Note that our Lord Jesus Christ did not say, 'if it causes you to sin God would remove it from you.' No, you have the responsibility to remove yourself from the sin trap or remove the sin trap from you.

I sense that another interpretation of this passage is that God may give us an alternative to or a way out of sin which may be as painful as losing an eye or a limb but would lead to life.

If one is fortunate to have another person stand in the gap as a watchman before God, then, the prayers can also bring His liberating arms into the situation to set the person free. The Holy Bible is full of examples where friends or parents or leaders cried out to the Lord and the recipient of the prayer was delivered.

Thank God for His mercy. When we come to Him, He forgives us. As we, in truth, acknowledge our sins and ask for His forgiveness, He gives it to us faithfully according to His promise in 1 John 1:8-9 which says, 'If we say that we have no sin, we deceive ourselves, and the truth is not in us. If we confess our sins, He is faithful and just to forgive us our sins and to cleanse us from all unrighteousness.'

The fear of God helps us not get into the evil in the first place. The words of Paul the apostle in Romans 6:1 come to mind here – "Shall we continue in sin that grace may abound?" Yes, grace is available but sin is to be avoided at all cost. It takes us into territories that are not for our own good at all.

Growing up as a young woman in the university I got involved in immoral activities that were contrary to my godly catholic upbringing. I thought that, as long as my parents were not aware of what I was doing, I would get away with it all and that whenever I stopped that behaviour, the Lord would welcome me back into His arms. The second part of this assumption was right but I had not been aware of other consequences of my sinful behaviour.

When I thought I had had enough and wanted to live for God, I found that I could not just walk away. I could not detach myself from the non-Christian relationship and the other party did not care about my faith. It was as though my inner being was stuck and could not let go; it was a very miserable time.

Then I was fortunate that God brought my husband to me at the time. Though he was not a committed Christian he had the hunger to grow close to God. Many years after having committed my life to Jesus as my Lord and Saviour, I was still having thoughts of sexual immorality filling my heart and occupying my thoughts.

One day, while I was in my kitchen preparing a meal

for my family, I heard the Lord say something that baffled me. He told me that I had the 'spirit of prostitution' living in me and that He had sent my husband to help me out. At this point in my life, I had thought I was a 'better' Christian than my husband. So, you can imagine that this information was not in agreement with my thoughts and I did not like it.

While I was trying to argue with the Lord, He went on to instruct me to stop for a minute and say a prayer right there to get rid of the prostitution spirit. I still did not quite understand the full meaning of what was going on. I didn't see my life before or after becoming a Christian to be in line with what the LORD referred to as the prostitution spirit. It appeared that the life of sexual immorality with my boyfriends, from whom I in return got the sense of being appreciated and valued, was a form of prostitution.

I might not have taken money from them but I took what I thought made me feel good from the experience. However, I prayed a simple prayer there in my kitchen and then carried on with my cooking. It was as though my mind then forgot about this prayer incident in my kitchen.

Two months later, the Lord reminded me that the immoral thoughts that used to fill my mind were gone, and I could identify that they stopped when I said that prayer. What am I alluding to by this story?

One should not take grace for granted because the enemy still gains access into our lives if we open the door through reckless living even in the midst of so much grace. It is for our own good then that the Lord asks us to abstain from sinful living. I was forgiven but not delivered from the evil spirit of prostitution till the Lord graciously stepped in and did it for me.

God would not leave us without options or a way out of temptation to go against what we know to be His heart's desire on the issue. In 1 Corinthians 10:13 we are told, 'No temptation has overtaken you except such as is common to man; but God is faithful, who will not allow you to be tempted beyond what you are able, but with the temptation will also make the way of escape, that you may be able to bear it.'

Again, the instruction is to cut it off and cast it from you. Cutting the offending issue or source of temptation off while leaving it within easy reach may not be enough to keep us from falling into the temptation. I have found this to be true in my personal experience. Removing it from one's vicinity or removing oneself from it is the advice.

Paul, the apostle, wrote in 1 Corinthians 6:18a, 'Flee sexual immorality' – essentially remove yourself from every opportunity to be involved in sexually immoral acts. This includes avoiding dressing or talking or walking in a sexually provocative manner in public places, as that would invite attention from those who fall into the trap. In 1 Timothy 6:10-11

Paul also writes, 'For the love of money is a root of all kinds of evil, for which some have strayed from the faith in their greediness, and pierced themselves through with many sorrows. But you, O man of God, flee these things and pursue righteousness, godliness, faith, love, patience, gentleness.' This means, fleeing evil and pursuing godliness. In Matthew 11:28-30 we read an interesting offer from our

THE FEAR OF GOD

Lord Jesus:

> "Come to Me, all you who labour and are heavy
> laden, and I will give you rest. Take My yoke upon
> you and learn from Me, for I am gentle and lowly
> in heart, and you will find rest for your souls. For
> My yoke is easy and My burden is light."

There is a yoke involved in following Jesus Christ, but He
has made it light. Another version of this offer is recorded
in Revelation 3:20, "Behold, I stand at the door and knock.
If anyone hears My voice and opens the door, I will come
in to him and dine with him, and he with Me."

Jesus seeks to yoke up with us, to partner with us.
Intimacy with Jesus is the ultimate answer to everything
in life. Like the water that quenches all thirst as He says
in John 4:14, "but whoever drinks of the water that I shall
give him will never thirst. But the water that I shall give
him will become in him a fountain of water springing up
into everlasting life."

In addition, He gives us grace in time of need – 'Let
us therefore come boldly to the throne of grace, that we
may obtain mercy and find grace to help in time of need'
– Hebrews 4:16. He knows any good that comes from us
originates from His Spirit.

In Romans 8:5 the Bible expounds on this – 'For those
who live according to the flesh set their minds on the things
of the flesh, but those who live according to the Spirit, the
things of the Spirit.' The Holy Spirit graciously provides us
with the antidote to the flesh.

Galatians 5:16-17 instructs us to, 'Walk in the Spirit,

and you shall not fulfil the lust of the flesh. For the flesh lusts against the Spirit, and the Spirit against the flesh; and these are contrary to one another, so that you do not do the things that you wish.' Struggling with sexual sin while in the university, I felt God's love drawing me back to Him all the time.

It was as though I needed Him to find a way out of the mess I was in against which I felt helpless. I did not know how to get this help though until I committed my life to God and received Jesus into my life as my Lord and Saviour. Still after that, it was through a process of daily yielding to the Holy Spirit, day-by-day, moment-by-moment, and bit-by-bit that I found victory over sin. As I am not yet perfected, the process still continues and by Him I gain more victory every day. Halleluiah!

When one enters a relationship with God through His Son Jesus Christ, He undertakes for the person as a Shepherd, as a Father. He makes with His people a covenant of victory that any child of God can tap into for any battle, physical or spiritual. In His relationship with the people of Israel, He demonstrated this over and over. One such account is recorded in 2 Chronicles 20:15-17:

> And he said, "Listen, all you of Judah and you inhabitants of Jerusalem, and you, King Jehoshaphat! Thus says the LORD to you: 'Do not be afraid nor dismayed because of this great multitude, for the battle is not yours, but God's. Tomorrow go down against them. They will surely come up by the Ascent of Ziz, and you will find them at the end of the brook before the

Wilderness of Jeruel. You will not need to fight in this battle. Position yourselves, stand still and see the salvation of the LORD, who is with you, O Judah and Jerusalem!' Do not fear or be dismayed; tomorrow go out against them, for the LORD is with you."

At a different setting, following the victory that God gave them over their enemies the Amalekites, the people of Israel concluded the story by acknowledging another covenant name of God as Jehovah Nissi (also YHWH Nissi). In Exodus 17:15-16 we read:

And Moses built an altar and called its name, The-LORD-Is-My-Banner (YHWH Nissi); for he said, "Because the LORD has sworn: the LORD will have war with Amalek from generation to generation."

As already said, we can tap into God's covenant promise to fight our battles when we face the battle of sin. When faced with the presence of something you desire but should not have, turn away and imagine you had not even seen it and that it was not available to you. Easier said than done but worth the try; and, God honours every effort we make at avoiding sin.

The Holy Spirit directs us and will make a way of escape when our heart is open to turning away from sin. Take for example, when someone says something that you would get offended about, in your mind, rewind the moment and imagine it had not even happened; in fact imagine the person had not even crossed your path at that moment, and move on.

I have tried this and it has worked in different situations, try it out for yourself and may the LORD help you as you do so. I have heard comments from different people about how God Almighty should not have allowed the temptation to come to Eve knowing that she would succumb to it. But just as it is today, the trials are there and we have to take responsibility for our responses to them.

When was the last time God disciplined you? Was it successful or have you put it aside for another day? For the sake of His unquenchable unyielding love, the discipline would usually return another day. Ephesians 5:5-6 tells us, 'For this you know, that no fornicator, unclean person, nor covetous man, who is an idolater, has any inheritance in the kingdom of Christ and God. Let no one deceive you with empty words, for because of these things the wrath of God comes upon the sons of disobedience'. It therefore makes sense that if the Father desires us to spend eternity with Him, He would work in and through us to get these disqualifying vices out of us.

Romans 1:21 says, '...although they knew God, they did not glorify Him as God, nor were thankful, but became futile in their thoughts, and their foolish hearts were darkened.' Isolating the spirit of man from God opens it to all sorts of pressures and conflicts. God is our rear guard. He watches over our boundaries and there is no going in or coming out of our lives that can take place without His say so.

In Isaiah 49:16 we read God's declaration which applies to all His children, "See, I have inscribed you on the palms of My hands; your walls are continually before Me." He watches over us and does not slumber; even when we ourselves slumber (Psalm 121:3-4).

We have been looking at how the fear of God delivers us from evil and sin. On the other hand, the fear of man is a reproach that also amounts to idolatry because it gives to man that which belongs to God. The Bible teaches that the fear of man brings a snare, but whoever trusts in the LORD shall be safe – Proverbs 29:25.

Also, in Job 28:28 we read, 'And to man He said, 'Behold, the fear of the Lord, that is wisdom, and to depart from evil is understanding.' We need to acknowledge God-ordained boundaries, even when we do not understand them; in fact, especially when we do not understand them and even when the option to go outside those boundaries appears harmless or of no apparent or immediate grave consequence. This is already well illustrated in the story of the fall of man in earlier chapters of this book.

In Matthew 5:10-12 we read from the teachings of our lord Jesus Christ:

> "Blessed are those who are persecuted for righteousness' sake, for theirs is the kingdom of heaven. Blessed are you when they revile and persecute you, and say all kinds of evil against you falsely for My sake. Rejoice and be exceedingly glad, for great is your reward in heaven, for so they persecuted the prophets who were before you."

Considering the above, you still never hear anyone pray to be persecuted for righteousness' sake so that they can have the kingdom of heaven. Nor does one pray to be reviled and persecuted for the Lord's sake in other that one may get a great reward in heaven.

I was reading through the gospel account of Matthew recently and came to chapter 3 verse 11 where John the Baptist said, "I indeed baptize you with water unto repentance, but He who is coming after me is mightier than I, whose sandals I am not worthy to carry. He will baptize you with the Holy Spirit and fire."

I had previously read this passage several times over and always had put the Holy Spirit and fire together to mean the same thing. At this instance I felt as though the Holy Spirit is teaching me something different. If the two meant the same thing, why are they spoken of separately? It could just be for emphasis but I have another angle to propose. The baptism of fire from the Lord is different from the baptism of the Holy Spirit. In the book of Malachi chapter 3 verses 2-3 we read of the coming Messenger (our Lord Jesus Christ):

"But who can endure the day of His coming? And who can stand when He appears? For He is like a refiner's fire and like launderer's soap. He will sit as a refiner and a purifier of silver; He will purify the sons of Levi, and purge them as gold and silver, that they may offer to the LORD an offering in righteousness."

Again, it is those whom you have allowed to share the personal space of your life, those whose opinion you value, those with whom you have established a certain amount or degree of familiarity or acquaintance, enough to give both you and them the privilege of each other's company, who will be used to affect your life.

Like Peter who could speak what the Spirit of God revealed to him but also what Satan wanted to say through him. Satan, copying God, sought for his wishes to be approved by Jesus who had just approved God's revelation from Peter.

Thus we must be on the look out not to be used as the devil's conduit but also watch out for those around us whom he seeks to use. Thus, one's spouse, brother, sister, children or friends would inevitably be the one to be used to further, advance or inhibit God's thoughts and purposes or Satan's in one's life.

Jesus encourages us on one hand to love everyone, otherwise referred to as our 'neighbour'. However, on the other hand, He wants us to be so set on giving God His due place in our lives, that we turn away from ungodly influence that our loved ones may be caught up with. In Luke 14:26 Jesus says, "If anyone comes to Me and does not hate his father and mother, wife and children, brothers and sisters, yes, and his own life also, he cannot be My disciple."

In verse 28 Jesus goes on to link this to the cost of following Him to the end, this may mean forsaking all if it stands in the way. One may not necessarily say to one's brother, sister or parents – 'Get thee behind me Satan" as Jesus said in response to His close friend Peter who was like family to Him.

But disagreeing with family tradition that is tantamount

to idolatry has brought some Christians to a place of family persecution, discord and disfavour. Would you stand your grounds in such situations?

It is one thing suffering persecution or rejection for one's faith from those to whom one is not close; but when it comes from family or close friends – it is a completely different situation. Home is usually the place where one would run to for comfort, strength and support in times of persecution - perceived to represent a place of safety and refuge. It follows then that persecution from within one's family can be one of the greatest challenges ever. Certainly, reports from people who have been in such situations have been heart breaking.

In Deuteronomy 32:35a God says, "Vengeance is Mine, and recompense." This implies that when persecution comes, it is not our place to respond but to yield the situation and circumstance to God and let Him sort the issues at hand out for us. Peter wrote some encouraging words for such times in 1 Peter 2:21-23:

> For to this you were called, because Christ also suffered for us, leaving us an example, that you should follow His steps: "Who committed no sin, nor was deceit found in His mouth"; who, when He was reviled, did not revile in return; when He suffered, He did not threaten, but committed Himself to Him who judges righteously.

This can be quite difficult. When I have been treated in a way I considered to be unfair, I have found it difficult to wish the person(s) well. God has helped me a lot in this area and I am better able to deal with such situations but the natural response is to seek redress for oneself. However, in the above statement, the Bible encourages us to commit ourselves to God who judges righteously.

This is another great example of the exercise of the fear of God. Giving Him His rightful place in such circumstances means that you have to give up the right, ability and urge to sort out the person(s) who has treated you unfairly or persecuted you and trust God to undertake for you.

Grace And The Fear Of God

Our God is gracious and patient; but what is grace? When we say we are living under grace what does it really mean? The definition of grace offered in Merriam-Webster dictionary is presented in the following expressions: unmerited divine assistance given humans for their regeneration or sanctification; a virtue coming from God; a state of sanctification enjoyed through divine assistance; approval, favour, mercy, pardon, privilege, disposition to or act or instance of kindness, courtesy or clemency, a temporary exemption or reprieve.

Grace should empower us to live beyond our natural abilities, to live beyond what those who do not have this grace can do. It is not for us to live below the standards of God's word which would mean that we miss out on the benefits of living by His wisdom.

Encouraging everyone not to refuse God's word, we are encouraged to use His grace appropriately in Hebrews 12:28-29, 'Therefore, since we are receiving a kingdom which cannot be shaken, let us have grace, by which we may serve God acceptably with reverence and godly fear. For our God is a consuming fire.'

My experience with my children during their teenage years comes to mind here. Often times I would tell them to undertake a particular task in a particular way. Commonly, they would ask why and offer to do it in a way that seemed easier and faster with less effort. I would try to explain why my option is preferable and they would argue.

Eventually they would do it their own way and it turns out a mess. 'I didn't know it would end up that way,' would be their response; but I had been trying to tell them just that. We sometimes do the same with the LORD. Our short-sightedness and partial understanding of events and their long-term consequences leave us poorly equipped to make certain decisions. When instructed by the LORD, we should choose to do it His way. Proverbs 13:13-14 teaches that:

> He who despises the word will be destroyed, but
> he who fears the commandments will be rewarded.
> The law of the wise is a fountain of life, to turn
> one away from the snares of death.

This also is another facet of the fear of God. Saying we have the fear of God and living in disregard for His commandments sounds like hypocrisy: a pretence of having a desirable or virtuous character, moral or religious beliefs or principles, that one does not actually possess. Sounds just as terrible as it really is.

This discuss brings to mind certain occasions when I have heard non-Christians refer to Christians as 'a bunch of hypocrites,' not understanding how or why a Christian may still be engaging in sinful activities. However, as the Christian progresses from one level of glory to the next, this should increasing not be the case.

In John 14:15 our Lord Jesus says, "If you love Me, keep My commandments." Again in verses 23-24 He says, "If anyone loves Me, he will keep My word; and My Father will love him, and We will come to him and make Our home with him. He who does not love Me does not keep My words; and the word which you hear is not Mine but the Father's who sent Me.'

Relating this to His experience, Jesus said in chapter 15 verse 10, "If you keep My commandments, you will abide in My love, just as I have kept My Father's commandments and abide in His love." To abide means to stick to, to hang on, to remain attached or close to, to dwell or stay with, to be established in.

The opposite is to fall away or become detached, disconnected or distanced from, withdraw, leave, abandon or turn away from. It follows that keeping the word or commandments of God is necessary for abiding in Him; while disregarding same leads to disconnection from Him. For emphasis I will also add what is written in 1 John 5:3-5:

> For this is the love of God, that we keep His
> commandments. And His commandments are
> not burdensome. For whatever is born of God
> overcomes the world. And this is the victory that
> has overcome the world-our faith. Who is he who
> overcomes the world, but he who believes that

Jesus is the Son of God?

Interestingly, these were the observations of the apostle John who referred to himself as the disciple whom Jesus loved (John 13:23). Grace is God's assistance to help us keep His commandments, live according to His will, walking in the Spirit rather than in the flesh. John 1:16 says of the Lord Jesus: And of His fullness we have all received, and grace for grace.

The fear of God complimented by His grace should help us live according to His word. Again, if I may use personal example to illustrate, one of my children when they were much younger responded so differently to getting things wrong that we quickly came to the conclusion that he was of a different spirit. When he found out he had done something wrong, it hurt him so much as though he absolutely hated doing wrong.

When he came to tell us about the issue, one could not help but hurt along with him; often I would console him on his suffering and find no place for caution as he had already suffered enough! This must be what King David meant when he wrote Psalm 51:17, 'The sacrifices of God are a broken spirit, a broken and a contrite heart—these, O God, You will not despise.'

I believe the fear of God and His grace should bring a godly sorrow as a consequence of sin, rather than an unhealthy attitude of accepting the sin and not being concerned with what our Father God thinks about it or its temporal or eternal consequences.

Grace is that extra empowerment to overcome the desire

of the flesh to dwell in evil; rather God warned Cain of this and encouraged him to rule over sin in Genesis 4:7, "If you do well, will you not be accepted? And if you do not do well, sin lies at the door. And its desire is for you, but you should rule over it."

The Will Of God And The Fear Of God

Murmuring, an expression of discontent and dissatisfaction, implies lack of willingness to submit to God's authority or plan. Cooperating with God's plan requires humility, because one may have to lay aside one's own ideas that, for seemingly cogent reasons, appear to that person to be excellent in the first place.

In 1 Peter 5:6-7 the Bible says 'Therefore humble yourselves under the mighty hand of God, that He may exalt you in due time, casting all your care upon Him, for He cares for you.' In the apostle Paul's letter to the Philippians, he talks of how our Lord Jesus humbled Himself so that He could carry out God's instructions for our salvation:

> Let this mind be in you which was also in Christ Jesus, who, being in the form of God, did not consider it robbery to be equal with God, but made Himself of no reputation, taking the form of a bondservant, and coming in the likeness of men. And being found in appearance as a man, He humbled Himself and became obedient to the point of death, even the death of the cross. Therefore God also has highly exalted Him and given Him the name which is above every name, that at the

name of Jesus every knee should bow, of those in heaven, and of those on earth, and of those under the earth, and that every tongue should confess that Jesus Christ is Lord, to the glory of God the Father. (Philippians 2:5-11).

As noted above, God elevated Jesus, but when Jesus is confessed as Lord, it is to the glory of the Father. This is how it should be with us. The Father enriches our lives, and these riches and the privileges arising from them should bring glory to Him.

As God's people we have received a privileged position of sonship through faith in His Son Jesus. However, rather than have everything at our feet, He still requires us to humble ourselves before Him for our needs which when met return glory to Him alone. Thus, we read in 2 Chronicles 7:14, "If My people who are called by My name will humble themselves, and pray and seek My face, and turn from their wicked ways, then I will hear from heaven, and will forgive their sin and heal their land."

In Deuteronomy 8:2, God led the people through the desert to humble them: 'And you shall remember that the LORD your God led you all the way these forty years in the wilderness, to humble you and test you, to know what was in your heart, whether you would keep His commandments or not.'

Why did they need humbling? The humble state reveals the state of the heart. You may have heard the saying; 'It's easy to abide by the law when things are going well.' The Bible continues further in verse 3, "So He humbled you, allowed you to hunger, and fed you with manna which you did not know nor did your fathers know, that He might make you know that man shall not live by bread alone; but man lives by every word that proceeds from the mouth of the LORD."

Difficult times can be evaluated in two perspectives that apply to most instances. Is it God's timing for one to go through that process or is it judgment resulting from one's earlier actions or even actions of generations past? For the latter options one can overturn the process through an act of repentance and confession or in the case of generational events, through prayers focused on releasing oneself from such.

It is the wisdom and discernment from the Holy Spirit that guides one as to which option applies to the specific circumstance. Ecclesiastes 8:5b-6 states that, 'And a wise man's heart discerns both time and judgment, because for every matter there is a time and judgment, though the misery of man increases greatly.'

We therefore ought to ask the Father which of the two options is applicable to any situation we see ourselves in so as to address it appropriately. Lack of understanding or wisdom concerning a situation leads to misplaced focus and delayed resolution. The word of God continues in Deuteronomy 8:6, "Therefore you shall keep the commandments of the LORD your God, to walk in His ways and to fear Him."

The use of 'therefore' at the start of the sentence in this reference implies that, having experienced the aforementioned humbling and chastening of the LORD, they should do what follows: obey God and fear Him. Furthermore, in verse 16b we read that God's purpose for humbling and testing His people was and remains "to do you good in the end."

This is also in line with His word in Romans 8:28, 'And we know that all things work together for good to those who love God, to those who are the called according to His purpose.' So even if one does not understand the origin of the trouble, we can trust our Father God to work all things together for us in it all. Halleluiah!

It is difficult, and even unwise, to try and interpret another person's times. Job's friends thought there was no other explanation for his hard times except his presumed disobedience to the LORD. Along the same lines the Bible advises us that mocking the poor man equates to mocking his Creator. God told Moses that He made the mute, the deaf, the seeing and the blind (Exodus 4:11). Proverbs 17:5 reads, 'He who mocks the poor reproaches his Maker; he who is glad at calamity will not go unpunished.' This applies to any form of mockery, not only of the financially deprived, but also those deprived or poor in any aspect of life.

One can therefore conclude that, mocking a person for his or her status or characteristics is a 'no-no' – unacceptable and unwise. You may choose to speak to the Maker to ask Him to alter the person's status to an improved status but bear in mind that it is up to Him what to do to His creation in line with His purposes. This is where God gives us the opportunity or privilege as priests to effect change in situations by praying for others – for His intervention in their lives.

As Christians we must resist the urge to mock the spiritually destitute or depraved. We must instead pray for them and correct them gently when the opportunity presents itself. Similarly, as those who lack the skills, health, strength, intelligence or even beauty that God Almighty has freely endowed you with come your way for help, as indeed they would, one must not mock but freely be a blessing with what one has been blessed with.

It would help to reflect on the truth that it could have been you on the deprived side of life; but God chose to have it the way it is. Holding God in high regard, as should be the case for a life that embraces the fear of God, includes treating those He chose to put at a relatively disadvantaged position compared to oneself with due regard and respect. In 1 Samuel chapter 1 we read of how Peninah mocked Hannah, not bearing in mind that it could have been her in Hannah's place instead. Do we stop and consider, "It could have been me in the other person's predicament?"

Why did God spare you from it? Was it so that you can oppress the other less fortunate or less-able person? Or did He place you in their vicinity as an opportunity for you to appreciate your God-given ability through helping those less able than yourself?

Jesus rightly put it this way, "Therefore, whatever you want men to do to you, do also to them, for this is the Law and the Prophets" – Matthew 7:12. On the same note, Lord Jesus goes on to say that when you give food for the hungry, drink for the thirsty, shelter for the homeless, clothing to the naked, visit the sick or the imprisoned, you do it to Him:

Then the King will say to those on His right hand, 'Come, you blessed of My Father, inherit the kingdom prepared for you from the foundation of the world: for I was hungry and you gave Me food; I was thirsty and you gave Me drink; I was a stranger and you took Me in; I was naked and you clothed Me; I was sick and you visited Me; I was in prison and you came to Me.' "Then the righteous will answer Him, saying, 'Lord, when did we see You hungry and feed You, or thirsty and give You drink? When did we see You a stranger and take You in, or naked and clothe You? Or when did we see You sick, or in prison, and come to You?' And the King will answer and say to them, 'Assuredly, I say to you, inasmuch as you did it to one of the least of these My brethren, you did it to Me.' (Matthew 25:34-40).

Note, the imprisoned, whether there for his own wrong-doing or not, the Lord still cares for him and wants us to do same. On the other hand, when we do not do the above charitable deeds, Jesus said it is Him that has been denied (Matthew 25:41-46).

This is a really serious issue with even eternal consequences. In addition, we are encouraged to make the glory of God the target of our actions, 'Therefore, whether you eat or drink, or whatever you do, do all to the glory of God' – 1 Corinthians 10:31. Can you glorify Him in the way you relate to the less able or less fortunate?

In response to the question regarding the reason behind

the blind man's blindness, the Lord Jesus answered, "Neither this man nor his parents sinned, but that the works of God should be revealed in him" – John 9:3. If it could happen to that blind man, what exempts anyone else from the same fate? How often do we thank God for our abilities? Instead it is the "How could a good God allow this to happen?" that one hears when it all goes wrong. We will revisit this later in the book.

Taking a different perspective as a sequel to the foregoing illustration anchored on 1 Corinthians 10:31, can God be glorified in the areas where you are less able or less fortunate than others? Romans 12:3 teaches us not to think of ourselves more highly than we ought to think, but to think soberly. Jesus taught His followers not to think themselves better than those who were suffering; rather, to repent so that they did not suffer likewise:

> There were present at that season some who told Him about the Galileans whose blood Pilate had mingled with their sacrifices. And Jesus answered and said to them, "Do you suppose that these Galileans were worse sinners than all other Galileans, because they suffered such things? I tell you, no; but unless you repent you will all likewise perish. Or those eighteen on whom the tower in Siloam fell and killed them, do you think that they were worse sinners than all other men who dwelt in Jerusalem? I tell you, no; but unless you repent you will all likewise perish" (Luke 13:1-5).

Worship Is The Ultimate Expression Of God's Lordship

When we do not have something, we get desperate and pray for the thing. When we lose something or do not get an extra help, there are complaints and then it is easy to forget to be thankful for what we have received. Being thankful for what we have received includes not using it for purposes that are against the wishes of the One who has given it to us.

This is an act of worship. Luke 14:16-21 gives an account of a man who prepared a feast and invited many people but each found an excuse not to honour the invitation. Whatever their reason, let us bear in mind that their refusal was also a refusal to honour the man and his entire household. Those invited to the feast were either going to see land and wife, going to the farm or going to get married. Again, bear in mind that the land and wife were given by the one inviting them to the feast – in this illustration, God, the One they cut out of their lives.

It is the epic example of ingratitude. The one who is mentally handicapped has not much problems because he has no ability to reason things out. With our intelligence though, how come we try so much to disprove the existence of the One who equipped us with the power to reason? This is the work perpetuated by the devil, also referred to as the ruler of this world (John 14:30 and John 12:31) and his agents.

You may wonder, like I have sometimes, 'how can people not get it?' It may seem so obvious but the power of the enemy is frequently overlooked and underestimated.

187

THE FEAR OF GOD

God warns us about him in several passages. In 1 Peter 5:8 the warning sounds out clear, 'Be sober, be vigilant; because your adversary the devil walks about like a roaring lion, seeking whom he may devour.'

This warning would be needless if there was no chance of the Christian being devoured by the devil. When Peter was with Jesus, Satan planned to sift him, Jesus had to pray for him (Luke 22:31). Satan had asked for permission to sift the one who was walking right beside the Master Himself.

Consider this, if a country rises and challenges the United States of America or Britain at this time when both nations represent significant military power in the world, they must have checked their ability to withstand the onslaught of retaliation from them. The enemy is described as wise by God Himself; so, he was not going against God as a fool would go against one much stronger than him.

However, his wisdom did him no favours in pushing him to think he could take the place of the One who gave him the wisdom in the first place. Just as only strong nations would defy another strong nation, the enemy must have been given the power by God with which he thought he could rise against the Almighty. Again one may think, "How stupid is that?"

What about today and now, how foolish to resist God's lordship and not yield to Him the things He has given us? God had given man freedom of choice to decide whether he chooses to follow His ways or to turn away from the same. The Bible says that the fool says in his mind there is no God (Psalm 14:1; Psalm 53:1), such a person has no concept of his own origin.

Note however that this is the power of the ruler of this world working on the mind of man, which is itself wicked beyond man's understanding, "The heart is deceitful above all things, and desperately wicked; who can know it?" (Jeremiah 17:9).

In Luke 12:16-21, Jesus tells a story:

> "The ground of a certain rich man yielded plentifully. And he thought within himself, saying, 'What shall I do, since I have no room to store my crops?' So he said, 'I will do this: I will pull down my barns and build greater, and there I will store my crops and my goods. And I will say to my soul, "Soul, you have many goods laid up for many years; take your ease; eat, drink, and be merry."' But God said to him, 'Fool! This night your soul will be required of you; then whose will those things be which you have provided?' "So is he who lays up treasure for himself, and is not rich toward God."

God is the One who, by giving us life, gives relevance to things around us – people and possessions alike. We ought not let what He gives distract us from Him the Giver.

Have you ever considered the interesting phenomenon of how the jobless find time for God, while the working person is too busy to commune with Him. I know, I have been there and honestly, without making a firm resolution to set time apart to commune with the LORD or to do the things He has called you to do, life events often do not lend you the time or space.

For example, my first book, Hope Breaks out with Singing was developed during a period of seven successive night vigils when I had no employed job to go to. It was not my plan to write the book but it was conceived when I set time apart for the LORD.

Again, writing this current book, I have set targets and deadlines that I did not eventually meet but they helped me make a conscious effort to get this book ready. I believe the LORD has continued to encourage me especially when at a prayer meeting a gentleman with prophetic ministry told me the LORD was asking about the book!! That got me even more stirred up towards finishing the book.

Later on, I recall searching for the draft copy to resume writing. Though I searched everywhere I thought it could be, I could not find it. I prayed to the LORD to help me find it. Then, in a dream shortly afterwards, a hand gave the pages of the draft to me; they were like the pictures I had seen of manuscripts on papyrus with uneven edges. I dusted it up in the dream. The very next morning, I went straight to where the draft was – a place I would never have looked for it. God is truly amazingly gracious!

Think for a moment, if we need to make some compromise regarding our time, why is it the time we spend with God that has to be given up? One could be busy but rearrange other life events to make certain that time is still set aside to commune with God for a healthy balanced life style. When we disregard our time with Him, we miss out quite a lot, sometimes without even realising it.

God is so serious about the issue of having prime place in our lives. In Exodus 23:13, He tells His people – the

Israelites, "And in all that I have said to you, be circumspect and make no mention of the name of other gods, nor let it be heard from your mouth." They were warned not to play around with other gods, not even their names, knowing that the heart of man can be influenced by the slightest distractions.

These days people wander into things that belong to other gods and think nothing of it. For example, many temples, dedicated to various gods, are intentionally visited by children of God as a form of recreation. Those who resist are frowned at as not being sociable.

It may not even be a 'temple' but other buildings, shrines or establishments dedicated to other gods. I was recently on a trip to Kawloon, Hong Kong, with colleagues to attend a conference, my first time in that part of the world. Part of the planned excursion included visits to temples dedicated to other gods. I steered away as much as possible but one of our meals was organised at one of these temples. I attended reluctantly but did so as a way of keeping among the group still not sure that it was the right decision.

I know the apostle Paul wrote about being all things to all men in other that one may win some (1 Corinthians 9:19-23). Still one has to do all things to the glory of God, whether we eat, drink or whatsoever we do (1 Corinthians 10:31). Each decision and choice has to be weighed individually with the guidance of the Holy Spirit because where it all matters eventually is before God, both now and in the hereafter. Joshua reminded Israel of God's command to them in Joshua 24:14-15:

"Now therefore, fear the LORD, serve Him in

sincerity and in truth, and put away the gods which your fathers served on the other side of the River and in Egypt. Serve the LORD! And if it seems evil to you to serve the LORD, choose for yourselves this day whom you will serve, whether the gods which your fathers served that were on the other side of the River, or the gods of the Amorites, in whose land you dwell. But as for me and my house, we will serve the LORD."

Psalm 5 verse 7 presents King David's contribution to this discourse: 'But as for me, I will come into Your house in the multitude of Your mercy; in fear of You I will worship toward Your holy temple.'

CHAPTER 4

THE CHURCH OF JESUS CHRIST AND THE FEAR OF GOD

*R*everence for the presence of God is anchored on the fear of God; without which, one may not give due reverence to His presence. When Jacob realised that he was in the presence of God at Jacob's ladder (Genesis 28:10-15), the experience influenced his subsequent actions as recorded in verses 16-22:

> Then Jacob awoke from his sleep and said, "Surely the LORD is in this place, and I did not know it." And he was afraid and said, "How awesome is this place! This is none other than the house of God, and this is the gate of heaven!" Then Jacob rose early in the morning, and took the stone that he had put at his head, set it up as a pillar, and poured oil on top of it. And he called the name of that place Bethel; but the name of that city had been Luz previously. Then Jacob made a vow, saying, "If God will be with me, and keep me in this way that I am going, and give me bread to eat and clothing to put on, so that I come back to my father's house in peace, then the LORD shall be my God. And this stone which I have set as a pillar shall be God's house, and of all that You give me I will surely give a tenth to You."

THE FEAR OF GOD

Without this revelation, Jacob would have just carried on as usual. A revelation of who God is and His presence brings a change in one's attitude. The fear of God is what dictates the nature of one's attitude.

It also builds an attitude of valuing the gathering of the saints as advised in Hebrews 10:23 – 'And let us consider one another in order to stir up love and good works, not forsaking the assembling of ourselves together, as is the manner of some, but exhorting one another, and so much the more as you see the Day approaching.'

This is especially true when bearing in mind that the Lord is there with us as promised in Matthew 18:20, "For where two or three are gathered together in My name, I am there in the midst of them."

The backbone principles of the Church take on new meaning to a life that is equipped by the fear of God. The attitude towards the breaking of bread and wine at the communion, regard for prayer & fasting, regard for the anointing of God, the baptism, the in-filling of the Holy Spirit, the gifts and fruit of the Holy Spirit, the calling not to conform to this world but to live a life led by the Holy Spirit, regard for one's calling/ministry/commission as a Christian are some examples.

Paul the apostle showed appreciation for his calling in 1 Timothy 1:12-15:

> And I thank Christ Jesus our Lord who has enabled me, because He counted me faithful, putting me into the ministry, although I was formerly a blasphemer, a persecutor, and an insolent man; but I obtained

mercy because I did it ignorantly in unbelief. And the grace of our Lord was exceedingly abundant, with faith and love which are in Christ Jesus. This is a faithful saying and worthy of all acceptance, that Christ Jesus came into the world to save sinners, of whom I am chief.

The revelation of God is made more real as the fear of God develops in us as both go hand in hand. This partly explains why people hear the same message and have different responses – one person shrugs it off and doesn't remember it the next minute while the other is awed and makes notes to revisit and recall, yet another commits it to memory and makes life changes based on what was received.

Derek Prince, an avid and well respected Christian writer one said, 'if you read (or hear) God's word and are not moved by it – you haven't grasped it.' The revelation of God is clearly indispensable to the Christian faith. Paul said in 2 Timothy 1:12, 'For this reason I also suffer these things; nevertheless I am not ashamed, for I know whom I have believed and am persuaded that He is able to keep what I have committed to Him until that Day.'

Ponder Time

Do you know the Lord?

My personal opinion is that creation, including man and angels, has not been given the capacity to comprehend or define the fullness of God Almighty.

The revelations He gives of Himself helps us gain understanding into that very aspect of Him that is revealed. Everything in creation has a definition, including angels of God, Satan and his demons, sun moon, stars and so on; but there is and will never be a complete definition of the Almighty God. No wonder some refer to Him as the Indescribable One.

The disciples of Jesus Christ had been with Him and seen many of His miracles – yet they asked, "Who can this be, that even the winds and the sea obey Him?" – Matthew 8:27. You may have experienced different responses to being introduced to people, or observed other people being introduced to each other.

Someone is introduced to another, the other stands up eagerly and the other sits until the other person is introduced; then, realizing that the other person is equally high ranking or higher ranking by societal values, they rise up quickly to their feet and the introduction continues.

Similarly, how one responds to the Lord depends of one's perception of who He is. Does he deserve a stand up and hand shake or just a nod of acknowledgement or a bowing of the head. The development of the fear of God within us helps us determine our response to Him.

The Fear Of God And Church Leadership

When Moses' father-in-law Jethro advised Moses to select men who would share the burden of judging the people of Israel with him, he said, "Moreover you shall select from all the people able men, such as fear God, men of truth, hating covetousness; and place such over them to be rulers of thousands, rulers of hundreds, rulers of fifties, and rulers of tens" - Exodus 18:21.

Moses heeded his father-in-law's advice and it worked well. Among the children of God, the fear of God ought to be applied as a criterion for appointing people into positions of leadership.

In everyday life the criteria usually follow the pattern of who shoves the others out of the way, who achieves set goals irrespective of the means of such achievements or whether they caused harm to others in the process.

Beyond having qualities such as good leadership skills, people management skills etc, leaders within Christian establishment should have the Jethro criteria applied just as Moses did. This does not mean that these people would always get it right. There are in fact real life accounts of several such people who have got it wrong, sometimes woefully wrong. However, it is a biblical principle and one that honours God.

The Bible teaches that when we turn from the principles of God Almighty and instead choose to trust others or trust in our strength, His judgment comes upon them making them unable to save or help us anyway. This exposes the weakness of human knowledge and wisdom – when it warps the person and makes him or her become a lord unto themselves. This is mentioned in Isaiah 47:10-15:

"For you have trusted in your wickedness; you have said, 'No one sees me'; your wisdom and your knowledge have warped you; and you have said in your heart, 'I am, and there is no one else besides me.' Therefore evil shall come upon you; you shall not know from where it arises. And trouble shall fall upon you; you will not be able to put it off. And desolation shall come upon you suddenly, which you shall not know. Stand now with your enchantments and the multitude of your sorceries, in which you have laboured from your youth – perhaps you will be able to profit, perhaps you will prevail. You are wearied in the multitude of your counsels; let now the astrologers, the stargazers, and the monthly prognosticators stand up and save you from what shall come upon you. Behold, they shall be as stubble, the fire shall burn them; they shall not deliver themselves from the power of the flame; it shall not be a coal to be warmed by, nor a fire to sit before! Thus shall they be to you with whom you have laboured, your merchants from your youth; they shall wander each one to his quarter. No one shall save you."

Here, it is pertinent to recall that the prophet Jonah could not be helped by the sailors who truly would have perished but Jonah persuaded them to throw him overboard – Jonah 1:10-16. They wanted to help him but were faced with opposition from God Himself; they eventually gave up.

The Holy Spirit is like our spiritual policeman. One of His several activities is to keep us on the 'straight and narrow,' not a popular phrase nowadays. This way, He protects us not only from harming ourselves but also from harming others. He also works in others to stop them harming us.

One day, I was thinking of this as I drove my car out of a shopping complex with my daughter sat beside me. My thoughts were so far away, I just managed to spot the police car across on the other side of the dual carriage way. I thought that was an interesting coincidence, I was just thinking of the "spiritual policeman".

So engrossed was I in my thoughts that I forgot to switch on my headlights. Then I wanted to check my speed and noticed the dashboard was darkened, only then did I realise my headlights were off. I quickly switched them on, thankful that the road was mostly deserted at that time of the night.

Within a few seconds of turning on my headlights, I noticed a police car behind me. It flashed its lights at us and indicated we should pull over. It turned out to be the police car I had seen earlier on the other side of the dual carriage way; they had turned round and come after us having noticed the headlights to be off.

The lady officer came to my window and asked, "Do you know why we stopped you, love?" "Yes," I answered. I explained that I had forgotten to put on my headlights and apologised for the mistake. "You need to be careful next time, it's just we don't want any accidents, with you getting hurt or other road users being involved if they crash into you," she said. "Yes, I will be careful. Thank you," I replied. We then parted ways as they continued on their patrol duty and I continued on my journey home. "Interesting," I thought.

The very first time a police person stops me on the road is when I'm thinking of the "spiritual policeman." Just to drive the point home that His policing stops me harming myself, or harming others; but also stops others harming me as I drive through the roads of life. I don't know about you but when I see a policeman on the road, my first instinct is to look at my speed, then check that I have got my seat belt on. Their presence in our vicinity should be reassuring because in keeping my speed down, I keep from harming myself or harming others.

Also as others drive safely, the road becomes a safer place for all. Similarly, when I am among people who are filled with the Holy Spirit, I feel safer because I expect them to be sensitive to His lead and to live by His standards. Granted, as human beings, many times we go against the Holy Spirit or the enemy uses our weakness when the "flesh" part of us, or the untamed human nature, gains the upper hand.

This is not to say that there are not people around us who though not Spirit-filled are living a disciplined life. There are and I am always pleased to come across them; but also saddened to know that according to the immutable word of God, they will not spend eternity in heaven without Jesus Christ.

Satan's ploy is usually the opposite of God's guidance. To Eve he said, and continues to say in a different format to us today, "You will surely not die" as a consequence of disregarding God's word. God had said to them, "...in the day that you eat of it you shall surely die" – Genesis 2:17.

The truth is – in doing God's will, one would 'surely not die.' It would not kill anyone to spend time in reading the word of God or to miss a meal in fasting and praying exercise, to be kind to the unfriendly neighbour, or to hold one's tongue and not have the last say in that argument. It most certainly would not kill anyone to hold back from committing adultery or fornication for that short-lived transient relief that often leaves a person feeling disgusted with him or herself later.

If you bear in mind that the sinful act is committed against God, the foregoing should apply to the one who chooses to acknowledge Him as God. This applies to one whose conscience has not yet been seared as described in 1 Timothy 4:1-2, 'Now the Spirit expressly says that in latter times some will depart from the faith, giving heed to deceiving spirits and doctrines of demons, speaking lies in hypocrisy, having their own conscience seared with a hot iron.' Furthermore, the Bible says in Romans 1:24-25:

> Therefore God also gave them up to uncleanness, in the lusts of their hearts, to dishonour their bodies among themselves, who exchanged the truth of God for the lie, and worshipped and served the creature rather than the Creator, who is blessed forever. Amen.

God says that His people are destroyed for lack of knowledge (Hosea 4:6). When you invite a Christian to partake in something that is clearly identifiable as sin, it is obvious and one may find it easier to hold back or resist such temptation.

However, when cunningly, the enemy or the source of the temptation uses God as the focus of the activity, people are more likely to be misled. This was the situation in Eve's case where Satan made 'being like God' the focus of the temptation.

For example, say a person tells me to steal from a poor person; I would see that as a sinful act against God. But, when the instruction is to steal from the poor so as to make the poor starve or experience lack so that they would call upon the Lord and serve Him, it sounds more acceptable than the outright wickedness that it really is.

In everyday life, people use "God" or what they consider to be their god as an excuse for perpetuating their wicked desires. I have heard sceptics remark that God has been behind several wars and the Bible lets us know that indeed He has; but men still wrongly use Him as an excuse to perpetuate their evil ways.

The hearts of men sometimes yield to the enticement of the enemy to imagine that their evil motive is indeed of God or in service of God. The Bible indeed tells us that men will kill Christians and claim to be doing it for God: 'They will put you out of the synagogues; yes, the time is coming that whoever kills you will think that he offers God service' (John 16:2). It has happened in times past and continues even in modern times.

In Acts 27:22-25, Paul encouraged his fellow sailors by expressing His confidence that His God would not let him down:

> "And now I urge you to take heart, for there will
> be no loss of life among you, but only of the ship.
> For there stood by me this night an angel of the
> God to whom I belong and whom I serve, saying,
> 'Do not be afraid, Paul; you must be brought

before Caesar; and indeed God has granted you all those who sail with you.' Therefore take heart, men, for I believe God that it will be just as it was told me."

Belonging to God is the best way to live; Paul's confidence is quite enviable. Make sure you do not yield yourself to another to serve them. Even if you have not consciously chosen to yield to evil, the Bible says that you are the servant of what you give yourself to (Romans 6:16).

The fear of God helps us to give Him His rightful place. It brings us to the place of having appropriate regard for His word. In Isaiah 66:2b God says, "But on this one will I look: on him who is poor and of a contrite spirit, and who trembles at My word." Clearly, God values those who tremble at His words, who gives due regard to His words.

Ponder Time

Do you tremble at God's words, or do you merely shrug them off and live as though God has no say in what you do?

In Jeremiah 2:19 we read God's rebuke to backslidden Israel – "Your own wickedness will correct you, and your backslidings will rebuke you. Know therefore and see that it is an evil and bitter thing that you have forsaken the LORD your God, and the fear of Me is not in you," says the Lord GOD of hosts.'

THE FEAR OF GOD

It follows that the lack of the fear of God among the people contributed significantly to their backsliding. Again, in Jeremiah 5:22-24 we read God's rebuke when Israel turned away and served other gods:

> 'Do you not fear Me?' says the LORD. 'Will you not tremble at My presence, who have placed the sand as the bound of the sea, by a perpetual decree, that it cannot pass beyond it? And though its waves toss to and fro, yet they cannot prevail; though they roar, yet they cannot pass over it. But this people has a defiant and rebellious heart; they have revolted and departed. They do not say in their heart, "Let us now fear the LORD our God, who gives rain, both the former and the latter, in its season. He reserves for us the appointed weeks of the harvest."'

The foregoing passages demonstrate that rebellion is born out of a lack of the fear of God. Like all of God's gifts, the fear of God is given to us out of His love and for our good. In Jeremiah 29:11 God states – 'For I know the thoughts that I think toward you, says the LORD, thoughts of peace and not of evil, to give you a future and a hope.' In Jeremiah 7:21-23, God reminded Israel of His instructions to their fathers:

> Thus says the LORD of hosts, the God of Israel: "Add your burnt offerings to your sacrifices and eat meat. For I did not speak to your fathers, or command them in the day that I brought them out

of the land of Egypt, concerning burnt offerings or sacrifices. But this is what I commanded them, saying, 'Obey My voice, and I will be your God, and you shall be My people. And walk in all the ways that I have commanded you, that it may be well with you.'"

He insists that His covenant with them to be their God was not anchored on their sacrifices; but rather, on their commitment to obey His voice. Referring to God, Psalm 119:74 says, 'Those who fear You will be glad when they see me, because I have hoped in Your word.' The fear of God should also dictate what we celebrate, what we approve and what we shrink from or disapprove.

For example, it would be difficult or impossible for a person with the fear of God to dance with joy or derive pleasure from listening to music that debases God or glorifies His enemies, or promotes the things that are against His word.

Without the fear of God, one can give in to the fact that the tune is pleasing to the ears and therefore choose to ignore the fact that the lyrics are against God. Similarly, it is the fear of God that makes us celebrate other people's testimonies when they speak of His wondrous works in their lives.

It follows that if you experience a stirring up of jealousy, anger or disgust when you listen to the testimonies of God's goodness in the lives of others, this is clearly not of God and one should repent of it and ask for God's grace to overcome it. Christians ought to share their testimonies of God's goodness as a means of encouraging and strengthening each other.

This is only possible when we have the fear of God. Psalm 35:27 adds to this discuss in stating, 'Let them shout for joy and be glad, who favour my righteous cause; and let them say continually, "Let the LORD be magnified, who has pleasure in the prosperity of His servant."

Furthermore, in Luke 1:50 we read, 'And His mercy is on those who fear Him from generation to generation.' The fear of God is a gift to His children to enable them fulfil the requirements of the covenant relationship they have with Him, for their own good and that of future generations. Jeremiah wrote about God's plan for His people when they are restored to Him in chapter 32 verses 38-41:

> They shall be My people, and I will be their God; then I will give them one heart and one way, that they may fear Me forever, for the good of them and their children after them. And I will make an everlasting covenant with them, that I will not turn away from doing them good; but I will put My fear in their hearts so that they will not depart from Me. Yes, I will rejoice over them to do them good, and I will assuredly plant them in this land, with all My heart and with all My soul.

When the Lord calls a person to do something, He makes His power available for the mission. He disregards the seemingly evident impossibilities because He focuses on His ability to do all things. This lines up with the passage, 'I can do all things through Christ who strengthens me'

(Philippians 4:13).

It is not unusual therefore for one to shrink back from a God-assigned mission initially; often because one perceives it to be beyond one's ability. However, to accomplish His purpose, we have to learn to lean on Him, to look beyond our abilities or inabilities and limitations and focus on His power and ability.

The fear of God encompasses the acknowledgement of the fact that God is way beyond our limitations. Let us review Ezekiel's answer when God asked him if the dry bones could live. He replied, "O Lord GOD, You know" implying that no situation is impossible with God (Ezekiel 37:3). Naturally, no one talks to dry bones. It may be imaginable to see a person talking to a set of dry bones, but to a multitude of them, the natural conclusion is nothing short of insanity.

In addition, the Almighty God has a reputation for employing weak people and turning them into victorious men or women of valour. He uses the foolish things of this world to shame the wise. In 1 Corinthians 1 vs. 25-29 we read:

> Because the foolishness of God is wiser than men, and the weakness of God is stronger than men. For you see your calling, brethren, that not many wise according to the flesh, not many mighty, not many noble, are called. But God has chosen the foolish things of the world to put to shame the wise, and God has chosen the weak things of the world to put to shame the things which are mighty; and the base things of the world and the things which are

despised God has chosen, and the things which are not, to bring to nothing the things that are, that no flesh should glory in His presence.

Now, let us reflect on the experience of Moses when God called him to deliver His people Israel out of slavery and the imposed bondage of Egypt's Pharaoh, the most powerful world ruler of their time (Exodus chapter 3).

Moses practically ruled himself out and told God to find someone else to lead Israel out of Egypt. Consider Gideon (Judges chapters 6&7). As far as we can see and understand, it seemed as though he was suffering from an inferiority complex.

Looking at it another way, you could say he was lowly. God saw him as a man of valour. From the 'tests' he put God through, one could tell he was not keen on taking the challenge of delivering the people of Israel from their enemies.

David on the other hand knew that God was the Almighty. He also knew that if a person was haughty enough to stretch his hand against God's people, indirectly stretching the hand against God – the person was already defeated. When David heard Goliath's taunt directed at Israel's army, he knew Goliath's downfall was settled. It was this knowledge that informed his declaration in 1 Samuel 17:45-47:

> Then David said to the Philistine, "You come to me with a sword, with a spear, and with a javelin. But I come to you in the name of the LORD of hosts, the God of the armies of Israel, whom you have defied. This day the LORD will deliver you into

my hand, and I will strike you and take your head from you. And this day I will give the carcasses of the camp of the Philistines to the birds of the air and the wild beasts of the earth, that all the earth may know that there is a God in Israel. Then all this assembly shall know that the LORD does not save with sword and spear; for the battle is the LORD's, and He will give you into our hands."

Giving God due reverence is a prerequisite to obedience to His word. Let us re-examine the case recorded in the twelfth chapter of Genesis involving the father of faith – Abraham. How many rich people today can be persuaded to leave their place and move to an unknown destination?

If one should go by the standards of our day, today's people or even people from generations past, as a rich man, he would have designed his home exactly the way he wanted it to be, with all the top range facilities of the day. To leave that for destination unknown – it is not difficult to imagine that many people would struggle to comply with a similar instruction!

Even those not so rich struggle to give things up. I have been there. I do not want to insult the experience of those who live in desperate poverty by referring to myself as poor with regards to standard of living, but I have been in position of what I personally regard as "lack" frequently. Even in these situations, it isn't easy to give up things to the Lord. It may not be physical things that He asks us to give up.

I recall when the Lord spoke to me to give up my sleep

at certain hours to pray. For some reason I initially started to disagree with Satan on the issue, having concluded that the message I received could not be from God. Eventually the Lord graciously helped me understand that Satan had nothing to gain from me praying at those hours. I then settled it in my mind that this was the Lord prompting me to prayer.

Then I tried to negotiate with the Lord. I offered to pray for the same length of time at a different time of the day, but I felt God say the other time was meant for me to do other things for Him and that the time He spoke about was what I should stick with. As I accepted the call I asked the Lord to help me co-operate with the Holy Spirit to make it happen and He did. He was so helpful to me that some of the time, I felt an arm around my shoulders encouraging me and leading me to my prayer spot in the house.

Lowliness does not equate to poverty, it is a matter of a heart being open to respond to God, giving Him His rightful place as the Almighty God – the One whose reign and authority overrides every other, including our desire to be in control of what goes on around us.

Before going on, I would encourage you my dear friend to stop and have a personal check at this point. I found myself stuck at this point; but this can easily be the biggest obstacle to success. We need to deny "self" and follow the Lord, yielding the control over our lives and decisions to Him. Consider King Saul, the LORD was not given the place of sovereignty in his heart which made it possible for him to consider giving in to the men's desire.

In 1 Samuel chapter 15, the Bible records that God

Almighty requested King Saul to be His agent of complete destruction upon the Amalekites but he executed this command partially. When confronted by the prophet Samuel, king Saul replied:

> "I have sinned, for I have transgressed the commandment of the LORD and your words, because I feared the people and obeyed their voice. Now therefore, please pardon my sin, and return with me, that I may worship the LORD." (1 Samuel 15:24-25)

When we don't give God His place in our lives, the opportunity or vacancy is created for another to take that place or position when the "right" situation or pressure arises.

We need to give to God all that pertains to us – body, mind, spirit and soul. He encourages us to serve Him with all these together, essentially, our whole being. Deuteronomy 6:5 says, "You shall love the LORD your God with all your heart, with all your soul, and with all your strength." When we fail to do this, we are not able to withstand the spiritual atmosphere that seeks to take over what we keep God out of.

While the Lord is gentle and wants us to give Him of ourselves freely, the devil is not so generous. That is why one may hear people speak about unauthorised possession by demons without the person's expressed consent but not by God. He urges us that each one should know how to possess his own vessel in sanctification and honour, not in passion of lust, like the Gentiles who do not know God

THE FEAR OF GOD

(1 Thessalonians 4:4-5) and that we present our bodies a living sacrifice, holy, acceptable to Him (Romans 12:1).

The Bible in addition offers the following warning in Romans 6:16, 'Do you not know that to whom you present yourselves slaves to obey, you are that one's slaves whom you obey, whether of sin leading to death, or of obedience leading to righteousness?'

The foregoing refers to either the King of the kingdom of light or the prince of darkness. There is no spiritual void even as there is no void in the natural. We submit to God and by His power, we mount a formidable resistance against the enemy (James 4:7). On our own, we can do nothing and that includes resisting the enemy.

The Fear Of God And Forgiveness

The serious nature of God's requirement of forgiveness stems from the fact that – if you do not forgive, God does not forgive you. If it was simply a reciprocal event, one could argue that the other person does not forgive and so I am not going to forgive him or her either – leaving both parties even.

However, if one accepts that the consequence of refusing to give forgiveness to those who offend us, is that the Giver of life who will judge the whole earth will not forgive us, then we can conclude that to forgive one's offenders is actually not optional. He is the One we owe a lot more than anyone can ever dream of owing another person.

Our Lord Jesus illustrated this very well in His reference to the two servants of the same master. One servant owed their master a huge sum which the master graciously forgave him and cancelled his debt. This servant however went and sent to prison another servant who owed him much less than he himself had owed. This was reported to their master who then commanded that he be put into prison till he could pay back every penny he owed (Matthew 18:21-35).

This clearly shows that all debt of forgiveness comes back to God; everyone needs his or her debt to be written off by Him. The Psalmist therefore states, 'But there is forgiveness with You, that You may be feared,' (Psalm 130:4). The fear of God helps us set God apart as the One to whom forgiveness belongs. This is why the scribes of Israel accused Jesus Christ of blasphemy when He told the paralytic that his sins were forgiven; the truth was, as God, Jesus had the power to forgive sin (Matthew 9:1-7).

If God be sovereign in our hearts, we would be inclined to disallow anything or person that would even suggest that we go against His will. "Don't even go there" seems to be the right phrase for what I am saying here. This stance needs to be affirmed moment by moment, day by day to prevent any laxity which could lead one into yielding grounds which ultimately leads to walking out on God's will.

My personal observation is that generally, a person would get involved in something that is known to be wrong when he or she believes he can get away with it. In the natural, if such a person escapes the police or law enforcement agents, they may not be prosecuted for the offence or made to take responsibility for the outcome. With God though, nothing is hidden.

THE FEAR OF GOD

In His patience He bears with us and one may feel that one gets away with the offence. The truth is that it is better to be made to face up to wrong doing in the natural and perhaps a godly-sorrow may lead to repentance with the ultimate outcome being redemption. Living with the wrong assumption that one can get away with disobeying God is terribly dangerous. Worse still, this could ultimately lead to the devastating eternal consequence of spending eternity in hell.

In Luke 6:37, our Lord Jesus Christ encourages us to be compassionate and not quick to judge others – "Judge not, and you shall not be judged. Condemn not, and you shall not be condemned. Forgive, and you will be forgiven."

Same requirement is applied to forgiveness and the judgment of others. It may well not make sense to us why the person acted in the offensive manner. One may think when assessing a person in a bad situation, "I would never do that." Well, how do you know? Even if you were in the same situation, you may not necessarily be from the same background or experiences.

Even the differences in genetic make up lead to different responses to same issues or events. Consider twins, they do not respond to same situations in same manner at all times, though they are exposed to similar influences. Therefore only God can truly judge the heart.

First Samuel chapter 2 verse 3b says, "For the LORD is the God of knowledge; and by Him actions are weighed." One would do well to leave such judgments to Him. Trying to figure out why those who offend us do so is often a futile exercise; hence, forgiving them and letting go is the way forward.

Boldness Through The Fear Of God

The fear of God will make us firm in our calling, not to be afraid of other people or adversity. It is paramount for a messenger to know the one who sent him in other to give the assignment due consideration.

If one is carrying out a project and has a poor revelation or appreciation of the person to whom one is accountable, the commitment to duty may be impaired. On the other hand, having given God His rightful place, when we serve, we can only serve to the best of our ability if we serve as unto God and not as unto man.

Man is not omnipresent and one may be tempted to be lax about one's duties when the person one is serving under is absent. However, when we bear in mind that God is omnipresent and that He asks us to render our duties as unto him, we would endeavour to put in our best in the position from which we serve (Ephesians 6:5-8 & Colossians 3:22-24).

When God called Samuel as a prophet, the first message He gave him was against the house of his mentor Eli the prophet. Eli sensed that the LORD had given such a message to Samuel and also sensed that the young prophet, not yet versed with the ways of God, would be reluctant to give the message. Eli then commanded Samuel not to withhold the word of the LORD from him (1 Samuel 3).

Consider also the calling of Moses to go and speak to the people of Israel who, as far as he could make out, had rejected him; and, to speak to Pharaoh about releasing

THE FEAR OF GOD

Israel having fled the presence of the preceding Pharaoh as a wanted man. Moses made lots of excuses including his slowness of speech at which point the Lord reminded him that He was his creator in the first place and had plans to use him in that manner, including with his slow speech (Exodus chapters 3&4).

In Isaiah 51:12-13, the LORD instructs us not to fear any other – "I, even I, am He who comforts you. Who are you that you should be afraid of a man who will die, and of the son of a man who will be made like grass? And you forget the LORD your Maker, who stretched out the heavens and laid the foundations of the earth; you have feared continually everyday because of the fury of the oppressor, when he has prepared to destroy. And where is the fury of the oppressor?" Essentially, the LORD says we have no business fearing any other being, and that this is only possible when we forget whom our God is.

At this point I would like to add a word that is in my spirit for teachers of the word in the house of God – in the church of Jesus Christ. When teaching His word, one should not alter its meaning or application to make it more acceptable to the listeners. The word of God is meant to encourage and strengthen His people and not for those who do not want to partake of Him and His ways.

I sense the Lord saying that those who do this with the intention of appearing more open or welcoming or inclusive, and to growing the number of their followers would not succeed in raising God-fearing Christians.

The Lord Jesus Christ Himself who is the builder of His church would personally reveal Himself to those whose hearts are set after Him, then they would realise the falsehood in such a house and His Spirit would stir them to leave any way to find a God-fearing gathering of His people. Let Him build His church.

God wants us to remember His ways and instructions; that He is the Lord. He knows that our hearts need to be reminded of His requirements for righteous living; thus, we have same word to read over and over – the Holy Bible. The twelve stones He instructed the leaders of the twelve tribes of Israel to take from the middle of the Jordan River constitute one example – Joshua 4:1-9.

They were instructed that when the generations coming after them asked what the stones meant, they were to reply, "The waters of the Jordan were cut off before the ark of the covenant of the LORD; when it crossed over the Jordan, the waters of the Jordan were cut off. And these stones shall be for a memorial to the children of Israel forever."

Another example is with the communion; Luke 22:19-20 reads, "And He took bread, gave thanks and broke it, and gave it to them, saying, "This is My body which is given for you; do this in remembrance of Me. Likewise He also took the cup after supper, saying, "This cup is the new covenant in My blood, which is shed for you."

In Deuteronomy chapter 8 for example, the LORD repeated instructions to His people not to forget what He had done for them. In verse 2 He says, "And you shall remember that the LORD your God led you all the way these forty years in the wilderness, to humble you and test you, to know what was in your heart, whether you would keep His commandments or not."

THE FEAR OF GOD

In verse 11 He reiterates by saying, "Beware that you do not forget the LORD your God by not keeping His commandments, His judgments, and His statutes which I command you today." Again in verse 18 the LORD says, "And you shall remember the LORD your God, for it is He who gives you power to get wealth, that He may establish His covenant which He swore to your fathers, as it is this day."

David remembered God's deliverance at the hand of the bear and the lion and put his trust in Him when he faced a giant. He said to king Saul, "Your servant has killed both lion and bear; and this uncircumcised Philistine will be like one of them, seeing he has defied the armies of the living God" – 1 Samuel 17:36. The human mind is made that way, making it imperative that we keep our hearts fresh with the word of God.

Have you come across people who progressed from very lowly positions in life unto privileged or affluent positions and then treat those less affluent than themselves terribly? Such a person should know what it is like to be underprivileged and one would expect that they would treat those persons with kind consideration, from a position of having experienced the same as them.

Remember the previous discussion about the servant who was forgiven his debt that was cancelled by his master and went straight out to persecute his fellow servant who owed him much less. The other servants seeing what happened rightly felt that this was inappropriate and reported back to their master who reviewed his debt and made him pay.

Keeping God's word and His victories in our

remembrance keeps the fear of God in us fresh and gives us boldness to do what He requires us to do to bring victory in our lives and glory to His name. Daniel 11:32b says, 'but the people who know their God shall be strong, and carry out great exploits.'

God's Faithfulness

God is rightly referred to as 'faithful' - with Him there is no need for plan B. In Genesis chapter 15 we read about Abram who raised the issue of his 'heir-lessness' with God who replied in verse 5, "'Look now toward heaven, and count the stars if you are able to number them." And He said to him, "So shall your descendants be."'

However, in chapter 16 Abram's wife Sarai, having evaluated the situation of her barrenness, wanted to see God's promise come to pass and persuaded Abram to go in to her Egyptian maid who subsequently bore a son – Ishmael. The LORD's response in the next chapter makes one to conclude that He had always wanted Abram's heir to come from Sarai his wife.

Certainly God knew Ishmael and loved him before he was conceived and knew that in Sarai's anxiety she would put in place the mechanics that would lead to his birth and He did not stop it, again leading one to conclude that God allowed Ishmael's delivery into Abram's household. One must consider also what would have happened if Abram stopped to ask God what he should do when Sarai presented the option of having an heir through Hagai.

The challenges of delayed conception and childbirth had pushed Sarai against the wall and opened her mind to option

219

B: help from her Egyptian maid. The writer of Hebrews acknowledges her faith in this difficult circumstance by writing, 'By faith Sarah herself also received strength to conceive seed, and she bore a child when she was past the age, because she judged Him faithful who had promised' (Hebrews 11:11).

In waiting to see God's purpose fulfilled in our lives, we must walk closely with Him and seek clarification where the choices are not clear-cut because He alone knows the end from the beginning. We are encouraged in the words of Hebrews 10:23 – 'Let us hold fast the confession of our hope without wavering, for He who promised is faithful.' We need the fear of God to give Him His due place and believe His promises.

I recall a while ago, I was waiting to catch a train home from work one day, I was considering whether to take the next train which was not direct and would require a change of trains before getting home, or to wait for the direct train which was due later. I decided to take the next train and change at the next station rather than wait around for the direct train.

As it turned out, the route had problems with faulty signals at a station ahead making me get home two hours later. I thought to myself that I should have gone on with the latter option, which would have been even more convenient. Because of the limits of our knowledge, we would encounter situations such as this where our poorly informed perceptions lead to wrong decisions.

Asking the LORD for wisdom and direction would save us a lot of unnecessary turns in life. We need to give Him

His rightful place as the all-knowing God. His plan A is what would bring the God-ordained best outcome.

Our Will Versus God's Will

Another problem I have noted personally but also perceived from interactions with other Christians is that it would seem we want to be 'free servants' to our God. Jesus Christ was Himself noted to have assumed the position of a bondservant of God (Philippians 2:7); even as was foretold to be the case in Isaiah 42:1.

I find myself adjusting situations to be comfortable and to suit me so much that one wonders whether the service rendered to God is on one's own terms or His terms. It is quite easy to slip into the comfort of what is acceptable to us, rather than do what is in line with the Father's heart. Paul the apostle repeatedly introduced himself as a bondservant of Jesus Christ.

Some examples are recorded in Titus 1:1, in Romans 1:1 and also along with Timothy in Philippians 1:1. Introducing himself in that manner implied he wanted those reading his letter to know that that was his foremost identity, his background and the stance, origin and basis of the contents of his letter, his viewpoint. Peter the apostle did the same in the second book of Peter 1:1 and so did Jude in the first verse of his letter.

Ponder Time

What about you – are you a bondservant of Jesus Christ?

THE FEAR OF GOD

The declaration of servitude to God seems to have lost its appeal. It does not override one's sonship in God, but affirms the willingness to give God His rightful place as Lord and Master.

Try something today, if you are a Christian, tell a Christian friend of yours that you are a bondservant of God and see what their response would be. With our Lord Jesus, He did not even do a thing without hearing or seeing the Father do it (John 5:19-30)! He concluded by saying, 'I do not seek My own will but the will of the Father who sent Me' – John 5:30b.

If one were to wait to know what the Father does, particularly at crucial points in life, before making decisions, how would one's emotions take it? This should provide good training for one's soul to keep the emotions still as one waits upon the Lord. The Lord is gracious in giving us insight into His will. The Holy Bible helps us in that it tells us what the Father wants and values. In addition, He also brings these things to our remembrance (John 14:26 and John 16:13-15).

I recall the time of waiting for the Lord to confirm who my husband was. This is a biblical exercise. Remember how Abraham's servant asked God to confirm to him who Isaac's wife was when he was sent to a far away land to find her; and He honoured that request. I had gotten to know my husband for sometime and we were starting to talk about getting married when I informed him I needed confirmation from the Lord, irrespective of how I felt about him.

Initially it sounded as though I was trying to make excuses not to commit to taking the relationship further.

Eventually, he realised I was serious. We actually went our separate ways until I got the revelation I needed. I had had dreams that became reality and I thought, as the decision about marriage was important, I should pray for the revelation in a dream; and, that was what I did. It was not an easy time at all. I had prayed about it most days and fasted some days.

By the time the revelation came, I had given up and even stopped praying about it. Having not seen my husband for quite sometime at this point, I asked the Lord to bring him my way so I didn't have to go looking for him, again He did so. It was a very exciting time for me. When we encountered obstacles along the way through the various processes required for the marriage ceremonies, God stepped in and made a way at each stage of the process.

In Colossians 1:15, we are told of the authority and power of Jesus Christ as the image of the invisible God. In the same chapter of Colossians, verses 16-17 speak further about Jesus:

> For by Him all things were created that are in heaven and that are on earth, visible and invisible, whether thrones or dominions or principalities or powers. All things were created through Him and for Him. And He is before all things, and in Him all things consist.

But, Philippians 2:7 says that He (wilfully) made Himself of no reputation, took the form of a bondservant, and came into the world in the likeness of men; all to fulfil the purpose of God. We also have been given the high position of sonship with God Almighty and will need to wilfully deny ourselves the glory of this privilege, take on the bondservant-hood and step into uncomfortable situations when that is required to serve the divine purpose of God. Romans 8:16-17 says

> The Spirit Himself bears witness with our spirit that we are children of God, and if children, then heirs-heirs of God and joint heirs with Christ, if indeed we suffer with Him, that we may also be glorified together.

Romans 8:19-21 further adds:

> For the earnest expectation of the creation eagerly waits for the revealing of the sons of God. For the creation was subjected to futility, not willingly, but because of Him who subjected it in hope; because the creation itself also will be delivered from the bondage of corruption into the glorious liberty of the children of God.

An evaluation of the Lord's prayer (Matthew 6:9-13) reveals that the first thing, following the acknowledgment of God as Father and praising Him, is – 'Your kingdom come. Your will be done on earth as it is in heaven,' before our own needs and desires get a mention.

Though holy, the Father does not wait for us to purify ourselves before encountering Him or we may never come. In the case of Israel, He visited them, and then asked them to purify themselves (Exodus 19:10-11). Here God asks for Israel to be consecrated in preparation for meeting with Him:

> Then the LORD said to Moses, "Go to the people and consecrate them today and tomorrow, and let them wash their clothes. And let them be ready for the third day. For on the third day the LORD will come down upon Mount Sinai in the sight of all the people."

The prophet Isaiah was happy and comfortable with the way things were in his life until he encountered God. He exclaimed, "Woe is me, for I am undone! Because I am a man of unclean lips, and I dwell in the midst of a people of unclean lips; for my eyes have seen the King, the LORD of hosts," (Isaiah 6:5). Any encounter with the holy God exposes the contrast between Himself and man. I remember standing by my window one day and appreciating God and His holiness with the song: 'Holy, holy, holy, Lord God Almighty.'

Then I heard a voice say, 'Holy – that means absence of anything wrong;' there is no wrongdoing in the holy God. I have heard someone say that people are reluctant to have an encounter with God because they fear they may need to change their way of living; and they do not want to do that. Like Isaiah realised his lips needed cleansing.

That is a bit like refusing to meet with the owner of a car dealership because he or she may offer to replace your old broken malfunctioning car, without charging you for it. Seriously, no analogy can reflect what a sinner meeting with the holy God means, but this is an attempt. In this case, the new life that God offers us, has been paid for by the blood of the sacrifice of His Son Jesus Christ. In Isaiah 1:16-20, God throws an open unconditional call to humanity:

> "Wash yourselves, make yourselves clean; put away the evil of your doings from before My eyes. Cease to do evil, learn to do good; seek justice, rebuke the oppressor; defend the fatherless, plead for the widow. Come now, and let us reason together," says the LORD, "Though your sins are like scarlet, they shall be as white as snow; though they are red like crimson, they shall be as wool. If you are willing and obedient, you shall eat the good of the land; but if you refuse and rebel, you shall be devoured by the sword"; for the mouth of the LORD has spoken.

It follows then that He calls us, knowing our state of sinfulness. However, He makes it clear that His purpose is to transform the scarlet to white; the crimson to wool and to spare us from being devoured by the sword. Good offer any day, except that the blindness from the forces of darkness try to obscure man's view of the unequalled offer from our loving God.

Let us review Peter's experience with the Lord Jesus as recorded in Luke 5:1-8. An experienced fisherman, Peter felt he knew when to quit fishing and felt he had got to that point having 'toiled all night and caught nothing' - verse 5.

Responding to the Lord's advice to launch out into the deep and let down the nets for a catch, he addressed Jesus as 'Master'; however, when he saw the outcome of his obedience – a boat-sinking load of fish – he had a deeper revelation of Him. "Depart from me, for I am a sinful man, O LORD!" Something had changed. One minute he was happy to stay with Jesus as he was, the next he was asking Jesus to depart from Him, with an expression of an increased awareness of his sinfulness.

It would appear that if, as followers of the Lord Jesus and children of God, we feel comfortable with sin, we should ask for a deeper revelation of who God is. The fear of God is all about knowing Him, giving Him His rightful place and ordering our everyday living according to His will.

The Holy Spirit works within us so that the awe associated with our revelation of the LORD is also accompanied by the revelation of His love and grace as well as the special position of sonship we have through our faith in the Lord Jesus.

Fear Of God And Evangelism / Witnessing

Concerning Noah, Hebrews 11:7 says, 'By faith Noah, being divinely warned of things not yet seen, moved with godly fear, prepared an ark for the saving of his household, by which he condemned the world and became heir of the righteousness which is according to faith.'

We are encouraged to regard God's word with godly fear; including obeying His instructions and standing by faith upon His word - that it will not fail. One can see that if as the word of God says, the last days would be like the days of Noah (Luke 17:26-27), one must embrace the same principles that Noah embraced to make it through - the principles of preparing a place of safety based on God's instructions, with godly fear.

When we give God's word its rightful place, we will witness to the lost, if we truly believe heaven and hell to be just as He says. Consider the situation with Lot and his sons-in-law for example. In Genesis 19:12-14 we read:

> Then the men (angels) said to Lot, "Have you anyone else here? Son-in-law, your sons, your daughters, and whomever you have in the city – take them out of this place! For we will destroy this place, because the outcry against them has grown great before the face of the LORD, and the LORD has sent us to destroy it." So Lot went out and spoke to his sons-in-law, who had married his daughters, and said, "Get up, get out of this place; for the LORD will destroy this city!" But to his sons-in-law he seemed to be joking.

Lot believed the angels' message that the LORD would destroy Sodom. Consequently, he tried to persuade his sons-in-law to embrace salvation along with the rest of his family but they would not take him seriously.

This is similar to what goes on today where several people think heaven and hell are not real. When as Christians we believe that the LORD will indeed commit to eternal death in hell all who do not believe in Jesus Christ, then we have to try to persuade those around us to escape the impending tragedy.

I have heard comments like, 'God is merciful and He

will not condemn people to such a place as hell.' But it is the same God today; He is not more or less merciful today than He was in the days of Lot. He will remain the same when the end of one's stay here on earth comes.

Actually, that mercy of God is what brings awareness of hell and brings those people who do not know God to us Christians so that we may help them escape it. Instead we make excuses and sometimes mislead those we should help; tragic, would you not agree?

The righteous judgment of God can have unpleasant consequences as He warns in His word. In Genesis 19:26 the Bible records how, contrary to the instructions given by the angels on assignment from God to destroy the city of Sodom and Gomorrah, Lot's wife looked back and became a pillar of salt.

The instruction was not accompanied by a warning regarding the consequences of disobedience. Similarly, when Uzzah (2 Samuel 6:6-9) reached out and touched the ark of covenant when the oxen carrying it stumbled, he was instantly struck down to death. Everyone knew the LORD had commanded that only the Levites were to set up things in the tabernacle (Numbers 1:51).

In addition, only the sub-tribe of the Kohathites was to carry the packaged sanctuary and its furnishings, I imagine that included the ark of God. Even then, they were not allowed to touch the holy things (Numbers 4:15). Uzzah was a descendant of Kish, a Levite but not a Kohathite. No one knew what the LORD would do should that instruction be violated.

Now, regarding salvation, the LORD states repeatedly in

229

the Holy Bible that eternal death and fire awaits those who reject His offer of salvation through His Son Jesus Christ. It would appear sensible that one should take that seriously and be focused on preaching the kingdom of God, with or without words, wherever one goes.

When His heart's desire is our priority, we will witness to the lost with or without words. 2 Peter 3:9 tells us, 'The Lord is not slack concerning His promise, as some count slackness, but is longsuffering toward us, not willing that any should perish but that all should come to repentance.'

Luke chapter 15 tells of how tax collectors and sinners drew near to Jesus Christ to hear Him and He ate with them to the amazement and disapproval of the Pharisees and scribes; how He responded by reflecting the Father's heart in the amazing stories of the lost sheep, the lost coin and the prodigal son.

When we do not rebuke our friends or those around us from pursuing the evil intents of their hearts, or we withhold godly advice when they seek our opinion, we become partakers with them in the offence and expose ourselves to needless troubles.

In Ezekiel 3:18, God puts it this way, "When I say to the wicked, 'You shall surely die,' and you give him no warning, nor speak to warn the wicked from his wicked way, to save his life, that same wicked man shall die in his iniquity; but his blood I will require at your hand." In verse 21, He continues, "Nevertheless if you warn the righteous man that the righteous should not sin, and he does not sin, he shall surely live because he took warning; also you will have delivered your soul."

The Church Of Christ And The Fear Of God

I remember reading the above passage and thinking to myself, 'Why does it have to be me who warns the next person about life and death, about obeying God's word to escape the consequences of disobedience? Why is it my responsibility?' In my spirit I sensed a reminder of the question Cain asked God when He enquired about his brother Abel (Genesis 4:9b), "I do not know. Am I my brother's keeper?"

Also, I am reminded of the Good Samaritan parable that was told by our Lord Jesus (Luke 10:30-37). In line with that parable, I observe that many people around me live their lives moving from a place of peace (Jerusalem) to a place of thieves and terror (Jericho) by their actions, which show disregard for whom God is.

Daily, one is faced with the decision to walk past people in such situations, like the priest who by chance came by the man who had fallen among thieves and had been wounded and stripped of his clothing. The man was essentially lying naked by the wayside. How true that is in our day that many lie naked and unclothed in spiritually wounded and shameful circumstances by the wayside of life. The priest passed on the other side. The Levite came and looked and also passed by on the other side.

The Samaritan however had compassion. He took of his own resources, his oil and his wine to address the man's wounds. The oil here can be seen as the presence of the Holy Spirit of God and the wine as His power to transform situations to bring a beautiful outcome.

As people of God, we are endowed with the oil and the wine required to be able to help those stripped and left naked by the wayside of this world. As the Samaritan took the man unto his animal, we have to be ready to be burdened with the spiritual needs of the people around us to take them to the One who will turn their life around and heal their wounds. The Samaritan knew it would cost him to help this man who would not be able to repay him; yet, he chose to take him on.

It would cost us money, time, pride, praying, rebuking gently at the risk of being told off or being rejected and called names or even being persecuted. The fear of God helps us overcome our self-consciousness or apathy in order to reach out to those around us, knowing that He expects us to look out for the 'neighbour' we meet on the highway of life. We can then trust God to protect us through whatever the consequences turn out to be.

The Fear Of God And Reverence For His Name

What is in a name? People are given names that appeal to their parents for various reasons, either because of an event surrounding their birth, related to their heritage or ancestry and so on.

Sometimes, an individual may choose to take on a name different from the one they were given at birth; the choice of name having different origins, commonly as a result of marriage or affiliation to a culture or religion. Adults are also given title names to reflect their activities, qualities or contribution to their community.

When God mentions His name in the Bible it is usually a revelation of His nature, what He has done, what He can do or what He promises to do, often as a result of His covenant with His people. Hence, some of the revelations of the name of God are referred to as His covenant names.

In Genesis 20:7, we read the third commandment that God gave to His people Israel saying, 'You shall not take the name of the LORD your God in vain, for the LORD will not hold him guiltless who takes His name in vain.' The phrase 'in vain' implies making of no effect, holding in disregard or derision, attributing no value or significance to an object or action.

This reminds me of the passage in 2 Timothy 3:5 by which the apostle Paul sent a warning as to what sort of people the Christians should avoid in the times ahead: 'having a form of godliness but denying its power. And from such people turn away!' In the context of the name of God, these would be people who speak of His name, but insist that it has no power whatsoever. They may even forbid the mention of the name.

We know that God gave His Son Jesus the name above every name by which Christians are to wage way against the enemies of God's kingdom in the exercise of their God-given authority. This is presented in Philippians 2:9-11:

> Therefore God also has highly exalted Him and given Him the name which is above every name, that at the name of Jesus every knee should bow, of those in heaven, and of those on earth, and of those under the earth, and that every tongue should confess that Jesus Christ is Lord, to the glory of God the Father.

THE FEAR OF GOD

Concurrently, beware of people who make long seemingly heartfelt prayers to God but refuse to seal it with the name of Jesus, not just in ignorance of the power in the name but in defiance of this requirement. Without the fear of God, one may not bother to pray in His name; or when they do – they think it is just a nice habit without knowing the impact of what they are doing.

The fear of God entails acknowledging Him and His name, and the power there in. In the absence of the fear of God, one would take His name in vain; this not being limited to those who make a swear word of His name. The covenant names of God are given for power to His people and an assurance of His provision for them.

A few examples of the names by which God Almighty is known include Elohim - God (Genesis 1:1); El Echad - The One God (Deuteronomy 6:4 & Malachi 2:10); Yahweh – LORD God, Jehovah (Genesis 2:4); El Yisrael – The God of Israel (Psalm 68:35); El Emet – The God of Truth (Psalm 31:5); El Elyon – God Most High (Genesis 14:18); Jehovah Jireh – The LORD Will Provide (Genesis 22:14); Jehovah Rohi – The Lord is my Shepherd (Psalm 23:1); Jehovah Rapha – The LORD who heals you (Exodus 15:26); Jehovah Ebenezer – Stone of Help (1 Samuel 7:12); Jehovah Tsidkenu – THE LORD OUR RIGHTEOUSNESS (Jeremiah 23:6);

Jehovah Shammah – THE LORD IS THERE (Ezekiel 48: 35); Jehovah Shalom – The-LORD-Is-Peace (Judges 6:24); Jehovah Nissi – The-LORD-Is-My-Banner (Exodus 17:15); Jehovah M'kaddesh – The LORD who sanctifies you (also the One who strengthens you for obedience -

Exodus 31:13 & Leviticus 20:8); Adonai – Master, Lord, LORD.

As in: The Lord of all the earth (Joshua 3:11) & The LORD (Isaiah 6:1) & The Lord GOD (Genesis 15:2); Jehovah Sabaoth – The LORD of hosts (Isaiah 1:24); King of kings and Lord of lords - 1 Timothy 6:15 & Revelations 19:16); El Hanne'eman – The Faithful God (Deuteronomy 7:9); El Hannora - The great, the mighty, and awesome God, who keeps covenant and mercy (Nehemiah 9:32); El Rachamim – Merciful God (Deuteronomy 4:31); El Roi – The God Who Sees Me (Genesis 16:13);

El Shaddai – Almighty God (Genesis 17:1); I AM, I AM WHO I AM – (Exodus 3:14, also John 8:24 & John 8:58); El Olam – The Everlasting God (Genesis 21:33); El-Channun – The Gracious God (Jonah 4:2); God who is love – (1 John 4:8); El Erekh Apayim avi ha-tanchumim – The God of Patience and Comfort (Romans 15:5); El Rachum – God of Compassion & El malei Rachamim – All Merciful God (Deuteronomy 4:31); El Hakkadosh – The Holy God (Isaiah 5:16 & Isaiah 6:3 & 1 Peter 1:15-16); El Qanna – A Jealous God (Exodus 20:5); El Gibbor – Mighty God (Isaiah 9:6); Man of War – (Exodus 15:3);

El De'ot – The God of Knowledge (1 Samuel 2:3); El Hakkavod – The God of Glory (Psalm 29:3); El Tsaddik – The Just and Righteous God (Isaiah 45:21); El Yeshuati – The God of my salvation (Isaiah 12:2); El Sali – God my Rock, God of my strength (Psalm 42:9); Immanuel – God-With-Us (Isaiah 7:14); El Chaiyai - God of my life (Psalm 42:8).[1]

---

1 Hebrew4christians.com

THE FEAR OF GOD

Calling on the name of the LORD dates back to the first generation of man as noted in Genesis 4:26, 'And as for Seth, to him also a son was born; and he named him Enosh. Then men began to call on the name of the LORD.' The Bible says that His name is a strong tower, 'The name of the LORD is a strong tower; the righteous run to it and are safe' – Proverbs 18:10.

David used several Psalms to express his trust in God for everything including provision, protection and security. He used the term 'tower' to describe the place of God as His protection. In Psalm 61: 1-5 he wrote:

> Hear my cry, O God; attend to my prayer. From the end of the earth I will cry to You, when my heart is overwhelmed; lead me to the rock that is higher than I. For You have been a shelter for me, a strong tower from the enemy. I will abide in Your tabernacle forever; I will trust in the shelter of Your wings. (Selah) For You, O God, have heard my vows; You have given me the heritage of those who fear Your name.

The fear of God, giving Him His rightful place, therefore includes embracing a reverential regard for His name – the fear of His name as referred to in the last verse above. Without that, we would miss out on the provisions God has made for us in His name. In Numbers 6:22-27, God gave instructions regarding how His people should be blessed by acknowledging Him as their source, putting His name upon them:

And the LORD spoke to Moses, saying: "Speak to Aaron and his sons, saying, 'This is the way you shall bless the children of Israel. Say to them: "The LORD bless you and keep you; the LORD make His face shine upon you, and be gracious to you; the LORD lift up His countenance upon you, and give you peace."' So they shall put My name on the children of Israel, and I will bless them."

Following from the above, putting God's specific covenant or revelatory name over a person or people is a way of blessing them and praying for Him to honour His name in the circumstance. The revelation of His name develops the fear of God in us, which in turn helps us to know that when we call on His name in prayer over a situation, the situation receives His name.

For example, for a person suffering from an illness, this would mean saying a prayer like, 'May Jehovah Rapha, the LORD who heals you, heal your body and raise you up from this sickness.' Romans 10:12-13 reads, 'For there is no distinction between Jew and Greek, for the same Lord over all is rich to all who call upon Him. For "whoever calls on the name of the LORD shall be saved."'

Acts chapter 4 verse 12 further encourages us that all salvation hinges upon His name alone, "Nor is there salvation in any other, for there is no other name under heaven given among men by which we must be saved." Having called upon the name of the LORD, the fear of God strengthens one's faith to believe that one would be saved – in, through and out of that situation.

Ponder Time

What is the LORD's name worth to you personally?

The Lord Jesus Christ encourages us doubly in John 14:13-14, "And whatever you ask in My name, that I will do, that the Father may be glorified in the Son. If you ask anything in My name, I will do it" and again in John 16:23-24,

"And in that day you will ask Me nothing. Most assuredly, I say to you, whatever you ask the Father in My name He will give you. Until now you have asked nothing in My name. Ask, and you will receive, that your joy may be full."

Bearing this in mind, on a different note, in Matthew 7:22-23, Jesus issued a warning regarding the consequences of one's actions or life style on their eternal destination when one's life is not aligned to His ways in spite of seeing miracles at the mention of His name saying, "Many will say to Me in that day, 'Lord, Lord, have we not prophesied in Your name, cast out demons in Your name, and done many wonders in Your name?' And then I will declare to them, 'I never knew you; depart from Me, you who practice lawlessness!'"

He expects us to be able to do these things in His name but to look beyond them to ensure our hearts remain faithful to Him. To conclude this discuss, let us look at another quotation of David in Psalm 20:7, 'Some trust in chariots, and some in horses; but we will remember the name of the LORD our God.'

Fear Of God And Salvation

The fear of God is important to keep our salvation because it keeps us from wilfully sinning against God and also from developing a seared conscience, which arises as a consequence of constantly ignoring God's instructions.

The fear of God keeps us from turning away from Him. When we embrace the salvation of God it will be strange to those who do not understand. Noah set about salvation the way God instructed him.

Imagine if he had built the ark according to the specifications that felt right and appropriate to him rather than building in accordance to God's specifications – would he have made it in the same comfort and shelter the ark provided over the several days of the flood and, with all those animals? God's ways are not our ways as indeed He says in Isaiah 55:8-9:

> "For My thoughts are not your thoughts, nor are your ways My ways," says the LORD. "For as the heavens are higher than the earth, so are My ways higher than your ways, and My thoughts than your thoughts."

For this reason, it is not surprising that our minds while being renewed may still have the tendency to not see "eye to eye" with the LORD. We need the fear of God to give His Word due consideration and align our lives accordingly even when it does not make sense to our minds.

We must resist the temptation to compromise with the word of God while still expecting to get the same results as if we were living in accordance to it. This leaves one exposed to the danger of calling Jesus Christ, 'Lord, Lord' and being told, 'Depart from Me, all you workers of iniquity' (Luke 13:24-27). This statement questions the impression that once one has made a commitment to follow Jesus, the person would always be saved.

What about the encouragement that one should work out his or her own salvation with fear and trembling (Philippians 2:12b)? Paul was commending the Philippians on their obedience when he said this. The statement implies some work or contribution is required from us in working out the full salvation package due us as believers in Christ Jesus.

Only the thief saved while on the cross did not have that responsibility as his life on earth, and hence any opportunity to work out the earthly aspect of the salvation package, terminated shortly after his conversion from darkness to light.

CHAPTER 5

THE FEAR OF GOD AND PRAYER

*T*he whole essence of prayer is acknowledging God as LORD over all. We as Christians are encouraged to enter His gates with thanksgiving and His courts with praise (Psalm 100:4). It is only by embracing the fear of God and giving God His due place that we can bring true unreserved praise, adoration and worship to Him.

The fear of God helps us to submit to Him in the place of prayer, trusting Him to answer and refusing to give up. In Luke 22:42 the Lord Jesus praying to the Father said, "Father, if it is Your will, take this cup away from Me; nevertheless not My will, but Yours, be done."

Our prayers therefore should be anchored on the will of God; we should endeavour to constantly seek to have an understanding of His revealed will and to pray accordingly. This is what keeps us from 'asking amiss' or saying prayers that seem unanswered as James commented in James 4:3.

God answers prayers. Our confidence in prayer should be anchored on God's faithfulness and His promises. For example, even when it seems as though we got it wrong in prayer due to our limited knowledge, He promises that the Holy Spirit would sort it out according to His will. Romans 8:26-27 explains this:

Likewise the Spirit also helps in our weaknesses.

> For we do not know what we should pray for as we ought, but the Spirit Himself makes intercession for us with groanings which cannot be uttered. Now He who searches the hearts knows what the mind of the Spirit is, because He makes intercession for the saints according to the will of God.

The Holy Spirit therefore is the only being capable of praying the perfect prayer one hundred per cent of the time. He is the 'Perfect Pray-er' (Pray-er hear representing one who prays).

When we trust the Holy Spirit in prayer as encouraged in the passage above, we can be confident that He has prayed beyond our limitations. He covers our blind spots. In addition, He gives us the gift of speaking in unknown tongues, which we can use in prayer to pray along with Him. We would do well therefore to work with Him to develop and use our ability to speak in tongues rather than being limited to praying only with our knowledge and understanding in familiar tongues.

Praying in tongues covers beyond what we know. That way, when one encounters an issue or situation that seems sudden and unexpected or unannounced, one can confidently declare like our Lord Jesus did at the tomb of Lazarus in John 11:41-42a, 'Father, I thank You that You have heard Me. And I know that You always hear Me..'

Answer to prayer belongs to God. Psalm 65 verse 2 says of Him, 'O You who hear prayer, to You all flesh will come.' We must trust in His love, mercy, compassion, faithfulness and righteousness. We must believe His word given to us that His thoughts towards us are of peace and not of evil, to give us a future and a hope - Jeremiah 29:11.

I used to think that God was waiting for me to make any mistake and He would whack me with His rod of discipline; thinking Him to be of no compassion and very intolerant of failures, sins or mistakes.

I also felt He was impatient with the prayers of mere mortals like myself. So, I often would pray quickly so as not to take up His time. I don't know if that perception was borne out of a sense that the rulers of the nations are themselves not easily accessible to the everyday person and could only be seen after a pre-arranged appointment for a brief 'interview' when they granted the individual the audience.

Contrary to that belief, 2 Chronicles 16:9a says that He is pacing about, searching with eagerness to show Himself strong on behalf of His people, 'For the eyes of the LORD run to and fro throughout the whole earth, to show Himself strong on behalf of those whose heart is loyal to Him.' Bear in mind that it is the devil that is searching for someone to devour or destroy and tries to convince men that God is the one doing so.

Hence Peter sends this warning, 'Be sober, be vigilant; because your adversary the devil walks about like a roaring lion, seeking whom he may devour.' Praised be the gracious loving Father who has this promise for His children in Psalm 37:32-33, 'The wicked watches the righteous, and seeks to slay him. The LORD will not leave him in his hand, nor condemn him when he is judged.'

Ponder Time

Is God Almighty a mean God or a loving God?

Whose report will you believe? In the Garden of Eden, Satan tried to paint the picture of God as the mean One and Satan as the helpful one by convincing Eve that God's plan was to withhold good from herself and her husband.

Psalm 84 verse 11 says that He will not withhold good from us, 'For the LORD God is a sun and shield; the LORD will give grace and glory; no good thing will He withhold from those who walk uprightly.'

It is the same God who has given us heaven's best, he will give us all things we need. In Romans 8:32 we read, 'He who did not spare His own Son, but delivered Him up for us all, how shall He not with Him also freely give us all things?' God invites us to come to Him at anytime and for any reason – with thanks or to lay down our burdens – or to obtain grace to deal with everyday issues.

He continues in Jeremiah 29:12-13 by saying, "Then you will call upon Me and go and pray to Me, and I will listen to you. And you will seek Me and find Me, when you search for Me with all your heart." Like many (if not all) of us, God wants to be sought after; promising to make Himself found by those who do so.

The fear of God within us enables us to give due value to God, releasing our hearts to seek after Him with our all, acknowledging that He is worthy of anything we could ever give up in pursuit of Him. In Psalm 65:5 we read,

'By awesome deeds in righteousness You will answer us, O God of our salvation, You who are the confidence of all the ends of the earth, and of the far-off seas.'

We should expect a response or answer from God not only by way of everyday events but also by awesome deeds. In Jeremiah 33:3, fondly referred to as God's telephone number, God firmly promises, "Call to Me, and I will answer you, and show you great and mighty things, which you do not know."

Hebrews 11:6 declares, 'But without faith it is impossible to please Him, for he who comes to God must believe that He is, and that He is a rewarder of those who diligently seek Him.'

Prayer is an expression of faith in the one to whom we pray. Prayer to God Almighty is an expression of faith in Him, in His ability to hear and to respond to the call of the one who prays. Even when it is difficult to believe, He still hears when one simply cries out, 'Lord, I believe; help my unbelief,' – Mark 9:24.

As the fear of God develops in an individual, appropriate to the revelation of whom God is, the greater and more significant consideration one would give to prayer. In Isaiah 45:19b the LORD also states, "I did not say to the seed of Jacob, 'Seek Me in vain'. " This is also in line with the words of our Lord Jesus in Matthew 7:7 - "Ask, and it will be given to you; seek, and you will find; knock, and it will be opened to you. For everyone who asks receives, and he who seeks finds, and to him who knocks it will be opened."

Speaking of Jesus, the writer of the book of Hebrews says

in Hebrews 5:7, 'who in the days of His flesh, when He had offered up prayers and supplications, with vehement cries and tears to Him who was able to save Him from death, and was heard because of His godly fear.'

This is another passage that demonstrates that the fear of God was a part of the life of Jesus Christ; and, it opens the door for prayers to be heard and for answers to be received.

In Matthew 11:28, Jesus says, 'Come to Me, all you who labour and are heavy laden, and I will give you rest.' In Revelation 3:20 He makes a hearty appeal, 'Behold, I stand at the door and knock. If anyone hears My voice and opens the door, I will come in to him and dine with him, and he with Me.' Because of the sacrifice of the cross of Jesus Christ, we are encouraged to come boldly before God to find grace to help. Hebrews 4:15-16 puts it this way:

> For we do not have a High Priest who cannot sympathize with our weaknesses, but was in all points tempted as we are, yet without sin. Let us therefore come boldly to the throne of grace, that we may obtain mercy and find grace to help in time of need.

It is noteworthy that there was no throne of grace available to man before the death of Jesus Christ. The LORD God fills the earth. What then does the Bible mean by 'Truly You are God, who hide Yourself, O God of Israel, the Saviour!' (Isaiah 45:15); or, 'Draw near to God and He will draw near to you' (James 4:8a).

Isaiah chapter 55 verse 6 also says, 'Seek the LORD

while He may be found, call upon Him while He is near.' And, Jeremiah 29:13 says, 'And you will seek Me and find Me, when you search for Me with all your heart.'

Also, Psalm 11:4 states that, 'The LORD is in His holy temple, the LORD's throne is in heaven; His eyes behold, His eyelids test the sons of men.' Consider the preparations made to invite reputable people, for example, Christian speakers or teachers of the gospel to visit a Christian gathering, such as a conference; often some persons needing a lot of persuasion.

Our God however, is the great I AM, yet He makes access into His presence well within our reach. Having said the foregoing, I know that my natural man often comes up with such ridiculous excuses when I want to pray.

For example, I may be doing little or nothing around the house at bed time and once I think, 'now I'm going to study God's word, praise Him and pray,' from nowhere comes a sudden feeling of tiredness and big giant yawns. So, it is not just the enemy who attacks us in prayer, it is our very own self that we need to overcome by the power of the Holy Spirit as well.

In contrast, I have had targets to meet and though having been up most of the night with the particular assignment, I have gotten up early next morning to pursue some other important business. I then ask myself why I do not get up early to spare few minutes with God in praise or prayer. My heartfelt prayer is that the Holy Spirit will enlighten me and build a strong desire for communion with God at the start of my day so that I can give God that prime time every day.

THE FEAR OF GOD

The fear of God opens us up to give Him His due place in our lives, to value His presence, give Him due honour, and ask His advice and help in every situation particularly when in trouble or need. I sometimes find that I have asked the people I see around me for their opinion or help before even speaking to God about the matter; or only speak to Him when help is not forthcoming from those around. It should be the other way round that we ask God first. The foregoing verses seem to challenge us to value, prefer, desire and pursue God's presence and opinion or will concerning the situations we encounter in life.

The Fear Of God Builds Up Our Faith In Him

To emphasise the Father's willingness to answer to our call, Jesus tells the story about the wicked judge concluding by saying that if the wicked judge could yield, how much more the Father who has committed to caring for us:

Then He spoke a parable to them, that men always ought to pray and not lose heart, saying: "There was in a certain city a judge who did not fear God nor regard man. Now there was a widow in that city; and she came to him, saying, 'Get justice for me from my adversary.' And he would not for a while; but afterward he said within himself, 'Though I do not fear God nor regard man, yet because this widow troubles me I will avenge her, lest by her continual coming she weary me.' " Then the Lord said, "Hear what the unjust judge said. And shall

God not avenge His own elect who cry out day and night to Him, though He bears long with them? I tell you that He will avenge them speedily. Nevertheless, when the Son of Man comes, will He really find faith on the earth?" – Luke 18:1-8.

Note that the Lord used the phrase - 'did not fear God nor regard men' to represent an unjust personality. Even the unjust are moved by repeated requests for help. Our God recognises that a cry for help usually requires a speedy response.

Hence, our Lord Jesus says He would answer speedily. One doesn't usually cry for help when there is no need. One might foresee a need for help and make plans to get help ahead of a possible need in the future, as is the case with insurance policies. We need to acknowledge God as whom He is – the Beginning and the End (Revelation 1:8 & Revelation 22:13) which means, He has seen the issues ahead before they come to pass.

Thus, at the point we cry for help, it is already done. That is why He can promise that while one is yet asking, He has already done it as we read in Isaiah 65:24, "It shall come to pass that before they call, I will answer; and while they are still speaking, I will hear."

If we, though wicked, can grant our children their requests; what compassion do we credit God with to hear us when we call upon Him? Luke 11:11-13 reads:

"If a son asks for bread from any father among you, will he give him a stone? Or if he asks for a fish, will he give him a serpent instead of a fish? Or if he asks for an egg, will he offer him a scorpion? If you then, being evil, know how to give good gifts to your children, how much more will your heavenly Father give the Holy Spirit to those who ask Him!"

As a parent, I feel disappointed when my child worries and stresses about issues he or she could have asked me about, or doubts when I say 'it is done'. In Luke 12:30-32 our Lord Jesus, discouraging His followers from worrying about what to eat or what to wear (Luke 12:22), puts it this way:

"For all these things the nations of the world seek after, and your Father knows that you need these things. But seek the kingdom of God, and all these things shall be added to you. Do not fear, little flock, for it is your Father's good pleasure to give you the kingdom."

We are further encouraged to rely upon the LORD in Philippians 4:6-7:

Be anxious for nothing, but in everything by prayer and supplication, with thanksgiving, let your requests be made known to God; and the peace of God, which surpasses all understanding, will guard your hearts and minds through Christ Jesus.

Mentioned briefly above, the greatest promise regarding

God's response to our prayers is found in Romans 8:32 – 'He who did not spare His own Son, but delivered Him up for us all, how shall He not with Him also freely give us all things?' Halleluiah!

It is all about Jesus and what He has done for us. Prayer is the greatest privilege given to man to effect changes through the power of God. It requires humility. Praying people acknowledge that their power lies only in their expression of dependence upon the Almighty God.

Prayer is an expression of faith in His means of addressing the issues of life. At the place of prayer we exchange our limitations with His limitless omnipotence referred to by our Lord Jesus in Luke 18:27 - "The things which are impossible with men are possible with God." Even when we seem to have the means for meeting our needs, we should still trust Him for everything.

Consider also building a fence around one's house, one would still need to rely on God for protection. A patient similarly should trust God rather than rely on the health care professionals to effect cure from an ailment. We have been endowed with various strengths and capabilities from the Father, yet He wants us to humbly seek His assistance and seek after the establishment of His kingdom authority over every situation. In Psalm 44:6, the Psalmist declares, 'For I will not trust in my bow, nor shall my sword save me.'

The bow and sword in this case have been provided by God; still, one is not to trust them to save independent of Him. Similarly David proclaimed in Psalm 20:6-7: 'Now I know that the LORD saves His anointed; He will answer him from His holy heaven with the saving strength of His right hand. Some trust in chariots, and some in horses; but we will remember the name of the LORD our God.' Again, chariots and horses are given by the LORD but one's expectation for deliverance should be focused on the LORD.

Psalm 147 verses 10-11 says this of our God, 'He does not delight in the strength of the horse; He takes no pleasure in the legs of a man. The LORD takes pleasure in those who fear Him, in those who hope in His mercy.' What God has given us - in our possessions as exemplified here by the strength of a horse, or our own abilities as referred to here as the legs of a man – are not impressive to Him.

In fact, they are not to His pleasure if they are not submitted and yielded to Him. Similarly, when the unity given to the descendants of Noah was not submitted to God's will, it paved a way for them to go contrary to His word. Rather, it seemed they applied this unity to reach the decision to stay together in one place rather than fill the earth as instructed by God. That was not to His pleasure.

In Genesis 11:4 the descendants of Noah said, "Come, let us build ourselves a city, and a tower whose top is in the heavens; let us make a name for ourselves, lest we be scattered abroad over the face of the whole earth." Thus, their intention was actually to prevent God's purpose for man as recorded in His instruction to Noah and his sons - Genesis 9:1, "Be fruitful and multiply, and fill the earth."

The fear of God goes beyond yielding to His will, it extends to an acknowledgement that one cannot do anything without His power or support. In Zechariah 4:6

the word of God declares, "This is the word of the LORD to Zerubbabel: 'Not by might nor by power, but by My Spirit,' says the LORD of hosts."

Again in John 15:5 our Lord Jesus declares, "I am the vine, you are the branches. He who abides in Me, and I in him, bears much fruit; for without Me you can do nothing." It is interesting the Lord did not say here that we would not do much; rather He states that without Him we can do nothing at all.

Let us for a moment reflect on the man in the illustrative parable given by the Lord Jesus - the man who, at midnight, went to ask his friend for three loaves of bread; food for another friend who had come to him from a journey (Luke 11:5-8). Seeking God repeatedly, even at inconvenient time, is seen as persistence. The man's approach was described as persistent not because he knocked repeatedly but because he went the extra mile to knock at midnight; bearing in mind that the hours of prayer according to the Jewish custom were during daytime.

The persistent knock on the friend's door; emboldened by the knowledge he had of his friend – his friend's riches, the strength of their friendship, his ability to honour his request, to honour and respect their friendship, perhaps previous times when his friend had helped him or helped others in similar situations.

He was persistent in spite of the clearly odd hour, though late and unsociable hour; he should have asked earlier but for some reason had not, confident in his covenant position with his friend he expected to get a positive response and not to be turned away empty-handed.

THE FEAR OF GOD

Sometimes at the place of prayer, the mind can come up with numerous excuses why one does not qualify for God to grant one's request. This man had excuses why his friend would not honour his request. Yet he persisted in his request. Bear in mind that this man, like an intercessor, was asking on behalf of another, not even for himself, yet he had the boldness to put forward his apparently poorly-timed request.

The fear of God gives Him His rightful place and enables us to believe His word. Without it, these passages would be no use to us. It brings us to the point of actually believing the covenant position that God has given us in Christ and brings us to the point of grace described in Hebrews 4:16, 'Let us therefore come boldly to the throne of grace, that we may obtain mercy and find grace to help in time of need.

The fear of God eliminates alternative options in our mind; as giving the LORD His rightful place means we decide and persist in faith, that there is no other source of help we would rather embrace. In Proverbs 3:5-6 we are further encouraged to trust in the LORD, 'Trust in the LORD with all your heart, and lean not on your own understanding; in all your ways acknowledge Him, and He shall direct your paths.'

Then comes the problem of lack of knowledge. A lack of knowledge and revelation of who God Almighty is, limits the development of the fear of God. The prince of this world knows this very well and uses blindness to prevent people from having a revelation of God. At the point of salvation this blindness is removed and one is then open to the instruction of the Holy Spirit.

This instruction is not automatic and we have to yield ourselves to it by making time to study the word of God, listen to Him and work with Him. In Hosea 4:6 the LORD addresses the issue of lack of knowledge quite firmly, "My people are destroyed for lack of knowledge. Because you have rejected knowledge, I also will reject you from being priest for Me; because you have forgotten the law of your God, I also will forget your children." The rejection of knowledge of the ways of the LORD is not only a limitation but also disqualifies a person from representing another person before Him as would be the place of a 'priest'.

For Christians, this would mean a limitation of the ability to express the priestly nature of our calling as a royal priesthood. Furthermore, Isaiah 5:13 adds to this discourse by stating: 'Therefore my people have gone into captivity, because they have no knowledge; their honourable men are famished, and their multitude dried up with thirst.'

Bearing the foregoing in mind, one must also acknowledge that knowing the truth does not equate to doing it. For example, what are you going to do with the revelation that the Lord gives you today on the issue of the fear of God through this book?

Interestingly, before the fall of Adam and Eve in the Garden of Eden, we do not find prayer; in fact it takes some time before we see a record or mention of prayer. We know that they acknowledged God as their source because they brought Him offering – Cain and Abel, perhaps something learnt from their parents. Genesis 4:3-5 records that:

And in the process of time it came to pass that

> Cain brought an offering of the fruit of the ground to the LORD. Abel also brought of the firstborn of his flock and of their fat. And the LORD respected Abel and his offering, but He did not respect Cain and his offering. And Cain was very angry, and his countenance fell.

In Genesis 4:13-15 we see the first petition made by man to God,:

> And Cain said to the LORD, "My punishment is greater than I can bear! Surely You have driven me out this day from the face of the ground; I shall be hidden from Your face; I shall be a fugitive and a vagabond on the earth, and it will happen that anyone who finds me will kill me."

The prayer seems to have been born out of a reluctance to bear the burden placed upon him by the LORD's punishment on his own and a realisation that his life was worth very little without God's grace as represented by His face in this context.

His parents made no attempt to seek God's mercy when their sentence for eating the forbidden fruit was pronounced; and, one can only guess what the outcome would have been if they had done so. Here we see that God relented and put a mark on Cain to ameliorate the suffering that would accrue consequent upon his punishment. So, from the very first prayer, God has shown mercy and grace whenever man called on Him to do so.

Though we pray, the determination of the answer must

be left with God. Without contradicting the teachings that God answers our prayers, and He does, one must be mindful of the fact that the outcome or the answer to prayer rests with God.

Our Lord Jesus' experience in the garden of Gethsemane is a good example. He concluded His prayer with, 'not My will, but Yours, be done,' Luke 22:42. Prayer commits the issue to God. As long as the issue remains one is encouraged to continue to commit it to Him in prayer, with thanksgiving. The Lord Jesus' example of the persistent widow's request for justice as detailed previously illustrates this.

Ponder Time

Thinking it through, consider - how many leaders of the world have you knocked on their doors?

As already stated above, prayer is also a great privilege. Just having the boldness to knock on a person's door, particularly people in leadership position, implies that one has been given a certain degree of proximity or access already. You need a connection, a contact from within the government. For every Christian, the connection we have is through our Lord Jesus Christ, the contact from within the presence of the Father.

It would appear that even after the fall, man's desire to take charge of the situation around and within him continued or remained, having contributed to the initial fall anyway. God gives us the desire and ability to take charge of issues in life as previously discussed regarding His first command to man in Genesis 1:28. But He still wants us to, and indeed He instructs us to, yield this to Him.

Therefore, when you see leadership that is effective - you see a leader who has managed to convince his followers to yield their 'desire to dominate' to him or her. The true follower then is one who acknowledges his or her God-given gifts and abilities to take dominion and chooses to yield these in other to be led by another. A clash of the two leads to rebellion and disunity.

What about fasting? To pray is one thing but to turn away from food that is available and for which one has the health and desire to eat it, in other to further humble oneself before God, is an even greater expression of faith. No wonder it isn't a popular topic!!

As discussed earlier, God Almighty often works on the principle of giving us something, whether gifts, ability or possessions, but then requiring us to yield that thing to Him. The ultimate example of this is the test Abraham faced with Isaac.

Why would He give us something and then want us to give it to Him of our own free will. Nothing we give to God is lost; even though it is out of what is already His that we give Him. This is affirmed by the statement in 1 Corinthians 4:7b, 'And what do you have that you did not receive? Now if you did indeed receive it, why do you boast as if you had not received it?'

It is natural to expect result with prayer – the Lord instructs us to do so. Asking without expectation is against the tenets of the Christian faith. In some instances, it appears

258

that God has not heard a prayer. When one's expectations of prayer are not yet manifest, one should seek God's wisdom and direction for the situation while still trusting Him.

In Isaiah 58:3, the LORD addressed Israel's expressed concern about His silence over their situation, 'Why have we fasted,' they say, 'and You have not seen? Why have we afflicted our souls, and You take no notice?' He went on to tell them what the problem was: they ignored mercy and God's instructions while seeking His face; this was deemed unacceptable to God.

The Psalmist in Psalm 66:18 acknowledged God's position regarding sin and prayer by saying, 'If I regard iniquity in my heart, the LORD will not hear.' These are just a few examples; the Holy Bible has a lot more. The commandment 'not to give up' stands, but to seek the wisdom of God in each situation, to be guided in prayer by Him; to prioritise God in prayer – embracing the fear of God.

God hears every prayer, certainly. In fact, before it is out of our mouth, He has answered - He always sees it coming. In Isaiah 65:24 the LORD declares, "It shall come to pass that before they call, I will answer; and while they are still speaking, I will hear."

Psalm 46:10 teaches us, 'Be still, and know that I am God; I will be exalted among the nations, I will be exalted in the earth!' The fear of God transforms one's knowledge of God to a reverential appreciation of who He is. It deals with the panic sensation, if after praying you are still in panic, ask the Holy Spirit to still the panic with the fear of God.

God Is For Us

We must believe what the LORD offers us in His love; that He truly wants the best for us. In Jeremiah 29:11 He declares: 'For I know the thoughts that I think toward you, says the LORD, thoughts of peace and not of evil, to give you a future and a hope.'

The popular sixteenth verse in John 3 encourages us with the assurance of His practically expressed love, "For God so loved the world that He gave His only begotten Son, that whoever believes in Him should not perish but have everlasting life."

He paid dearly to make available to us the things that we need, the things that we seek from Him – why then would He unduly withhold them from us even for a moment? Again, repetitive as it may sound, it is always worth bearing in mind what the Bible says in Romans 8:32, 'He who did not spare His own Son, but delivered Him up for us all, how shall He not with Him also freely give us all things?'

The Fear Of God And His Word

Words we speak or listen to while waiting for the manifestation of God's promises or answer to our request - can build or tear down our faith. Knowing and having a divine revelation into the word of God is an indispensable asset in these situations.

Rightly, the word of God is referred to as the belt of truth that girds the waist (Ephesians 6:14). Just as the natural physical belt holds our garments in place in the centre of our physical body, so that we are not exposed to the elements of nature that may harm us, such as rain, cold, sun, snow, sand to mention a few; the truth holds our guard up in the core of our being so we do not suffer harm from exposure to life's challenges.

It is the same truth administered by the ministers of God that gives us stability and stops us being blown all over by different doctrines:

> And He Himself gave some to be apostles, some prophets, some evangelists, and some pastors and teachers, for the equipping of the saints for the work of ministry, for the edifying of the body of Christ, till we all come to the unity of the faith and of the knowledge of the Son of God, to a perfect man, to the measure of the stature of the fullness of Christ; that we should no longer be children, tossed to and fro and carried about with every wind of doctrine, by the trickery of men, in the cunning craftiness of deceitful plotting (Ephesians 4: 11-14).

I recall my experience in a time of waiting when I received a message from a well-meaning friend that really discouraged me and shook my faith, thankfully only for a moment.

The message came from someone who repeatedly affirmed he had nothing against the Christian faith but gave several reasons why one should not spend time and effort pursuing fellowship with God rather than pursuing excellence by human strength and effort.

The speaker condemned Christian leaders who encouraged their followers to give God their best time of maximum strength first thing in the morning instead of using that time on self-enhancing activities and so on. I was in a situation where I knew I did not have of myself what it took to advance me to the next level that I was aspiring to and I had been seeking God's grace to see me through.

After a moment I stopped and asked myself, 'what does the Holy Bible say?' I started to recall how God had promised Israel that they would inhabit houses they had not built and inherit vineyards they had not cultivated (Deuteronomy 6:10-13). He also went on to warn them in Joshua 24:13-14 that the embrace of the fear of God would keep them from turning away from Him in that time of abundance that they had not worked for:

> "'I have given you a land for which you did not labour, and cities which you did not build, and you dwell in them; you eat of the vineyards and olive groves which you did not plant.' "Now therefore, fear the LORD, serve Him in sincerity and in truth, and put away the gods which your fathers served on the other side of the River and in Egypt. Serve the LORD!'"

In Biblical records, Israel was not popular because they seemed to appear from nowhere and lay claim on other nation's property stating that their God had given them the place. Currently, this may be a contributory factor in the conflict between them and other nations of the world.

Bearing this in mind, as well as other Bible passages where God came through beyond the individual's natural strength including David as he faced Goliath (1 Samuel

17), Joshua and the unskilled armies of Israel against strong cities like Jericho and Ai (Joshua chapters 7 & 8),

Gideon unskilled at battle with his handful of unskilled soldiers against the Midianites (Judges 7) and King Hezekiah of Israel against King Sennacherib of Assyria and his strong army (2 Chronicles 32) to mention a few; I encouraged myself in the LORD and found strength and faith to hold on to God till the victory was manifested physically.

Praise God that we do not only get what we are able to achieve by our own efforts. Along the same lines the Holy Bible makes a statement that suggests that the one who gains the victory is not necessarily the best of them all – 'I returned and saw under the sun that—the race is not to the swift, nor the battle to the strong, nor bread to the wise, nor riches to men of understanding, nor favor to men of skill; but time and chance happen to them all (Ecclesiastes 9:11).

Time is one thing that man has no control over, even when it seems that things work out in a timely manner as planned; it is only because God allowed it to happen that way. Thus, the Psalmist in Psalms 31:14-15 declares:

But as for me, I trust in You, O LORD; I say, "You are my God." My times are in Your hand; deliver me from the hand of my enemies, and from those who persecute me.

That is certainly reassuring and we need to constantly remind ourselves of this truth. Chance can be viewed as the opportunity that one has to be in the place with favourable conditions for winning. As an example, the very intelligent person who lies very sick in the hospital bed at the time of an academic competition or examination has not got any chance of scoring high in it.

It is equally crucial that in the waiting time, one should guard one's heart and tongue. Proverbs 18:21 says, 'Death and life are in the power of the tongue, and those who love it will eat its fruit.' The word of God in Numbers 14:28 is to be borne in mind every time the tongue speaks: "Say to them, 'As I live,' says the LORD, 'just as you have spoken in My hearing, so I will do to you.'"

This does not only apply to negative speech but we can expect the LORD to honour the blessings, including His word that we speak over lives, nations and situations! While it was a threat (which He duly carried out) towards Israel, it can actually be a promise to hold onto in prayer and in the time of waiting.

In Matthew 15:11 we also read the teaching of our Lord Jesus, "Not what goes into the mouth defiles a man; but what comes out of the mouth, this defiles a man." With regards to guarding the heart, the Holy Bible says in Matthew 12:35-37:

> "A good man out of the good treasure of his heart brings forth good things, and an evil man out of the evil treasure brings forth evil things. But I say to you that for every idle word men may speak, they will give account of it in the day of judgment. For by your words you will be justified, and by your words you will be condemned."

Waiting for the physical manifestation of the answer to one's prayer or for the manifestation of God's promise tests the word of the Lord, an exercise to develop the fear of God in us. Of Joseph, Psalm 105:19 recorded, 'Until the time that his word came to pass, the word of the LORD tested him.'

As said earlier – as long as the issue remains – one ought to persist in prayer and keep presenting the situation or issue to Him. King David quit fasting only when the issue he prayed about had been dealt with and could no longer be changed, though not the outcome he wanted. 2 Samuel 12:19-22 presents a record of his experience:

> When David saw that his servants were whispering, David perceived that the child was dead. Therefore David said to his servants, "Is the child dead?" And they said, "He is dead." So David arose from the ground, washed and anointed himself, and changed his clothes; and he went into the house of the LORD and worshiped. Then he went to his own house; and when he requested, they set food before him, and he ate. Then his servants said to him, "What is this that you have done? You fasted and wept for the child while he was alive, but when the child died, you arose and ate food." And he said, "While the child was alive, I fasted and wept; for I said, 'Who can tell whether the LORD will be gracious to me, that the child may live?' But now he is dead; why should I fast? Can I bring him back again? I shall go to him, but he shall not return to me."

Interesting is it not? One may consider that King David should have stopped praying when he heard God's verdict on the matter - that the child shall die (verse 14). Knowing the LORD to be compassionate and merciful, he persisted in prayer. This time the LORD had heard his prayer but had another plan – to raise the next child to inherit the throne.

Unfortunately, King David did not pray for the rest of God's judgment to be reversed and his family suffered as was foretold by the prophet in verses 10-12 of the same chapter. Contrast David's experience with King Hezekiah's where God reversed His word that had told him - to prepare for death; but rather, in response to his prayer, He added 15 years to his life instead (2 Kings 20:1-7).

The apostle Paul prayed till the Lord said, "My grace is sufficient for you, for My strength is made perfect in weakness" - 2 Corinthians 12:7-10.

Our Lord Jesus, while He knew that the Father's will was for Him to die on the cross for the salvation of all of mankind, prayed in the garden of Gethsemane, yielding His anguish and burden to God the Father and submitting to His will. Our Lord Jesus received the grace to yield to the Father's will and the angels ministered to Him at this time. He encourages us to cast our burden on Him, we receive grace to live beyond the burden's ability to hinder our God-given mission.

When we pray, God's peace guards our hearts and minds through Christ Jesus (Philippians 4:7) irrespective of whether the situation changes or not. Hebrews 4:16 also adds to this discuss by saying, 'Let us therefore come boldly to the throne of grace, that we may obtain mercy and find grace to help in time of need.'

When the prophet Samuel came to the people of Israel, the regard they had for God's word is seen in 1 Samuel 16:4 - 'So Samuel did what the LORD said, and went to Bethlehem. And the elders of the town trembled at his coming, and said, "Do you come peaceably?"'

Ponder Time

The days when people trembled at the sighting of a prophet are they gone or still with us?

Somehow, we have convinced ourselves that God's word from His prophets will always bring us joy; the godly sorrow is often no longer expected as a tool for restoration of God's people. The prophetic expressions are not purely for encouragement or edification. Rather, like all that God's word is intended to do, they are also for reproof, correction and instruction in righteousness:

> All Scripture is given by inspiration of God, and is profitable for doctrine, for reproof, for correction, for instruction in righteousness, that the man of God may be complete, thoroughly equipped for every good work - 2 Timothy 3:16-17:

Proverbs chapter 3 verses 7-8 reads, 'Do not be wise in your own eyes; fear the LORD and depart from evil. It will be health to your flesh, and strength to your bones.' When God threatened to rain hail on Egypt – as the seventh of the ten plagues sent in the process of securing Israel's release from Egypt, He even added a provision for escape for whoever would acknowledge His ability to fulfil His word.

The Holy Bible records two responses among Pharaoh's servants; note here that there were no undecided persons nor was there the option to make no choice and be indifferent. Exodus 9:20-21 tells us that, 'He who feared the word of the LORD among the servants of Pharaoh made his servants and his livestock flee to the houses. But he who did not regard the word of the LORD left his servants and his livestock in the field.'

Verse 25 relays the outcome: 'And the hail struck throughout the whole land of Egypt, all that was in the field, both man and beast; and the hail struck every herb of the field and broke every tree of the field.' These were not believers nor people who had chosen to enter into covenant relationship with God; but having seen how God had fulfilled earlier threats, they gave due regard to His word and saved their animals and servants.

The fear of God births a reverent response to His word. The opposite of that is to have no regard for His word – to not be moved by His word. Consider Peter's encounter with our Lord Jesus. Peter said, 'Nevertheless at Your word I will let down the net' – Luke 5:5b. Here he showed due regard for the word of God, setting his wisdom and expertise aside.

Prayer Challenges The 'Whatever Will Be, Will Be' (Que Sera Sera) Stance

In many ways, praying about a situation, asking the LORD to intervene and effect a change on it equates to challenging the situation. The more of God we know, the greater the revelation we have of whom He is, the more we would rise up to challenge the situations that are contrary to His divine will for our lives or the circumstance under consideration. By equipping us to give the Almighty God His due place, the fear of God emboldens one to 'dare' to challenge such situations with the power that is in praying to Him.

Compare this with the experience of people who do not know their rights or entitlements; they generally do not put up a fight when it is denied them, unlike those who know their entitlements. The LORD says even his own people are destroyed for lack of knowledge (Hosea 4:6).

The following is a popular quotation heard repeatedly quoted in Christian gatherings:

> You lust and do not have. You murder and covet and cannot obtain. You fight and war. Yet you do not have because you do not ask. You ask and do not receive, because you ask amiss, that you may spend it on your pleasures - James 4:2-3.

Matthew chapter 21 verse 22 then says, "And whatever things you ask in prayer, believing, you will receive." In Mark 9:23, Jesus Christ teaches that all things are possible – we only have to believe. Easier said than done eh? But …. the power to believe is given us by His Holy Spirit.

269

THE FEAR OF GOD

Romans 12:3 teaches how we rely on Him for our faith – measure by measure, 'For I say, through the grace given to me, to everyone who is among you, not to think of himself more highly than he ought to think, but to think soberly, as God has dealt to each one a measure of faith.'

Looking again at Matthew 21, now verse 21, we read, 'So Jesus answered and said to them, "Assuredly, I say to you, if you have faith and do not doubt, you will not only do what was done to the fig tree, but also if you say to this mountain, 'Be removed and be cast into the sea,' it will be done.' Therefore, one can conclude that our responsibility in prayer is to ask (according to God's will) and believe.

Let us revisit the illustrations given about the woman and the judge and the man asking for refreshment for his guest at a late hour. They could have settled for what they had but chose not to, rather to challenge the situation by asking for help.

It is my experience that people generally try to make the most of the situation and yield it to God in prayer only when it gets beyond one's perceived ability to bear it. We ought to challenge the situation with prayer as soon as we perceive that it is not in line with what we know to be God's plan; whether for us personally, for people close to us, people we know or do not know, for example when interceding for nations.

The Lord Jesus said to His disciples, "Pray that you may not enter into temptation," (Matthew 6:13, Luke 22:40 & 46) implying that one should embrace preventive prayers as well not just waiting for situations to turn sore before praying. The Lord foresaw Peter's fall and challenged it with prayer (Luke 22:31-32). In Ezekiel 22:30-31, God Almighty sought a person to challenge the situation in Israel with prayer and found none:

> "'So I sought for a man among them who would make a wall, and stand in the gap before Me on behalf of the land, that I should not destroy it; but I found no one. Therefore I have poured out My indignation on them; I have consumed them with the fire of My wrath; and I have recompensed their deeds on their own heads," says the Lord GOD.'

The fear of God brings boldness in the place of prayer. The Psalmist in Psalm 119:38 boldly asked for the word of God to be established in his life due to his fear of God - "Establish Your word to Your servant, who is devoted to fearing You."

Travelling on the train often, I have made an interesting observation. If I put my bag on a nearby seat, usually no one would ask to sit on it. However, if I leave the seat clear and put my bag elsewhere, almost certainly, someone would come to take the seat. And vice versa, I observed that I tend to do the same.

Occasionally, when the train is full – people would ask you to take your bag off the seat for them to sit down. I for one think – 'I have paid for the seat and every other person has equally paid for just one – not two seats,' so I ask for the seat. It feels at times like challenging the other person's right to have their bag or item occupy the seat, which should or could be one's to sit on.

When we know the Lord's ability to deliver us from a

situation, or the fact that the thing is already paid for and also that He is willing for us to have it, we can boldly challenge the situation through prayer; not challenging God, but the situation.

Another illustration comes to my mind. When I want to ask my husband for something, I consider - does he have it at his disposal to give to me? If yes, then I ask. I do not usually ask if he is willing. This is a separate issue from God's will or purpose.

For example, coming home on the train, I phone my husband asking if he is free at the time I should be arriving. If he is, then I simply ask him to pick me up having made the assumption that he would not rather be doing something else or expect me to make my way home when he is available to do it for me. I often do not ask if he is willing.

This is interesting when you consider the man who asked the Lord to heal him if He was willing. We must tailor our expectations based not only on what the Lord is able to do but also on what His divine will for us is.

When we disregard God's word, we weaken our faith in Him and also hinder our growth in faith. If we disregard His word in our everyday activity, when we come to pray, our heart would find it difficult or impossible to trust in His word.

If we succeed in convincing ourselves, concerning one issue or the other in the Bible, that the LORD does not really mean what He has said, in prayer or considering His promises, we would find it difficult to convince ourselves that He means what He has said He would do for us also.

In the Bible, the LORD is seen to tell His people

repeatedly, "Do not fear." And, this is often followed by the reason not to fear, which relates to who God is to us, His promises and our position in Him. For example, in Jeremiah 46:28, we read the command to Israel saying, "Do not fear," which is followed by, "for I am with you." When we do not know the One who is with us, that instruction will have little or no effect on our fear.

Looking at an illustration in life, imagine my computer starts to malfunction and my 14 year old son says, 'mum let me have a look at it for you.' I would usually let him have a look and this is because he has shown much more experience at handling such things than myself. Even so, I would be peering from over his shoulders to make sure he does not touch something that could make the situation worse.

However, on the other hand, when I take my computer to the computer company 'PC World' to evaluate a problem, I do not even ask who would be looking at it or the person's experience at such things. I would just leave it with them and they would contact me when they have finished assessing it.

Our ability to leave our cares or fears to God is similarly anchored on our ability to trust Him with the issue at hand. We must choose to give value to all His word, as long as we know it is His word and not to be selective because, as already said, not doing so tends to erode our faith and trust in Him. In many places in the Holy Bible we are told that God did something great so that the people could fear Him. For example, in Exodus 20:18-20 we read:

Now all the people witnessed the thunderings, the

lightning flashes, the sound of the trumpet, and the mountain smoking; and when the people saw it, they trembled and stood afar off. Then they said to Moses, "You speak with us, and we will hear; but let not God speak with us, lest we die." And Moses said to the people, "Do not fear; for God has come to test you, and that His fear may be before you, so that you may not sin."

You could ask Him to compliment the work of the Holy Spirit by doing something that would steer your heart in same way, so that you can develop a healthy fear of God.

As previously mentioned, God is watching out and searching throughout the whole earth to show Himself strong on our behalf (2 Chronicles 16:9a), not on behalf of the angels and certainly not on behalf of the devil. His power is there to facilitate us in the purpose He has ordained for us, not to harm us. His display of His power strengthens our faith, and builds the fear of God in those who observe this display of His power.

The Fear Of Man Versus The Fear Of God

While King Saul was still ruling over Israel, God prompted the prophet Samuel to go and anoint another person as king. Understandably, Samuel was fearful of what King Saul's response would be. He conveyed this fear to the LORD God, "How can I go? If Saul hears it, he will kill me."

God gave Samuel a way out. Note that He did not chide Samuel or dismiss his concern. "Take a heifer with you, and say, 'I have come to sacrifice to the LORD' (1Samuel 16:2). The LORD gave Samuel the divine counsel and wisdom that he needed for that moment.

We should turn to God when doing His will means stepping into 'perilous high waters'. His wisdom and counsel will see us through victoriously rather than yielding to the fear of man and disobeying God as this would not be in our best interest.

In the prophecy of Zechariah after the birth of his son John the Baptist, he commented, "To grant us that we, being delivered from the hand of our enemies, might serve Him without fear, in holiness and righteousness before Him all the days of our life" – Luke 1:74-75.

It would appear that at the time he was speaking, the enemies of the Jewish nation had prevented free service of God making the people afraid due to persecution from the authorities. The fear of oppression and threat of isolation as well as the desire to 'belong' can hinder or diminish the service that one gives to God.

Consequences of putting others before God stem from the fact that people are imperfect and not all-knowing, as God is. Though God may choose to give us godly counsel through people, we should check every counsel against His word. Let His word always be our final guide.

I recall a situation while in the university; I had a friend whom I encouraged to join in prayer with me especially as exams were approaching. She later needed godly counsel on an issue I was struggling with myself and I gave her a wrong advice but that was because I was genuinely misled myself.

THE FEAR OF GOD

Hence, do not think because a person is a believer in Jesus Christ that he or she would always give godly counsel. If in doubt ask another person or better still, ask the Lord and search the scriptures for the correct directive to follow.

Consider Moses' older brother Aaron. Exodus 32 tells the story of when the people of Israel were waiting for Moses at the foot of Mount Sinai, how they persuaded Aaron to make a god for them in the form of a moulded golden calf. When challenged for his actions by Moses, Aaron replied in verses 22-24:

> "Do not let the anger of my lord become hot. You know the people, that they are set on evil. For they said to me, 'Make us gods that shall go before us; as for this Moses, the man who brought us out of the land of Egypt, we do not know what has become of him.' And I said to them, 'Whoever has any gold, let them break it off.' So they gave it to me, and I cast it into the fire, and this calf came out."

We can see from the fore-going passage how Aaron yielded to the pressure of the people and did what he knew was against God. As refreshing as it may be to point the finger at another person's mistake, one must consider and evaluate our personal issues to see if we are falling into same offence regularly.

For instance, by yielding to wrong influence of friends or family to get involved in something that God frowns upon. Our Lord Jesus on the other hand, recognizing Satan as the one putting pressure on Him, though speaking through Peter, rebuked Satan directly rather than trying to see how He could please Peter by yielding to his voice.

Yielding to the voice that the enemy uses essentially equates to yielding to the enemy not to the physical owner of the voice whether friends, colleagues or family. As already stated, one ought to bring every thought into captivity to the obedience of Christ. This is part of our commission as Christians, for which we have been appropriately equipped:

> For the weapons of our warfare are not carnal but mighty in God for pulling down strongholds, casting down arguments and every high thing that exalts itself against the knowledge of God, bringing every thought into captivity to the obedience of Christ.

King Saul's experience on this issue is recorded in the fifteenth chapter of 1 Samuel. The LORD gave him the following instruction:

> "I will punish Amalek for what he did to Israel, how he ambushed him on the way when he came up from Egypt. Now go and attack Amalek, and utterly destroy all that they have, and do not spare them. But kill both man and woman, infant and nursing child, ox and sheep, camel and donkey." (1 Samuel 15:2-3)

It would appear that King Saul had good intentions to carry

out God's instruction because he did not ask any questions about whether to spare anything or any persons. What he actually did was recorded in verse 9:

> But Saul and the people spared Agag and the best of the sheep, the oxen, the fatlings, the lambs, and all that was good, and were unwilling to utterly destroy them. But everything despised and worthless, that they utterly destroyed.

The key phrase in the verses above is "unwilling." This suggests that they overruled God's instruction with their wisdom. King Saul's partial obedience was seen as rebellion, stubbornness, failure to obey or to heed and a rejection of God's word (verses 22-23).

God sent the prophet Samuel to King Saul to tell him what he had done and the consequences he had to bear for it including being replaced as Israel's king, this not being averted despite Samuel's all night grieving and crying before God on Saul's behalf. King Saul's explanation was, "I have sinned, for I have transgressed the commandment of the LORD and your words, because I feared the people and obeyed their voice" (verse 24).

Every time I read this story, I have two reactions to its implications. I shudder at the thought of how often my life has reflected partial obedience to God's word, often without any iota of remorse. I would often make excuses centred around the phrase: 'The LORD understands.'

On the other hand, I marvel at the LORD's mercy; that when prompted by the Holy Spirit I acknowledge my disobedience, He forgives me completely and spares me the consequences of my actions in the natural, and I believe, also in the spiritual. Of course, the LORD understands when we are weak, but He expects us to look to him for strength rather than yield to our weakness.

Again, the striking word in that report is – unwilling. They may have had apparently good reasons from the human point of view for not being willing to destroy the Amelekite king and the best of the animals, but that was not theirs to decide; they had specific instructions from God that they needed to have followed.

We are not given the details of the discussions that led to the partial obedience, but they clearly acted as they thought right. Conviction only came to Saul after Samuel told him what God had in store for him in response to his partial obedience.

I can site several examples of partial obedience in my life. I remember a time when I had a disagreement with my husband. As usual – I was 'right.' However, the LORD spoke into my spirit to go and apologise.

After much hesitation – I went to my husband and had a discussion with him about the issue. I told him what I felt he did wrong, why I was upset and even that I was ok with it, in other words, I said I had forgiven him. As I walked away, the word in my spirit was – that is no apology. I had to go back and apologise. I think my husband being a Christian makes it a bit easier. His response was not of pride or victory but he seemed subdued by the realisation that I was obeying the LORD in what I was doing, though not enjoying the experience myself.

More interestingly, God's response was that Saul's

actions reflected the state of his heart. In verse 11, He said to Samuel, "I greatly regret that I have set up Saul as king, for he has turned back from following Me, and has not performed My commandments." Note that the turning back preceded the action of disobedience.

In verse 23, Samuel told Saul that he had rejected the word of the LORD, and in turn, He also had rejected him from being king. This was the point when Saul came to the realisation of what had actually happened.

The turning away was also evident in Saul's language, referring to the LORD as 'the LORD your God' rather than 'the LORD my God' when he was speaking to Samuel in verse 15. One needs to come to the 'I have sinned' point of acceptance of departure from God's ways, just as Saul did, in other to move forward through restitution.

In response to the authority questioning why the disciples continued to preach in the name of Jesus having been instructed not to do so, the apostle Peter said in Acts 5:29, "We ought to obey God rather than men."

Furthermore, the writer of Hebrews in verse 31 of chapter 10 said, 'It is a fearful thing to fall into the hands of the living God.' Considering the foregoing, wisdom dictates that we obey God rather than men when the two parties disagree. In Proverbs 24:21-22 we read:

> My son, fear the LORD and the king; do not associate with those given to change; for their calamity will rise suddenly, and who knows the ruin those two can bring?

In Matthew 23:13-36, the Lord Jesus Christ repeatedly

pronounced woe on the scribes and Pharisees because they were concentrating on putting up a good front before people without having the interest of God's kingdom at heart. For this attitude, He also called them hypocrites.

It always sounds more interesting when someone else's mistake or slip-up is being analysed; why not bring it closer to home? When was the last time that God corrected or disciplined you? Was it successful? Or have you put it aside for another day? For the sake of His unquenchable, unyielding love, the discipline would usually return another day!!

In Romans 1:21-23 the apostle Paul talks about how those who, though they knew God, did not give Him His due place, '..although they knew God, they did not glorify Him as God, nor were thankful, but became futile in their thoughts, and their foolish hearts were darkened. Professing to be wise, they became fools, and changed the glory of the incorruptible God into an image made like corruptible man and birds and four-footed animals and creeping things.'

When we give God His rightful place in our hearts and in everyday living, we can be thankful, knowing that even in the face of delays in seeing His promises fulfilled, He is still faithful who has promised (Hebrews 11:11b).

In the twenty-third chapter of the book of Matthew, Jesus teaches in detail about making God the focus of our decisions and actions. Essentially, one's decision should be weighed according to how it rates before God. This is a core issue for a life governed or directed by the fear of God.

In verses 2-3, He encouraged the people to respect

THE FEAR OF GOD

the authority of God, which the scribes and the Pharisees represented – "sitting in Moses' seat." This they were to do even if they did not agree with their leaders' life styles. In verses 4-7 Jesus speaks of how the scribes and the Pharisees overburdened the people with regulations that they themselves were not ready to abide by and how they lived their lives with the approval and praise of men as their main focus. He was against their hypocrisy, eye service and self-centredness.

The fear of God demands that we do not flatter people in their wrongdoing even when they are in a position of authority. If we are unable to caution them about their ill behaviour, we should not commend what God condemns about it. He then went on to discourage people from assuming a position of dominance over others but to acknowledge and yield only to the authority of God as the ultimate authority.

In verses 9-10 He admonished: "Do not call anyone on earth your father; for One is your Father, He who is in heaven. And do not be called teachers; for One is your Teacher, the Christ." There is ample evidence in the Bible that Jesus recognised parental authority and was not advocating people disobeying or disregarding their natural parents. The message theme is captured in verse 12, 'And whoever exalts himself will be humbled, and he who humbles himself will be exalted.' The Lord was teaching them that one should live a life that reserves all praise and adoration for the Almighty.

This goes beyond the confession of the lips to touch every aspect of life, yielding to His authority as the ultimate. Knowing God's authority to be the ultimate helps us place other authorities in their rightful position under Him. Colossians 1:15-16 says of Jesus:

He is the image of the invisible God, the firstborn over all creation. For by Him all things were created that are in heaven and that are on earth, visible and invisible, whether thrones or dominions or principalities or powers. All things were created through Him and for Him.

Again in Revelation 19:16, He is called the KING OF KINGS AND LORD OF LORDS. Therefore when a situation arises presenting a conflict between the LORD's requirements and those of a king, the LORD should be the One given due preferential regard; the fear of God is always above the fear of the king – whatever the circumstance.

When God sent the prophet Samuel to King Saul (1 Samuel 15) and similarly sent the prophet Nathan to King David (2 Samuel 12), both had to deliver God's message to the kings with God-given wisdom. Contrast this with the false prophets referred to in Micah chapters 2 and 3, who chanted peace (chapter 3 verse 5) to please the people. Their hearers ended up not being saved from God's judgment.

Job 31:23 records Job's thoughts: "For destruction from God is a terror to me, and because of His magnificence I cannot endure." If God has permitted destruction upon a person, it is unimaginable what hope can be found in that situation, practically none. The One to save, is seen as having authorized the captivity in the first place.

Dr Ravi Zacharias and Vince Vitale recently coauthored a bestseller on why God allows suffering; and, I would recommend this to anyone who wants more in-depth study on that subject.[1] It is worth mentioning that my recommendation based on biblical principles is to keep focused on God, on Jesus, the author and perfecter of our faith:

> Therefore we also, since we are surrounded by so great a cloud of witnesses, let us lay aside every weight, and the sin which so easily ensnares us, and let us run with endurance the race that is set before us, looking unto Jesus, the author and finisher of our faith, who for the joy that was set before Him endured the cross, despising the shame, and has sat down at the right hand of the throne of God (Hebrews 12:1-2).

Knowing that God is with us in troubled times, keeping His promise of never leaving nor forsaking us, is key to overcoming in trials. Consider a child being handed over by the parent to a person to afflict him or her.

This reminds me of my observation when I worked in the paediatric surgical specialty when the parents gave consent and presented their child for surgery - an affliction of some sort; the expectation being that the surgery would rid the child of a medical condition and get them to a state of better health, equipping the child to maximize his or her potentials in life. Many of these brave parents left the

---

1 Ravi Zacharias and Vince Vitale. Why Suffering? Finding Meaning and Comfort When Life doesn't Make Sense. Hachette Book Group, USA, 2014.

anaesthetic room in tears after the child had been put under general anaesthesia often times on the parent's knees for the very young children. How our Father God must hurt for us as well (not that He goes away and cries over it) when He has to let us come through some trials to become better equipped for our kingdom calling.

The Holy Bible states that He is afflicted when we are afflicted (Isaiah 63:9a). He knows the end point, unlike Job and the rest of us; so, we would do well to trust Him for a good outcome.

THE FEAR OF GOD

CHAPTER 6

THE FEAR OF GOD – MY BEAUTIFYING VIRTUE

*T*he Merriam-Webster dictionary definition of the word virtue includes the following: conformity to a standard of right, morality; a particular moral excellence, a beneficial quality or power of a thing, manly strength or courage, valour; a commendable quality or trait, merit; a capacity to act, potency; chastity, especially in a woman. Proverbs 31:24-31 describes the virtuous woman as one with qualities that make her stand out in a good way:

> She makes linen garments and sells them, and supplies sashes for the merchants. Strength and honour are her clothing; she shall rejoice in time to come. She opens her mouth with wisdom, and on her tongue is the law of kindness. She watches over the ways of her household, and does not eat the bread of idleness. Her children rise up and call her blessed; her husband also, and he praises her: "Many daughters have done well, but you excel them all." Charm is deceitful and beauty is passing, but a woman who fears the LORD, she shall be praised. Give her of the fruit of her hands, and let her own works praise her in the gates.

Being endowed with the fear of God produces in one's life

an enviable state of being. Imagine being able to live a life
not dominated by sin; a life that takes God at His word and
trusts Him with everything. One would like to say: 'That's
me!'

However my day-to-day responses to life's challenges
tell me, 'Not quite.' And that's ok because I know it is a
journey. I am pleased with the cultivation of the fear of
God in my life by the work of the Holy Spirit, and yes, it
is a journey.

The fear of God develops in us the virtues that give God
His rightful place above all things. As already liberally
illustrated, the Holy Bible enumerates several benefits and
blessings that accompany a life that lives out the fear of
God. Psalm 112 is one of such passages and it reads:

'Praise the LORD! Blessed is the man who
fears the LORD, who delights greatly in His
commandments. His descendants will be mighty
on earth; the generation of the upright will be
blessed. Wealth and riches will be in his house,
and his righteousness endures forever. Unto the
upright there arises light in the darkness; he is
gracious, and full of compassion, and righteous. A
good man deals graciously and lends; he will guide
his affairs with discretion. Surely he will never
be shaken; the righteous will be in everlasting
remembrance. He will not be afraid of evil tidings;
his heart is steadfast, trusting in the LORD. His
heart is established; he will not be afraid, until he
sees his desire upon his enemies. He has dispersed
abroad, he has given to the poor; his righteousness

endures forever; his horn will be exalted with honour. The wicked will see it and be grieved; he will gnash his teeth and melt away; the desire of the wicked shall perish.'

Psalm 128 also enumerates several blessings that adorn the life of anyone who fears God:

'Blessed is everyone who fears the LORD, who walks in His ways. When you eat the labour of your hands, you shall be happy, and it shall be well with you. Your wife shall be like a fruitful vine in the very heart of your house, your children like olive plants all around your table. Behold, thus shall the man be blessed who fears the LORD. The LORD bless you out of Zion, and may you see the good of Jerusalem all the days of your life. Yes, may you see your children's children. Peace be upon Israel!'

All very desirable blessings one must agree. God so much wants us to live by the fear of God that He places premium rewards for those who choose to comply.

Repentance

The virtue of repentance is anchored on the fear of God, which empowers us to acknowledge and denounce sin while running to God for restoration rather than hiding from Him.

At this point, an evaluation and comparison of the

experiences of Adam and Eve versus King David would illustrate the point. After the temptation and fall of Adam and Eve, they ran from God's presence. He caught up with them and demanded they face up to their failings.

King David on the other hand is recorded over and over as acknowledging his sin before God and asking for forgiveness and restoration. Psalm 51 is a typical example among many of such psalms of David.

The love of God draws us to Him, the fear of God keeps us with Him and helps us realise that even when we fail, the only way out is to return to God. It helps us realise there is no other way but God. Consider the story told by Jesus about the prodigal son. He was already a son, but he returned to his Father only when he came to the conclusion that his father's place was his only hope.

The fear of God teaches us that God is the only way out, even when we mess everything up. Peter the apostle of our Lord Jesus denied Him three times, then later cried for help and was restored. Judas on the other hand betrayed Jesus but was driven to suicide. One wonders what would have become of Judas if he had repented and asked for forgiveness. I feel he would have been forgiven and restored too. However, the supernatural details of Judas' fate are not given to us and I would not speculate any further on his case.

Obedience

Isaiah chapter 50 verse 10 reads, "Who among you fears the LORD? Who obeys the voice of His Servant? Who walks in darkness and has no light? Let him trust in the name of the

LORD and rely upon his God." The fear of God invariably births obedience to His word. Proverbs 8:13a says, 'The fear of the LORD is to hate evil.' It follows therefore that the tendency to knowingly embrace evil is a manifestation of the absence of the fear of God.

In Proverbs 23:17-18 we read, 'Do not let your heart envy sinners, but be zealous for the fear of the LORD all the day; for surely there is a hereafter, and your hope will not be cut off.'

The fear of God provides an answer when one is tempted to be envious of sinners. In viewing prosperity in life, one is encouraged not to envy those who do not fear God but appear to do well, rather to be led by the fear of God while being mindful of the truth that life continues beyond the grave.

Proverbs chapter 3 verse 7 offers this advice, 'Do not be wise in your own eyes; fear the LORD and depart from evil.' Here, again, we see that the fear of God is a tool for working out our salvation in holiness.

In recognition of God's sovereignty, when teachings from others or even our own ideas seem good, we ought to put them through a scrutiny based on God's word. By so doing, we would depart from evil. We cannot rely on the wisdom of man. Recall another advice in Proverbs 16:25, 'There is a way that seems right to a man, but its end is the way of death.' The apostle Paul offers this advice in Galatians 1:6-10:

> I marvel that you are turning away so soon from Him who called you in the grace of Christ, to a different gospel, which is not another; but there

are some who trouble you and want to pervert the gospel of Christ. But even if we, or an angel from heaven, preach any other gospel to you than what we have preached to you, let him be accursed. As we have said before, so now I say again, if anyone preaches any other gospel to you than what you have received, let him be accursed. For do I now persuade men, or God? Or do I seek to please men? For if I still pleased men, I would not be a bondservant of Christ.

Consider the example from the account of the man of God referred to in 1 Kings chapter 13. He was instructed by God not to eat bread, nor drink water there, nor return by the same way he came. However when an older person beguiled him claiming to be a prophet and hearing from an angel, the man of God unfortunately yielded to him, believing his word to be true.

This was seen as an act of disobedience for which he paid with his life. Interestingly, the older prophet knew that he was deceiving the man of God. This is a display of the wickedness of the heart of man as written in Jeremiah 17:9, "The heart is deceitful above all things, and desperately wicked; who can know it?"

Philippians chapter 2 verse 12 instructs us all, 'Therefore, my beloved, as you have always obeyed, not as in my presence only, but now much more in my absence, work out your own salvation with fear and trembling.' The fear of God facilitates the Christian practical living.

In 2 Corinthians 7:1 we read, "Therefore, having

these promises, beloved, let us cleanse ourselves from all filthiness of the flesh and spirit, perfecting holiness in the fear of God.'

Following Israel's restoration the LORD said, "Jacob shall not now be ashamed, nor shall his face now grow pale; but when he sees his children, the work of My hands, in his midst, they will hallow My name, and hallow the Holy One of Jacob, and fear the God of Israel. These also who erred in spirit will come to understanding, and those who complained will learn doctrine" (Isaiah 29:22-24).

The fear of God is part of His blessings to His children who return to Him; I believe, to equip His people to serve Him faithfully and fruitfully.

Ponder Time

Would Father God let me get away with sin and turn a blind eye?

God loves me too much to let me be carried away by anything, and that includes His gifts and blessings. Consider the father of faith - Abraham. In Genesis 18:1-12 we read of how the LORD visited him and his wife Sarah and gave them the promise of a son of their own. This was Abraham's greatest desire at the time.

In chapter 15 when the LORD visited Abraham and told him of how He was his shield and his exceedingly great reward, Abraham's response showed how much he desired and valued having a son of his own. "Lord GOD, what will You give me, seeing I go childless, and the heir of my

THE FEAR OF GOD

house is Eliezer of Damascus?" – Genesis 15:2.

Further on in chapter 22, having given a son Isaac to Sarah and Abraham, a very welcome and highly-valued gift one must appreciate, God asks for him to be given up as a sacrifice! To be cut up by Abraham's hand, bleeding and set on fire!! I have tried to imagine what was going on in Abraham's mind at this time, it seems to be beyond my grasp completely.

Interestingly, in response to Abraham's obedience to this 'impossible' request, in verse twelve God speaks to him "…for now I know that you fear God, since you have not withheld your son, your only son, from Me." In line with what we read in Psalms 112 and 128 above, God swore to bless Abraham for his display of the fear of God saying:

> "By Myself I have sworn, says the LORD, because you have done this thing, and have not withheld your son, your only son - blessing I will bless you, and multiplying I will multiply your descendants as the stars of the heaven and as the sand which is on the seashore; and your descendants shall possess the gate of their enemies. In your seed all the nations of the earth shall be blessed, because you have obeyed My voice" (Genesis 22:16-18).

'Show Me you fear Me,' God seems to have said to Abraham. Quite contrary to today's commonly heard declarations: "God knows I love Him, He knows I appreciate Him." God loves to see obedience that is born out of utmost regard for Him and His word; and, He rewards this.

Ephesians 5:8-10 encourages us to find out what is

acceptable to the Lord and to use that as our guide:

> For you were once darkness, but now you are light
> in the Lord. Walk as children of light (for the fruit
> of the Spirit is in all goodness, righteousness, and
> truth), finding out what is acceptable to the Lord.

'Finding out' implies actually searching to elucidate or bring to light or bring to one's knowledge; not just waiting passively for the matter to be made known or revealed to the person. In 2 Corinthians 5:9, the desirable virtue of obedience – living a life that embraces what pleases God - is further emphasized by the apostle Paul saying, 'Therefore we make it our aim, whether present or absent, to be well pleasing to Him.'

Humility

Living a life that embraces the fear of God invariably creates an atmosphere, spiritually and physically, where the virtue of humility develops and thrives. Romans 6:16 challenges us as follows, 'Do you not know that to whom you present yourselves slaves to obey, you are that one's slaves whom you obey, whether of sin leading to death, or of obedience leading to righteousness?'

Yielding equals servitude. If you do not want to be a servant to the thing or way of life, then, do not yield to it. In Ephesians 5:21 Paul encourages us in 'submitting to one another in the fear of God.'

If the fear of God is embraced and established in the gathering of God's people, submission would follow while quarrelling and power tussles would be much reduced if not done away with altogether. Going further on this issue, Proverbs chapter 22 verse 4 instructs us that, 'By humility and the fear of the LORD are riches and honour and life.' Here we can see that the fear of the Lord works together with humility; together, they are the keys to true riches, honour and life. God's way leads to life, even though it may not even seem right or even pleasant to our minds sometimes.

As mentioned above, Proverbs 16:25 teaches us that, 'There is a way that seems right to a man, but its end is the way of death.' In conclusion of this segment, it is worth bringing to mind that God's ways are not our ways; and, if we wait to understand Him before yielding to them, we may never get there. Written in Isaiah 55:8-9:

> "For My thoughts are not your thoughts, nor are your ways My ways," says the LORD. "For as the heavens are higher than the earth, so are My ways higher than your ways, and My thoughts than your thoughts."

The Fear Of God Facilitates The Expression Of Our Love For Him

The fear of God equips us to express our love for God practically; the two working together to produce obedience to His word. The fear of God empowers us unto obedience to Him; cultivating a life style of obedience to God as an act of love, we live out our love for the Lord in our obedience.

In John 14:15-16, Jesus our Lord and Master says, "If you love Me, keep My commandments. And I will pray the Father, and He will give you another Helper, that He may abide with you forever..."

Also in John 14:23-24, Jesus continues to stress the benefits of a practical expression of our love for Him, "If anyone loves Me, he will keep My word; and My Father will love him, and We will come to him and make Our home with him. He who does not love Me does not keep My words; and the word which you hear is not Mine but the Father's who sent Me."

Here He promises special revelation and knowledge of God's ways to those who keep His word as an expression of their love for Him. I suppose every Christian wants the Lord Jesus to manifest Himself to him or her. Thinking this through, just like in the relationships between humans, there are varying degrees of commitment. One does not go about saying, 'I love you' to everyone.

Loving the Lord is not a casual event that just happens because one is in church with other Christians. One would need to yield to the Holy Spirit who draws us into this special relationship and develops a love for Him in our hearts. Hence, Romans 5:5b says that, 'the love of God has been poured out in our hearts by the Holy Spirit who was given to us.'

It would therefore be sensible to ask the Holy Spirit to 'upgrade' our love of God when we struggle to yield to Him. Along similar lines, in Psalms 25:12, the LORD promises that to the person who fears Him, He will teach in the way He chooses. Further along, verse 14 also states, 'The secret of the LORD is with those who fear Him, and He will show them His covenant.'

This connotes a revelation of the ways and covenant of God which is given specifically to those who fear Him and not available as common knowledge to all men.

Conversely, our Lord Jesus speaks of the consequences of not abiding in Him, this relating to those who are already in Him but later cast out as a branch. In John 15:5-6 He says:

> "I am the vine, you are the branches. He who abides in Me, and I in him, bears much fruit; for without Me you can do nothing. If anyone does not abide in Me, he is cast out as a branch and is withered; and they gather them and throw them into the fire, and they are burned."

In verse 10 Jesus continues, "If you keep My commandments, you will abide in My love, just as I have kept My Father's commandments and abide in His love." This is similar to the foregoing, telling us that He had to do same: keeping the Father's commandments as an outward expression of His love which is a pre-requisite for abiding in His love.

Power For Kingdom Living

Romans 8:6-9 tells us that pleasing God is not possible without the help of the Holy Spirit:

> For to be carnally minded is death, but to be spiritually minded is life and peace. Because the

carnal mind is enmity against God; for it is not subject to the law of God, nor indeed can be. So then, those who are in the flesh cannot please God. But you are not in the flesh but in the Spirit, if indeed the Spirit of God dwells in you. Now if anyone does not have the Spirit of Christ, he is not His.

In Romans 12:2 the Bible teaches us: 'Do not be conformed to this world, but be transformed by the renewing of your mind, that you may prove what is that good and acceptable and perfect will of God.'

This good, acceptable and perfect will of God is that our spirit is brought back into unity with Him. This can only take place as we embrace the presence of Jesus and cultivate intimacy with Him. The fear of God is a tool used by the Holy Spirit to enable us to achieve this.

The Bible in Galatians 5:16-17 reads, 'I say then: Walk in the Spirit, and you shall not fulfil the lust of the flesh. For the flesh lusts against the Spirit, and the Spirit against the flesh; and these are contrary to one another, so that you do not do the things that you wish.'

Also, verse 24 says that 'those who are Christ's have crucified the flesh with its passions and desires.' The fear of God is our tool for this daily maintaining the flesh in its crucified state. His grace is sufficient to help us overcome our weaknesses. In 2 Corinthians 12:9 we read, "My grace is sufficient for you, for my strength is made perfect in weakness."

The prophet Nehemiah chided the people of Israel for

oppressing the poor among them in the time of famine. In Nehemiah 5:9, he encouraged them to change their behaviour, pointing out that as God's people, their bad behaviour – in this case the ill-treatment of the poor – was causing reproach to His name among those who did not acknowledge Him as God, "What you are doing is not good. Should you not walk in the fear of our God because of the reproach of the nations, our enemies?"

In verse 15, Nehemiah explains the reason he was a different type of governor, not like his predecessors - 'But the former governors who were before me laid burdens on the people, and took from them bread and wine, besides forty shekels of silver. Yes, even their servants bore rule over the people, but I did not do so, because of the fear of God.'

The fear of God enables us live different because it helps us to discipline the flesh so that it is brought under the control of the Holy Spirit. It then follows that we should ask the Lord to develop the fear of God in us. In everyday living, one hears of temptations that topple men and we expect people to live above the failings or shortcomings of the flesh when they do not have the empowerment afforded by the Spirit of God through the fear of God.

The Virtue Of Faith

Hebrews 11:7 states, 'By faith Noah, being divinely warned of things not yet seen, moved with godly fear, prepared an ark for the saving of his household, by which he condemned the world and became heir of the righteousness which is according to faith.'

The fear of God preserves us in faith and covenant relationship with God. In Jeremiah 32:38-40, speaking of Israel's restoration, God says:

> "They shall be My people, and I will be their God; then I will give them one heart and one way, that they may fear Me forever, for the good of them and their children after them. And I will make an everlasting covenant with them, that I will not turn away from doing them good; but I will put My fear in their hearts so that they will not depart from Me."

This covenant-sealing promise of God is mediated by the Holy Spirit in the new covenant that every Christian has with God through Jesus Christ.

Giving God His Rightful Place

Leaving God's place to Him is an expression of the presence of the fear of God. I recall an evening when I was taking a ride on the bus to my residence in Norwich (UK). I started to celebrate God's goodness to me and how being His child gives me such peace as could not be described with words; the self-value that comes from knowing that He loves me.

I then prayed in my heart that the Lord should bring my way people who needed to experience that peace and self-value so that I could give the same to them. I heard the Spirit speak into my spirit that it is not my place to do that for anyone. Rather, my duty would be to direct such a person to Him.

THE FEAR OF GOD

The Lord sees it as His place to satisfy the needs of His creation, physically but more especially spiritually. He may choose to use us as people to do that but that would be His choice. What a lesson that was for me - do not play 'God' to anyone.

Another example is with salvation. The Bible says in Psalm 3:8a, 'Salvation belongs to the LORD.' This is further strengthened by Revelation 7:10 which says, "Salvation belongs to our God who sits on the throne, and to the Lamb!"

Also, Isaiah 43:11 reads, 'I, even I, am the LORD, and besides Me there is no saviour.' As a young person growing up, I used to think that if I was unable to convince someone else to become a Christian – I had failed; it was my fault.

As I read the Bible and listened to Christian teachers and leaders, I began to understand differently. God is the Saviour. He works through people, like you and I, to point others in His direction, and the Holy Spirit enables those who come to God to take that step as they open their hearts to Him.

Just as He used people at different stages of my journey to draw me closer and closer to Him till I made that decision. Conversely, one cannot take the glory or honour for anyone who responds to God by becoming a Christian in response to our encouragement. God is the Saviour. The fear of God teaches that we do not take to ourselves what belongs to Him. This extends to other issues like worship and tithes as well as credit for answered prayers.

Giving the Lord His rightful place includes encouraging those around us to look to Him, to trust Him, rather than looking to us for their help or provision. This is especially important for leaders or pastors.

Effective Witnessing And Evangelism

The fear of God equips the Christian to be a more effective witness for Him. The Holy Bible puts it this way in 2 Corinthians 5:10-11:

> For we must all appear before the judgment seat of Christ, that each one may receive the things done in the body, according to what he has done, whether good or bad. Knowing, therefore, the terror of the Lord, we persuade men; but we are well known to God, and I also trust are well known in your consciences.

God is the only way to Himself. Jesus, God the Son, declared Himself to be the only way to the Father: "I am the way, the truth, and the life. No one comes to the Father except through Me" - John 14:6. Just as one's spirit or heart is best placed to know that person in the natural man, the Holy Spirit best knows the Spirit or heart of God.

First Corinthians chapter 2 verse 11 puts it this way: "For what man knows the things of a man except the spirit of the man which is in him? Even so no one knows the things of God except the Spirit of God." If we believe God's word concerning the eternal destiny of unbelievers, we are strengthened and encouraged to evangelise to them, with or without words.

As already referred to above, Hebrews 11:7 reminds us

that, 'By faith Noah, being divinely warned of things not yet seen, moved with godly fear, prepared an ark for the saving of his household, by which he condemned the world and became heir of the righteousness which is according to faith.'

If Noah had not believed God, he would not have built the ark or persuaded others to join him in it. Also, believing God, Lot tried to persuade his sons-in-law to leave Sodom and Gomorrah with him. They did not listen though and perished in the fire (Genesis 19:14).

Good Health

Proverbs 3:7-8 admonishes us, 'Do not be wise in your own eyes; fear the LORD and depart from evil. It will be health to your flesh, and strength to your bones.' In addition, Proverbs 10:27 teaches that the fear of the LORD prolongs days, but the years of the wicked will be shortened.

Contentment

There may be needs but the person who lives by the fear of the Lord has the promise of contentment. Psalm 34:9 states, 'Oh, fear the LORD, you His saints! There is no want to those who fear Him.'

The LORD takes personal or perhaps 'extra' responsibility for those who fear Him. Psalm 33:18-19 says, 'Behold, the eye of the LORD is on those who fear Him, on those who hope in His mercy, to deliver their soul from death, and to keep them alive in famine.'

Protection

There is protection in living by the fear of God. Proverbs 19:23 states, 'The fear of the LORD leads to life, and he who has it will abide in satisfaction; he will not be visited with evil.'

Knowing that one has acted according to the will of the Almighty God brings a peace and contentment that cannot be explained by natural means. Contrast this with the sin that leads to death and separation from God as Adam and Eve discovered. Psalm 34:7 promises us that, 'The angel of the LORD encamps all around those who fear Him, and delivers them.' God's protection is here promised, both physically and spiritually.

Healthy Relationships

The fear of God facilitates the cultivation of healthy interpersonal relationships. In Leviticus 25:17 we read that, as part of the instructions they were given regarding the year of Jubilee, Moses told Israel, '"Therefore you shall not oppress one another, but you shall fear your God; for I am the LORD your God."'

Also in encouraging them to treat each other well, knowing that each of them belonged to Him as His servant whom He brought out of Egypt (verse 42) God says in verses 35-36, '"If one of your brethren becomes poor, and falls into poverty among you, then you shall help him, like a stranger or a sojourner, that he may live with you. Take no usury or interest from him; but fear your God, that your brother may live with you."'

THE FEAR OF GOD

The poor among them who sold himself to serve another was to be treated as a servant or a sojourner not as a slave (verse 39). In verse 43 the LORD says, "'You shall not rule over him with rigor, but you shall fear your God.'" The fear of God was their basis for treating each other appropriately.

It would seem as though one could not expect anything good from a person who did not fear God. In the story told by our Lord Jesus in illustrating the benefits of persistent prayer (Luke 18), He spoke of the judge who did not fear God or regard man, and how the widow's persistent request for justice made him yield to her - (Luke 18: 4-5) 'And he would not for a while; but afterward he said within himself, 'Though I do not fear God nor regard man, yet because this widow troubles me I will avenge her, lest by her continual coming she weary me.'

The story makes more sense and gives us more boldness to pray when we appreciate that having no fear of God meant that no one expected anything good from this man; yet if he could give in to the widow's persistent request, how much more the One who loves us and gives us all things in His Son Jesus.

Jesus says, "And shall God not avenge His own elect who cry out day and night to Him, though He bears long with them? I tell you that He will avenge them speedily. Nevertheless, when the Son of Man comes, will He really find faith on the earth?" - Luke 18:7-8.

We are encouraged as Christians to submit to one another in the fear of God. The fear of God curbs prejudices against others and enables us treat others well to fulfil the commandment to love one's neighbour as oneself. This would be impossible otherwise. The fear of God equips us to treat others right and fairly.

The instruction to Christians written in Colossians 3:22 reads, 'Bondservants, obey in all things your masters according to the flesh, not with eyeservice, as men-pleasers, but in sincerity of heart, fearing God.'

Thus, any establishment or industry that is filled with men or women who fear God can expect good, honest, faithful and trustworthy service from them. In fact, we ought to pray for everyone with whom we have partnership agreement of any sort, that the fear of God would guide his or her decisions and activities. This should apply whether it is a relationship with one's spouse, children, social or business partners.

Encouraging the Roman Christians to keep a balance between being subject to the governing authorities and submission to God, the apostle Paul wrote, 'Render therefore to all their due: taxes to whom taxes are due, customs to whom customs, fear to whom fear, honour to whom honour' - Romans 13:7.

In 2 Chronicles 19, we read of how Jehoshaphat, king of Judah appointed judges and said to them (verse 7), "Now therefore, let the fear of the LORD be upon you; take care and do it, for there is no iniquity with the LORD our God, no partiality, nor taking of bribes."

King Jehoshaphat also appointed Levites, priests and chief fathers of Israel for the judgment of the LORD and for controversies. In verse 9 of the same chapter he said to them, "Thus you shall act in the fear of the LORD, faithfully and with a loyal heart." For those who are employers, how about praying for the fear of the LORD to guide your employees, should that result in them serving 'faithfully and with a loyal heart,' how wonderful your enterprise would turn out!!

Moreover, if we as Christians could serve faithfully and with a loyal heart before our employers, how truly blessed they would be and what a magnificent witness of the LORD's greatness that would be!!! Furthermore, just as these leaders, we should pray for our leaders in different spheres of life to be endowed with the fear of God so that they can be loyal and faithful. Nations across the world suffering the scourge of corruption among their leaders would definitely benefit from this.

The fear of God can also be seen as a moderator of our relationship with older people. In Leviticus 19:32 we see another example where the law was given and obedience was encouraged by the exercise of the fear of the LORD – 'You shall rise before the grey headed and honour the presence of an old man, and fear your God: I am the LORD.'

Acceptance By God

Acts chapter 10 verse 2 speaks highly of Cornelius, the centurion who is here described as a devout man, one who feared God with all his household, who gave alms generously to the people, and prayed to God always.

An angel was sent to him during a session of prayer who informed him that his prayers and alms had come up as a memorial before God and advised him to invite the apostle Peter to his house. At Peter's preaching, Cornelius' household received the Holy Spirit baptism and were thereafter baptised in water.

When Peter heard of the visitation that Cornelius had received from the angel he commented in amazement, "In truth I perceive that God shows no partiality. But in every nation whoever fears Him and works righteousness is accepted by Him" - Acts 10:34-35.

In Psalm 15:1, King David asked the question: "LORD, who may abide in Your tabernacle? Who may dwell in Your holy hill?" Then he gives some options and in verse 4 he wrote, "In whose eyes a vile person is despised, but he honours those who fear the LORD." The one who is approved of God despises evil and honours those who fear Him. The full chapter states:

> LORD, who may abide in Your tabernacle? Who may dwell in Your holy hill? He who walks uprightly, and works righteousness, and speaks the truth in his heart; he who does not backbite with his tongue, nor does evil to his neighbour, nor does he take up a reproach against his friend; in whose eyes a vile person is despised, but he honours those who fear the LORD; he who swears to his own hurt and does not change; he who does not put out his money at usury, nor does he take a bribe against the innocent. He who does these things shall never be moved - Psalm 15.

When someone stands for what God requires because of the fear of God, He esteems that person highly; but also anyone who honours the one who fears Him. Along the same vein, one should be mindful of how one comments when it is not clear why a person who fears God chooses to do things differently.

A good example is when one chooses to dress different from others who are scantily clad, avoidance of alcohol or refusing to take advantage of the weaknesses of others, one ought not to mock such a person, or join with those who do so. Rather, as Christians, we should encourage a person who dares to be different in an environment where the majority embrace practices that do not reflect the fear of God.

CHAPTER 7

CONCLUSION

*T*he fear of God is an indispensable tool in the armoury of every child of God, not only because of the numerous benefits it confers but more importantly because God demands it of us. Without it, the Christian walk would be hindered and deep intimacy with the Lord would be unattainable.

In 2 Timothy 4: 1-8, Paul the apostle refers to our Lord Jesus Christ as the One who will judge the living and the dead at His appearing. The fear of God extends to giving due regard to the word and instructions of the One who will judge what is right or wrong.

In my home, I lay down the ground rules determining what is acceptable and what is not. If a member of the family takes instructions from elsewhere which does not agree with my instructions, that person runs the risk of facing consequences determined by myself in response to their actions not according to the judgment or opinion of the one whose instructions were preferred.

Thus, anyone acknowledging the Lord as the righteous Judge (2 Timothy 4:8), should at all times seek to live according to His judgments and instructions, irrespective of what others propose to be the right instruction.

The fear of God makes one to laugh at the face of the enemy because one knows who is in control (See 1 Samuel 2:1-10). In Psalm 23, King David observed that the presence of the enemy was no deterrent to God's grace and provisions. In verse 5 he said, 'You prepare a table before me in the presence of my enemies.' God is always ahead of the enemy.

For every enemy punch thrown our way, God Almighty has a seven-fold restoration plan (See Proverbs 6:30-31), if we would hold on to Him.

The fear of God emboldens one's heart in prayer and stops murmuring; thereby preventing an unnecessary forty-year round-the-mountain trip, similar to that experienced by the nation of Israel after their exodus from the bondage of Egypt.

This book would not be complete without information on how to pursue after a life that embraces the fear of God. As stated in the introductory chapters, the Holy Spirit – also known as the Spirit of the fear of the Lord, who lives in every Christian, is the One who endows one with and helps us grow in the fear of the Lord. He would enable us with this if we ask Him.

It may be that you are not yet a Christian and would like to be one. You can do this by talking to a Christian and asking advice on how to do it. Also you can talk to Jesus Christ directly about this in a prayer, an example is suggested below:

Dear Jesus Christ, I believe that You are the only begotten Son of God, and that You left Your throne in heaven to come to the earth and pay for my sins on the cross. I am a sinner; forgive me my sins, which I now confess before You. I forgive anyone who has offended me.

Please come into my heart, save my soul, be my Lord and Saviour. Give me Your Holy Spirit to develop the fear of God in me and help me now as I start this new journey of turning my back on everything that is against You. Thank You for saving me. I make this prayer in Your name Jesus, Amen!

Big massive congratulations if you said the prayer above. I pray that God will help you find a local church where, through fellowship with other Bible-believing Christians, you can grow in loving God and living a life led by the Holy Spirit through the fear of God.

THE FEAR OF GOD

ABOUT THE AUTHOR

Dr. Ngozi Joy Nwokoma is a Medical Practitioner. By the grace of God she made a commitment to become a disciple of Jesus Christ at a Full Gospel Business Men's Fellowship meeting in 1994. She is married to Dr. Chinwe Nwokoma; they are blessed with three lovely children and live in Doncaster UK.

Dr. Ngozi Nwokoma is one of the leaders of the Overseas Fellowship of Nigerian Christians, Doncaster branch. She has a passion for encouraging people to trust God and develop a personal relationship with Him through prayer and to keep focused on Jesus Christ, particularly in and through the challenges of life. This passion is also expressed in her first book titled '*Hope Breaks out with Singing.*'

To contact Dr. Ngozi Nwokoma with your feedback or orders, email: **trinitybooks@writeme.com**.